TALES OF TWO LONDONS

TALES OF
TWO LONDONS

Stories from a
Fractured City

EDITED BY
Claire Armitstead

A

Arcadia Books Ltd
139 Highlever Road
London W10 6PH

www.arcadiabooks.co.uk

First published by OR Books, New York and London 2018
This edition published 2019
Copyright © The contributors 2018

ISBN 978-1-911350-60-6

Typeset in Caslon
Printed and bound by TJ International, Padstow PL28 8RW

Arcadia Books distributors are as follows:

in the UK and elsewhere in Europe:
BookSource
50 Cambuslang Road
Cambuslang
Glasgow G32 8NB

in Australia/New Zealand:
NewSouth Books
University of New South Wales
Sydney NSW 2052

CONTENTS

INTRODUCTION

Claire Armitstead

THE 100TH EPISODE of the TV home-building programme *Grand Designs* featured what appeared to be one of the most reckless architectural makeovers by a private individual that London had ever seen. More than a century of rubble – and over 200 dead pigeons – had to be cleared from the nine-storey Victorian water tower before the new owners could even take a proper look around. The whole project had to be finished within eight months, because small-time property developer Leigh and his partner Graham didn't own the land around its base.

They had bought the derelict Grade II-listed building for £380,000 and, by the time it was finished in 2012, had spent nearly £2m more in their potentially ruinous race against the clock. Great story, and oh so photogenic. Giggling sheepishly to camera, they revealed that they had set their hearts on the 100-foot tower after spotting it from their flat high up in one of London's flashy new skyscrapers.

The water tower is in Kennington, a short hop from the Elephant and Castle roundabout, and I was born in its shadow – in a hospital that no longer exists. 'She felt so wonderful, making little alive noises, when half an hour before she wasn't there', wrote my mother in a flimsy blue airmail letter to my father, who was 3,000 miles away at the time. Were I to have opened my eyes, the first faces I would have seen were those of the two Lambeth midwives Miss Hurter and Miss Pickles, into whose capable hands I slithered, 'crying lustily', at 2.30am on 2 December 1958.

There's no such happy record of seven-year-old Charlie Chaplin's arrival at the same address 62 years earlier. When the comedian was admitted with his brother in 1896, after their mother became unable to care for them, the imposing red and yellow brick building was a workhouse containing 820 destitute Londoners. By the time I bowled up, it had been transformed into a general hospital, which continued to serve the largely working class population of the Elephant and Castle until the mid-1970s.

Like any city, London is constantly evolving. *Tales of Two Londons* is the third in a series of anthologies that seek to investigate the history, symptoms and consequences of inequality in particular locations. The first two, both edited by John Freeman, focused on New York and America. This third collection concentrates on London at a time when it has felt fractured and embattled as rarely before in peacetime.

The vote in 2016 to leave the European Union has profoundly shaken individuals and institutions across the capital. The majority of Londoners themselves voted to remain and were bewildered by the assumption of many leave voters outside the capital that they were an out-of-touch metropolitan elite. Now, many long-term residents, either born or with family origins outside the UK, are questioning whether they have a future here at all.

The morale of this international city was briefly revived by its refusal to be cowed by a series of attacks by alienated and radicalised men, several of them born and raised in the UK. At Finsbury Park Mosque, as at Borough Market and on Westminster Bridge, ordinary people responded with courageous acts to help one another and personalised messages on stickers and handmade posters.

And then came the Grenfell Tower inferno, with its appalling reminder of how contemptuously many of London's poorest citizens have been treated over decades of privatisation and mismanagement – in this case by a local authority in one of the city's richest areas. As an anonymous resident of Kensington and Chelsea put it, in a powerful open letter written days after the fire and reproduced here: 'A tower block full of disadvantaged neighbours has now been repurposed as a human chimney.'

The most dangerous thing a society can do is to deny a voice to the individuals that live in it. As Jon Snow pointed out in an important lecture responding to the Grenfell fire, the warnings were there, but for the umpteenth time in recent history, the media was not listening. 'Why didn't we enable the residents of Grenfell Tower, and indeed the other hundreds of towers like it around Britain, to find pathways to talk to us and for us to expose their stories?' he asks.

In order to do so, the journalist, the editor, the curator or the anthologist has to seek out and listen to voices outside conventional arenas of received opinion. To voices like that of Grenfell Tower blogger Edward Daffarn, who predicted a catastrophe eight months before it happened, but also to poets and storytellers who may express themselves in new or unfamiliar ways. The award-winning poet Daljit Nagra provides an eloquent example in an eight-line poem about a religious convert, as does Kurdish activist Memed Aksoy, through a blistering fable of a young London immigrant stripped of his mother tongue. Aksoy, a graduate of Goldsmiths, University of London, who arrived in the UK at the age of ten, was determined to use his art as a writer and filmmaker to expose injustice. He was killed while documenting the battle for the Syrian city of Raqqa just weeks before this anthology went to press. His final message said simply: 'I'm currently in Rojava, northern Syria, doing some charity work and don't know when I'll be back but I'd like to help in any way I can.'

To hear people like Memed, we need to confront the tyranny

of tone: the convention that any work of art or literature should speak in an even voice, paint within a clearly co-ordinated cultural palette. For how can any one voice, any one palette represent a city of more than 8 million people, nearly 37 per cent of whom – according to the latest census in 2011 – were born outside the UK?

This anthology sets out to mirror London's diversity by ensuring that more than a third of the voices are of those not born in the UK. It aims to reflect the fact that any city is the sum of its people, and the intelligence they offer is various and sometimes oblique. How do the triumphs of community activism square with the curse of gentrification? What is it like to give birth shortly after arriving in a strange city? How does Londoners' love of cats and dogs feel to someone who has lost everything? Memoir, reportage, history and several different genres of poetry keep company in its pages, hopefully sparking off each other in challenging, invigorating and inspiring ways. Several contributions were produced through a network of creative writing schemes for new immigrants and refugees in the city, including the Brave New Voices programme run by the writers' charity English PEN, an organisation which will receive the royalties earned from this collection.

Two years ago, Poles became the UK's largest migrant population. In a devastating book of reportage, which is in the process of being translated into English, the award-winning Polish journalist Ewa Winnicka toured the country, seeking out the testimony of people like Marcin, a one-time advertising executive employed as one of 90 Poles and 'a handful of Lithuanians' under the management of piratical Albanians, to process the capital's rubbish in a depot just outside the city limits. 'I have the impression he has stared into the jaws of hell,' writes Winnicka. Pedants might quibble that Dartford isn't yet formally part of London, but you only have to look at the location of its airports – Gatwick, Luton, Stansted as well as Heathrow – to be reminded that this is a metropolis that has always pushed its noisy, dirty work to, and beyond, the city limits.

In 'The City as a Warzone', film and opera director Penny Woolcock and youth worker Stephen Griffith offer a shocking account of what is going wrong at street level, chronicling an epidemic of knife crime, in which young men are stabbed to death outside the shops where their well-heeled neighbours obliviously go to buy olives and high roast coffee. London's rich and poor often inhabit the same streets but simply don't see each other. 'Is there a connection between grotesque inequality and petty criminal activity, between state-sanctioned violence and small turf wars?', Woolcock asks, adding, 'What I know is that if white middle-class kids were killing each other on the streets of London, we would see them very clearly.'

But we both appal and surprise ourselves, and the 'better self' of this edgy, overcrowded city is beautifully captured by Arifa Akbar and John Crace in memoirs of unlikely friendships forged in shared houses or on football terraces. Ali Smith recalls the thrill of her first encounter with a city of restaurants where she heard 'more languages spoken in one brief walk down a street than I'd heard my whole life so far', while the poet and playwright Inua Ellams captures the vivacity of late-night homegoers:

Elephant & Castle is a coral reef, resplendent,
rippling with daredevil kids too schooled
in cool to check the pickpocket whose wrist-flick
shimmers like a blade. A shoal of girls clothed
in tinsel dresses burp and bubble with ale,
their cheap garments ripple like fish scales.

Sometimes fiction is best-placed to capture the nuances of city life: the sly humour of Kinga Burger's short story 'I Have a Friend Who Is Polish, He's Very Nice' skewers the coincidence of Poland's ascendancy to the UK's biggest minority with the Brexit vote a year later, while Helen Simpson's 'Double Whammy' personifies the dark forces beneath the veneer of a networked European city in the story of a day in the life of a wholefood company executive. The suave banter of Andrew O'Hagan's north London literati counterpoints the bemused lilt of Lisa Smith's elderly Jamaican, locked up in a Peckham police cell on New Year's Eve.

As Duncan Campbell writes, we have always blamed immigrants for our crimes. Yet, since London's earliest days, when Romans feasted on oysters and garum sauce beside the deep water docks that enabled it to become a centre of international commerce, it has been a city of incomers, enriched by the generations who have disembarked and decided to make it their home. Our language is a creole. We eat curry and kebabs, and drink lattes on café verandahs. Shakespeare, who added 1,700 words to the language in a theatre just south of the Thames – then a marshy overspill of brothels and bearpits – would not understand any part of that previous sentence.

The Thames is a psychic as well as a historical and geographical divide; it begins and ends this collection just as, from its earliest days, it has defined the city itself. This can have unintentionally comic results: the intelligence agencies, MI5 and MI6, glowering at each other from opposing banks, their ideological differences mirrored in their architectural styles; the flashy new cable car that flies its sponsor's colours high above the river, beginning and ending in an empty car park.

There is a happenstance about where people find themselves in a city that is reflected in many pieces in this anthology; but also very visible is the fact that we all develop footprints that are unique to us. I've been a northeast Londoner for most of my adult life and I don't go to south London much. I was born in Lambeth Hospital because my parents lived abroad and my uncle was a doctor there. Births, operations and deaths have dominated my relationship with the ribbon of land that meanders east along the Thames from Westminster Bridge to the Elephant and Castle and on to London Bridge, where I watched the New Year's Eve fireworks set fire to the sky on my father's final night in a creepily empty private hospital wing above the railway station.

It was only in researching this introduction that it occurred to me that my intensely medicalised relationship with south London might be partly responsible for my resistance to it. It hasn't all been bad. One of my earliest memories, recovering in Lambeth children's ward, aged five, after having my tonsils removed, is of how sore it was to laugh at the 'naughty boys' tobogganing up the ward on their dinner trays, pursued by a nurse with what looked like a wedding cake balanced on her head. (This wasn't a happy-gas hallucination: Lambeth nurses were proud graduates at the Nightingale Home and Training School, and were identifiable at the time by the implausible architecture of their caps.)

My last visit was with my mother in the early 1970s for a consultation about a suspicious lump in her breast. We arrived early, so she treated me to a glass of cider in the pub just outside the gates. By the time it was decided that surgery was needed, Lambeth Hospital had closed and all its services had been transferred to the shiny white citadel of St Thomas's on Westminster Bridge Road.

Memories make a city just as they make a person. As Alex Rhys-Taylor writes in a colourful piece on the history of *al fresco* eating in Petticoat Lane market: 'Where once there were cook shops vending Huguenot *pommes frites* and kosher fried fish, a Greek-Cypriot-owned fish and chip shop heats up its oil, slices its potatoes and prepares fillets for frittering. By lunchtime, the result is a constellation of aromas that make a mouth-watering testament to half a millennium of everyday eating in London.'

For those who care to look and to listen, as the poet Ruth Padel does in the opening poem, there are rivers under roads, and stories written into every stone (not only in the great cemeteries explored by David McKie). If we choose to follow them they often lead us in unexpected directions – which returns me to my own journey back to the place where I was born.

It turns out that Leigh's water tower is one of two buildings that survived demolition. Some quick Googling reveals that it failed to sell when it was put on the market for £4.75m in 2013, provoking a spate of newspaper stories about the 'curse of Grand Designs'. A few keystrokes later I discover that it is now an Airbnb charging £175 a night per room and that Leigh has become a 'superhost'.

After making contact in the guise of a tourist looking for a city break, I confess to my mission and ask for a meeting. The response is curt: 'You will know more than me. I am not from here. I don't know more than what's already online (or more than you).' Did you give up on finding a buyer or decide you liked it here? I persevere; after all, it's not the most exclusive location for a 21st century mega-maison. 'It was for sale for 4 weeks, 5 years ago,' Leigh snaps back, before my request is removed from the site, terminating the conversation.

My doctor uncle was so devoted to the hospital that he spent a large chunk of his retirement struggling to write its history, 27 yellowing chapters of which survive in my aunt's Clapham attic. In a brisk reminder not to get too sentimental, he reported on the rigid segregation of its workhouse era, which divided inmates into 'several classes in each sex for aged, able-bodied of good character, and two subdivisions of able-bodied of bad character, together with accommodation for a limited number of boys and girls.'

The story he tells is still partially visible when I cycle down to Kennington one sunny morning in late summer. The old pub where my mother and I sat and drank cider is boarded up, but the entry pillars survive, as does the surprisingly grand 'Master's

House', where the workhouse manager once lived. Above a flow-erbed planted with stripy yuccas and bright pink pelargoniums, a tablet is set into its wall:

THIS STONE WAS LAID ON THE 3rd OF APRIL 1871, BY JOHN DOULTON, ESQ, CHAIRMAN OF THE BOARD OF GUARDIANS.

Doulton, the eponymous founder of the famous porcelain company was by then a grandee in his 70s – a walking advertisement for the social mobility of the industrialised 19th century city. He had begun his working life as an enterprising pottery apprentice making salt glaze sewer pipes.

I arrive expecting to find an enraging example of gentrification, but London is not always as straightforward as that. New, low-level housing is discreet and classy, but reggae music wafts from an open window, and part of the site has been preserved for community medicine. Miss Hurter and Miss Pickles, who brought so many babies of all classes and creeds into the world, would have approved of the Mary Sheridan Centre for Child Health and the South London Sickle Cell and Thalassaemia Centre.

Leigh's made-over water tower might be the TV era's match for those magnificent follies of an imperial age when Victorians had more money than sense, but it still stands on public land, and cycling around its base, I catch a glimpse through 'the largest sliding glass doors in the UK' of the Airbnb superhost preparing lunch in his state-of-the-art kitchen. The Master's House is now a cinema museum. As I head back north across the river, I remember Charlie Chaplin as the little Tramp, rescuing an orphan in his first full-length feature film, *The Kid*. The international comedy star made movie magic out of his melancholic time as a Lambeth workhouse waif.

WALKING THE FLEET

Ruth Padel

You're standing where the hidden river
swills out into Thames. In Roman times
a major waterway of redbrick mills
on the estuary tide. In Anglo-Saxon days
a tidal inlet   *Flēot*   feeding private homes
breweries   Saint Pancras Church   and tanning yards.
Then a River of Wells leading
to the holy healing fountain
Clerkenwell. Today a sludgy dream-stream
cemented over but still flowing
under Old Seacoal Lane
the Holbourne Viaduct and four miles of city.
Memory is not only what you've lost
but knowing what you had   and you still do.

MY HOUSE IN HARRA

Omar Alfrouh

My house in Harra is like a fort, ten bedrooms
A large painting of my mother and father
hanging on the wall
welcoming whoever walks through the door
My house in Harlesden is small
Three bedrooms for six people
But I am trying to feed it yoully rice and tabola
and kabsa and aeraan and tea
and my sister and brothers, grandparents and uncles
The kabab used to mean we were together
Now it means we are apart
I want to come back to all the tables
where my family gather
I want to die where I was born

TOP RANKING

Ali Smith

LONDON, **THE SLEEPER** train in the clear cold of the air and the dark of evening in Inverness railway station, the municipal smell of the cabin and the little lid over the sink, the slow-going sound of the shunt of trains somewhere down the map god knew where in the middle of the night, everything outside dark, then the brightness and the smoothness of the flooring underfoot, Euston station and me making my father take me to see *New York, New York* (he fell asleep, it was long) in the afternoon in a cinema in the city of cinema, of BBC-everything, of glamorous Underground cinema posters, glamorous even the escalators.

London, the thunk and swing and pang-panache and twinge of the opening bars of 'Uptown Top Ranking' by Althea and Donna upending all the dirges, sending 'Mull of Kintyre' by Wings dwindling away down the charts and me on a hotel bed (in a hotel in Paddington whose restaurant was staffed by people from all over the world and whose burgers were named after pre-decimal coins, the penny, the halfpenny, the sixpence, the shilling) listening to it literally happen, on a radio coming out of the hotel bedhead in the actual city where it was being broadcast, in London, city of restaurants called Golden Egg, Spaghetti House.

London, and my brother Gordon (who lived and worked down there) walking me over a bridge (Waterloo Bridge) the sun on the river (the river) towards a theatre, the theatre was National, that night it was *Death of a Salesman* then the next night it was international, Italian, it was *Accidental Death of an Anarchist* we saw and I was thrilled to the core with the life in it.

London, where the people on the Tube gently eyed me, sand-shoes tied by their laces to the straps of my rucksack, like I might well be a runaway.

London, where street after street never ended, went on for miles and miles.

London, where I heard more languages spoken in one brief walk down a street than I'd heard my whole life so far.

Far have I travelled and much have I seen.

Love is all I bring, inna me khaki suit and ting.

GRENFELL TOWER: AN ATROCITY IN THREE ACTS

Jon Snow, Grenfell Action Group, Anonymous

Act One: the Best of Times, the Worst of Times
(Jon Snow, 23 August 2017)

ON THE MORNING of 14 June 2017 in the middle of one of the very wealthiest boroughs in one of the richest cities in the world, a fire engulfed the 24-storey Grenfell Tower.

Even now we do not know the true number who died. The authorities say at least 80 people perished, the surviving residents say many more.

When journalists woke that terrible morning and Googled 'Grenfell Tower', they found a blog published eight months before. It raged at the Tenant Management Organisation and highlighted the dangers of the building and the disconnect between the tenants and the landlord.

A chronicle of death foretold not by any journalist but in a blog by the leader of the action group for those who lived in the tower.

Where are the once strong local papers that used to exist and served to inform national journalists? Gone. Yet the Grenfell residents' story was out there, published online and shocking in its accuracy. It was hidden in plain sight, but we had stopped looking. The disconnect complete.

Amid the demonstrations around the lower part of the building after the fire there were cries of 'Where were you? Why didn't you come here before?'

Why didn't any of us see the Grenfell action blog? Why didn't we know? Why didn't we have contact?

Why didn't we enable the residents of Grenfell Tower, and indeed the other hundreds of towers like it around Britain, to find pathways to talk to us and for us to expose their stories?

In that moment I felt both disconnected and frustrated. I felt on the wrong side of the terrible divide that exists in present day society and which we all, in the media, are major players.

In July, the new leader of Kensington and Chelsea Borough Council admitted that she had never been up one of the residential towers that her administration was responsible for, despite at the same time being in charge of children and families.

Understandably it caused something of a stir, and then I wondered how many of us has ever been up a local authority housing tower block?

We can accuse the political classes for their failures, and we do. But we are guilty of them ourselves.

We are too far removed from those who lived their lives in Grenfell and who, across the country, now live on, amid combustible cladding, the lack of sprinklers, the absence of centralised fire alarms and more, revealed by the Grenfell Tower.

How much time had we devoted to social housing in this year since the EU referendum, when day after day we found ourselves filling the airwaves with negotiating positions of Theresa May, Boris Johnson, David Davis (the Brexit Bulldog), Jeremy Corbyn and the rest, before serious negotiations had even begun?

Not just Brexit, consuming the airwaves with so much

political flatulence. Stuff which we know from viewing figures, whether you are pro- or anti-Brexit, bore and frustrate the viewer.

And I haven't even mentioned the antics of Trump yet. Sapping airtime that could have and should have been devoted to subjects nearer the hearts of those who watch.

We have learned that lesson this year.

I am still haunted too by my own link with what happened at Grenfell Tower.

On 20 April this year, I was involved with Bill Gates in judging a schools debate, a competition in London. It was the final of a countrywide championship organised by the charity Debate Mate, an organisation that does fantastic work democratising that skill so often associated with the elite – public speaking.

I was there to judge the best floor speech. I had little difficulty in deciding. The winner was Firdows Kedir, a remarkably poised hijab-wearing 12-year-old from west London. She was confident. She used language beautifully. Bill Gates grasped her hand and gave her the award.

On 19 June, a mere two months later, reporting from Grenfell, I spotted a picture of Firdows on a 'missing' poster. She and her entire family of five are believed to have been incinerated together on the 22nd floor of Grenfell Tower. Two weeks ago it was confirmed that remnants of Firdows and her father had indeed been found, in their flat, and that their identities had been confirmed using DNA.

Firdows had been described as 'the most intelligent, wise and eloquent girl.' I was fortunate to witness that firsthand and since then I often think, 'What might have she become?' What were her life chances, once she'd been picked out in this way? Could she have prevailed over the fractures in our society and succeeded?

Britain is not alone in this – our organic links within our own society are badly broken, in part because the echelons from which our media is drawn do not for the most part fully reflect the population, amongst whom we live and to whom we seek to transmit information and ideas.

Grenfell speaks to us all about our own lack of diversity, and capacity to reach into the swathes of Western society with whom we have no connection.

Like my fellow journalists, I have spent many hours around Grenfell. I have come to know a number of the survivors, and I speak to them regularly by phone or email.

They are so casually written off as nameless migrants, scroungers, illegals, and the rest, when actually – and it should be no shock to us – the tower was full of talent. Not least the wonderful and talented Khadija Saye, who died with her mother, on the verge of a major breakthrough as an artist. Or community leaders like Eddie Daffarn, who survived the inferno, and who wrote that warning blog on 20 November, 2016.

Could things have turned out differently had a local reporter been aware of Eddie Daffarn and his blog at Grenfell Tower, and seeped his warnings of danger and devastation out into the media mainstream before it was too late?

Extracted from Jon Snow's James MacTaggart Memorial Lecture at the 2017 Edinburgh International Television Festival.

Act Two: Playing with Fire!
(Grenfell Action Group blog, 20 November 2016)

It is a truly terrifying thought but the Grenfell Action Group firmly believe that only a catastrophic event will expose the incompetence of our landlord, the Kensington and Chelsea Tenants Management Organisation (KCTMO), and bring an end to the dangerous living conditions and neglect of health and safety legislation that they inflict upon their tenants and leaseholders.

We believe that the KCTMO are an unprincipled mini-mafia who have no business to be charged with the responsibility of looking after the everyday management of large scale social housing estates, and that their sordid collusion with the RBKC Council is a recipe for a future major disaster.

The Grenfell Action Group believe that a major fire disaster was narrowly averted at Grenfell Tower in 2013 when residents experienced a period of terrifying power surges that were subsequently found to have been caused by faulty wiring. In October 2015 a fire ripped through another KCTMO property, the 14-storey Adair Tower in North Kensington, causing mass panic and resulting in a number of residents being taken to hospital suffering from smoke inhalation. Had it not been for the swift actions of the London Fire Brigade, the consequences of this fire could have been much worse.

In the aftermath of the Adair Tower fire the London Fire Brigade found that the KCTMO had not been looking after the safety of residents properly and issued an Enforcement Order compelling them to improve the fire safety in the escape staircases and to provide self-closing devices for all the tower block's front doors. A further fire brigade audit of the neighbouring Hazelwood Tower (located alongside Adair Tower) found similar breaches of health and safety legislation. What is shocking is that a decade ago a fatality occurred due to a fire at Hazelwood Tower, and the fire investigation team ordered that the grilles on the fire escape staircase be covered over. This never happened and it is believed that uncovered grilles at Adair House acted like a chimney and were responsible for the accelerated spread of the fire and smoke damage.

In the last 20 years, and despite the terrifying power surge incident in 2013 and the recent fire at Adair Tower, residents of Grenfell Tower have received no proper fire safety instructions. They were informed by a temporary notice stuck in the lift and one announcement in a recent regeneration newsletter that in the event of a fire they should remain in their flats. There are not and never have been any instructions posted in the Grenfell Tower noticeboard or on individual floors as to how residents should act in a fire. Anyone who witnessed the recent tower block fire at Shepherds Court, in nearby Shepherd's Bush, will know that the advice to remain in our properties would have led to certain fatalities, and we are calling on our landlords to reconsider the advice that they have so badly circulated.

The Grenfell Action Group predict that it won't be long before the words of this blog come back to haunt the KCTMO management, and we will do everything in our power to ensure that those in authority know how long and how appallingly our landlords have ignored their responsibility to ensure the health and safety of their tenants and leaseholders. They can't say that they haven't been warned!

Act Three: Give It Back
(An Open Letter from a Resident of Kensington and Chelsea, 16 June 2017)

In 2014, I received my Kensington and Chelsea council tax bill and a letter from the leader of the council, Nicholas Paget-Brown, explaining that all residents who pay council tax in full would 'receive a one-off payment of £100', to be deducted from the bill. This bonus, the letter continued, was due to the council's careful management of its finances over the years, 'consistently delivering greater efficiencies while improving services'. Austerity, K&C style: you give to the rich while taking from the poor (nobody with discounted bills or claiming from the council tax support scheme was eligible to share in the bounty of the town hall bluechips).

On a Conservative website, Paget-Brown further explained that 'thanks to an overachieving efficiency drive', the council was 'well ahead of [its] savings targets for the year.' Triple A credit status, how nice. In deciding what to do with this surplus, he continued, 'we have taken the view that it is simply wrong to discount from our calculations whose money this was in the first place. In short, we think the right place for it is back with our residents.' A few months later, in May 2014, the local election returned a huge majority of Conservative councillors. Business as usual.

For years, the Royal Borough has got away with bribing the electorate with its own money. For years, the Royal Borough has been running huge underspends in its revenue budgets, which it then transfers into capital reserves. The underspend in the 2016-17 adult services budget alone is £1.9m. Apparently, adult services in the area are doing so well they don't need the money. And every other social service must be performing brilliantly, as the council's projected reserves of £167m by the end of 2016-17 has climbed to a staggering £209m – that's £42m surplus to requirements. How many sprinkler systems is that?

A tower block full of disadvantaged neighbours has now been repurposed as a human chimney. As the toxic ash of Grenfell Tower's vanity cladding falls over the neighbouring streets, we are left with the acrid truth in our throats: regeneration in the Royal Borough is in fact a crime of greed and selfishness.

I took the refund. At the time, I felt uncomfortable with this decision and the ways in which I justified it to myself. And then I forgot about it, until the smoke drifting into my flat in the early hours of Wednesday woke me up. Today, I gave it back. It wasn't ever mine to keep. I handed it over in cash to a vicar running a refuge for the victims of the fire in a local church. I explained that it was not a donation, not a charitable act, that it was guilt money and he was doing me a kindness by taking it off my hands.

Please, if you can afford to, give it back. But not to the council, which seems to have trouble identifying those – 'our residents' – who might actually need it.

NOTTING HILL'S LAST STAND

Ed Vulliamy

TAKE A RIDE along the River Thames, one of the great waterways of Europe. Not long ago, you made your way from elegant Chelsea reach through real London, still echoing Dickens, past the original Oxo building and wharves – even the old brick space, used as an underground car park, like an adventure playground beneath Blackfriars, reaching down to the river's edge like a pebble beach. Not long ago, you wound around the loop past the Rotherhithe, Wapping and Millwall reaches – atmospheric Peter Ackroyd, Mayhew terrain. The destruction and redefinition of Canary Wharf is an old story, but what about the rest: the Shard, Gherkin and Walkie-Talkie; places like 'Bermondsey Spa' in estate agent parlance: then mile after mile of tacky, cheaply-built but pricey Lego-brick apartment blocks? And back along the Chelsea embankment, a horror of eyesores for billionaires to buy.

'NOSTALGIA!' – you can hear them shriek, as though it were a war crime to mourn the loss of beautiful things, or those of which memory is made. 'STANDING IN THE WAY OF PROGRESS!' But what exactly does 'progress' mean; is it not just as meaningless as 'nostalgia', only the other way round? Why are the Westfield shopping centres by necessity better, and finer, buildings, than the old Smithfield, Billingsgate and Covent Garden markets?

The people doing all this were called 'property speculators' back in the day, but are now euphemistically described as 'developers'. In fact, they are vandals: if you were to propose the kind of wanton destruction currently in 'progress' in London for 19th century buildings in Paris, New York, Stockholm, Budapest, Rome, Amsterdam, they'd think you were mad and they'd be right.

Crucially: What does all this mean for people raised and living in London or trying to, and people arriving without too much money? All this is just the shop window. Demolition, speculation and 'development' are just the visible money-go-round, the overt money-laundering and money-making on display. What the brazen destruction, the ruthless 'development' and rebuilding of new skylines hides is the real story: 'social cleansing', as it has come to be known. It is about getting rid of people: the raising of property prices and rents – and wanton granting of licences to speculators – to the point that few people from and in the city can afford to live in London any more. In recent years, according to data on entitlement to free school meals, 50,000 families have been physically removed from the capital as the result of the destruction of social housing. Tens of thousands more simply cannot afford to stay, as rents are driven sky-high by the speculators' 'buy-to-rent' strategy.

So London becomes a medieval city, devoid of its working- or middle-class. Only those blessed with fortunes, or able to scrape by, can remain: the super-rich and a troglodyte subclass, increasingly immigrant, paid slave wages to clean their offices by night, serve coffee to their bored, pampered wives and wash their toilets. And so proceeds apace the great hidden death of London: the ravaging of community, the bonfire of authenticity, the physical devastation of community spaces, affordable housing, former council estates, community assets and meeting places – in particular, pubs. Yes: pubs, taverns: focal points of any community since Chaucer's time and before, places where people meet, greet and chew the fat, take a look at the world over a drink or two, watch football, listen to music, laugh and chatter; places where human beings can be just that, where life goes on, where a community's heart beats.

The place in which I was born has suffered as badly as anywhere: Notting Hill, west London, where the burnt-out shell of Grenfell Tower is clearly visible as I write. The spine of the area is Ladbroke Grove and the junction where it meets Lancaster Grove has since 1865 been the site of a pub, the Kensington Park Hotel, known locally by the letters that have adorned its corner wall for longer than I can remember: KPH.

It was a very special meeting place – the heartbeat of its community, an urban village green, a place that stood for fun, conviviality, community and authenticity. Just one pub, one story – but it could be so many others, and so many other places or stories. It stood for and epitomised so much that was good about London, but is now irreparably lost, crushed by the stampede of greed.

When I first went for an underage drink at the KPH in 1970, aged 16, it was quite a roughhouse and one of many of its kind locally, where the five layers of community that made up the neighbourhood could meet and mingle effortlessly: the indigenous cockneys, the Irish, Spanish, West Indians and newly arrived bohemians.

I was born, in 1954, on the street in which Jimi Hendrix would die, a few doors down, 16 years later – Lansdowne Crescent, W11. It was a ramshackle street then, all peeling stucco and rows of bells beside every front door. The building in which my parents were renting a flat when I came into the world is the only one left in the street that remains in the hands of the Notting Hill Housing Trust.

A contemporary free glossy magazine called 'The Hill' describes the Notting Hill of my youth to its wealthy readers as 'a no-go area for sure'. That's not how I remember things. I think – and this is not nostalgia – that Notting Hill was a rather special place to grow up. The area had its well-established white working class, many of whom lived in grinding poverty, as described in the memoir of Labour politician Alan Johnson. But it had been largely built by the Irish, who had begun arriving in the mid-19th century and continued to do so. It was settled in the 1940s by refugees from the Spanish Civil War. And later, during the '50s, by those arrived from the West Indies on boats, the *Windrush* and *Irpinia*, shipped in to provide a cheap workforce in the bold new Welfare State. All these people amounted to a whole greater than the sum of their parts, infusing Notting Hill with a special effervescence, a unique sense of community and *mélange*.

Yet among my first memories were the race riots of 1958, 'teddy boys' streaming out of Ladbroke Grove station to attack our local black people. I recall my mother going up to four of them who were setting about a young black boy against the grille across the lift shaft at then scrappy Holland Park Tube, and saying, rather imperiously: 'What on earth do you think you're doing?' They slunk off. Mum asked the black boy if he was okay; he thanked her and slunk off too (I realise now that she was brave to engage them, aged 30, with a toddler). The headquarters of Colin Jordan's National Socialist party on Princedale Road had two swastikas on the frontage; one day, some gallant fellow backed a lorry into the Nazi HQ, or at least intended to – but missed and hit Mr Benton's shoe-shop instead.

But this was the worst of it, the rest far better. Fascist Oswald Mosley's attempt to cash in on the riots and contest the seat of North Kensington in 1959 was catastrophic for a good reason: there was genuine, unforced and unconscious conviviality between the peoples of Notting Hill, long before anyone invented the word 'multicultural', let alone 'diversity'.

The latest influx of white jazz-generation bohemians like my parents were 'cash-poor, book-rich' as the saying went, and – ironically, now – Ladbroke Grove was the only place in London they could afford, post art-school, post-World War Two. Mum and

Dad were warned by some about the dangerous area in which they met and settled. But as their children we fitted in fine, apart from the objections of a few skinheads who resented 'fuckin' 'ippies' – and even the fuckin' 'ippies were permissible if they supported Third Division Queens Park Rangers as avidly as we did.

As we reached our teens, Portobello Road became the Haight-Ashbury of Europe. Pink Floyd rehearsed in a local church and Joe Boyd, who had produced Bob Dylan at Newport, moved in from America to record them, and stayed. Hawkwind and the Pink Fairies played for free under the Westway on Saturdays. The underground papers *Oz* and *International Times* set up shop, as did 'Release' to help with, and campaign over, drug use and abuse. The Mangrove became the epicentre in Britain for a new soul culture, and black civil rights. The Mountain Grill became the canteen for the London underground scene. Mick Jagger filmed *Performance*. The Angry Brigade plotted in the shadows, and squats along Freston Street declared independence from Britain – the republic of 'Frestonia' – in the shadow of a new high-rise, Grenfell Tower.

Portobello market itself was a carnival: freaks in Sergeant Pepper military dress uniforms, agitprop papers for sale, along with the usual cockney fruit 'n' veg vendors. The Notting Hill Carnival was a small-scale community affair, led by steel bands and old-school 'Trojan' reggae. Pash's music shop on Elgin Crescent was an apparently permanent jam session on instruments he had often bought from Vietnam draft resisters who'd arrived here on the run from America. Where else but this place would Hendrix die, tragically, 18 days after I'd seen him play at the Isle of Wight?

It lasted at that pitch for about another decade: in 1978, The Clash played the warm-up gig for their worldwide '16 Tons Tour' by playing to 150 people in Acklam Hall at lunchtime on Christmas Day. How did my brother and I get to be among those deemed worthy by the Clash to be among the audience they wanted for that occasion? Well, you had to be in the right place late on Christmas Eve, when the band put news out by word of mouth: you had to be in either the Elgin or the KPH when the whisper went round. Ah, yes, the pubs.

No place contained – and has since those days energised and preserved – all this history quite like the pubs. And no places better guarantee the passage of that past into the future. The pubs were where we lived. They were the pulse, the urban pow-wow tent. The places where lifelong friendships and decisions were made; ambitions sworn and resolutions broken; bets lost and sweethearts won; livers trashed, pints pulled, chasers downed, kisses locked and punches thrown.

We had: the Prince of Wales, which connected Portland and Princedale Roads (a social mix, became trendy after Liverpool poet Brian Patten made it his local); the Portland Arms at Clarendon Cross (rough, white, fun). The Zetland was by Avondale Park opposite the 19th kiln, part of a tile factory, against which people still used to huddle and keep warm (rough but great honky-tonk piano). There were the Britannia on Clarendon Road (very rough) and the Duke of Wellington, corner of Elgin and Portobello (shut by the police for drug-dealing, enough said). We also had The Pelican on All Saints Road (hippies, local blacks and Afghan Black; plus rum and other hard liquor); The Elgin on Ladbroke Grove and The Castle on Portobello Road.

The change began during Margaret Thatcher-time, when the word 'yuppie' was coined, and the first 'hooray-Henries' and 'Sloane Rangers' arrived, seduced and urged by the pushers: Foxtons, Marsh & Parsons, Faron Sutaria et al. In an Orwellian twist, an estate agent's office right next door to the KPH now displays the icons of that which they destroyed: vinyl LP album covers of Hendrix, the Beatles – not for playing, just commodities.

Sometimes I wonder why it took the rich so long to find and 'invest in' our area. Look at it their way: it was the perfect place for up-market vandals to trash, with all that peeling but elegant stucco, those green communal gardens and squares, those little cafés and pubs to turn into gourmet-gastro-bistro whatever, or just close and 'convert' into 'condominiums' or 'lofts'. But once they'd found our neighbourhood, and realised they preferred it to Hampstead, Chelsea or Kensington W8, they came, they saw, they conquered.

By the turn of the century and release of *Notting Hill*, that saccharin-sickly film starring Hugh Grant and Julia Roberts, bankers and other people who make money out of money and nothing else had arrived in force, attracted, ironically, by the peace of Notting Hill which they shattered and the architecture which they wrecked with their basement-building. They turned our quiet streets into a bedlam of subterranean excavation, heaving and hauling to build their private gyms, cinemas and pools. Many of the new 'homeowners' in the area do not even live here, but treat our houses as tax-free stocks and shares for addition to portfolios purchased by offshore trusts. Others 'buy to let', further ratcheting up already giddy levels of rent. Some do move in – and flaunt it. With the crisis for the rest of Britain in 2008, the bankers duly went berserk, and launched a final assault on our community. One invitation to a seminar, circulated through letter boxes in selected streets by something called Ogilvy Wealth Management, promised that 'fortunes are made during a boom, dynasties during a recession'.

These vultures need flesh to pick, and pubs were among the tastiest easy-pickings. The Prince of Wales became luxury flats. The Portland Arms is now a pedicure place for bankers' wives called the 'Cowshed'. The Zetland closed and the site now houses a capital asset management firm. The Britannia changes serially from one bistro to another and is currently closed. All the others up Ladbroke Grove and Portobello were by 2016 similarly 'gastroided' or in one way or another ruined.

All, that is, but the KPH, which stood alone, uniquely authentic, a litmus test, a parable, a metaphor for it all. A last beach, a final stand – in its small but crucial and epic way – by one notion of London against another, one way of life against another. A stand by conviviality and authenticity – the *mélange* – against mediocrity and uniformity. By community and democracy – and fun, good fun – against the dictatorship of money.

It was built about two decades after wealthy James Weller Ladbroke began to construct what he intended to be a fashionable suburb with the added attraction of a racecourse called the Hippodrome. He succeeded: in the opening chapter of *The Forsyte Saga*, one of the family finds 'a spacious abode and a great bargain' in Ladbroke Grove. My own great, great grandfather, the architect Lewis Vulliamy, had added his contribution to the area in 1845, designing – and supervising the building of – St James Norland Church, on a grand square to the west.

I wonder what they talked about in the KPH when it first opened its doors in 1865. The American Civil War? – possibly. The election, just won by Lord Palmerston's Liberal Party? – likely so. The first definition of a dog-breed standard? – quite probably – it was bestowed on the pointer. Insurgent events in Ireland, for sure: recent famine had driven many here to build Notting Hill, and there would be an uprising in 1868.

As years rolled by, regulars at the KPH would have celebrated the turn of the 19th to the 20th centuries (as they would later do the turn of the 20th to the 21st), discussed the death of Queen Victoria, no doubt monitored the Easter Rising and bloody birth of Ireland during and after the first of two world wars. A theatre opened upstairs above the bar in 1929, for musical shows, plays and meetings. Then came depression and the Spanish Civil War, when those who had escaped to Notting Hill would have followed and talked about the bombing of Guernica. Then our own blitz by the Luftwaffe, throughout which the KPH pub remained proudly open. They'd have celebrated the Armistice and probably welcomed the building of the Welfare State in the late 1940s, during which serial killer John Christie was, reportedly, a barman at the KPH. His neighbour Timothy Evans, wrongly hanged for Christie's crimes, was a regular.

When the Spanish arrived in the 1940s, the KPH's doors opened to them, as it did to the West Indians a decade later – although a meeting by Oswald Mosley's fascists was also held in an upstairs room at the pub during his disastrous election campaign of 1959. Once the '60s came, Tom Jones sang his first London concert in the first-floor theatre. He was paid ten pounds, and recalls the evening as a happy and successful one. These were bold days, for Swinging London and new ideas: the Notting Hill Housing Trust was a revolutionary concept in its day from which many of the KPH's clientele would almost certainly have bene fitted. On the slipstream of the hippie era, during the heyday of punk and ever since, among the regulars was Mick Jones of the Clash.

Let's admit it: many people agreed that a few years ago, the KPH was not quite the asset to the area that its past deserved. It was always fun to visit, great for football, and the old crowd would never – could never – go anywhere else. But it was run down. Even the barman with tattoos from the Long Kesh internment camp in Northern Ireland thought it was getting a bit grubby. It needed an injection of vim, a lease of life, an idea.

And who better to inject that vim than the man who had revived the Glastonbury and Reading festivals; who brought Bob Dylan to Finsbury Park, and Johnny Cash, Paul McCartney and Roy Orbison to his Mean Fiddler venue in Harlesden: Vince Power. When word went round that the one-time king of music could possibly be interested in the tatty old KPH, the excitement along Ladbroke Grove was palpable.

In early 2013, Power was given power of attorney (no pun

intended) by the licensee, Patrick Burke, who was too ill to manage the pub himself. And Vince cast a spell over the place, though it wasn't really like that: it took time, money, hard work – plus faith in the future of the pub, and in the community's faith in it too. It was faith well placed.

'I fell in love with it,' said Power. He cleaned it up but kept the original features, installed a pizza oven and coffee machine, reopened it as a profitable meeting place – and added his passion: live music. Among those who came to play here were Vin Gordon, the main trombonist on the classic reggae scene who formed part of the Wailers and Heptones; Mick Eve, sax man with Georgie Fame's Blue Flames who met Hendrix on his first day in London and played with him; Mary Coughlan, the great Irish jazz singer – and many others. Plays were performed upstairs, children's parties thrown, there was a yoga club. KPH was a crucial venue for the Portobello Film Festival and played a central role in the Notting Hill Carnival.

In July 2013, however, freehold was bought from Punch Taverns by SWA Developments, fronted by its CEO Steven Archer, whose father was reprimanded by the Football Association for selling Brighton & Hove Albion's Goldstone Ground in 1997 in a way that secured profits for his DIY empire, but almost none for the club. According to court papers, SWA now sought to change the ground floor of the KPH 'from a public house to another commercial use' – later denied by SWA, although it did open negotiations with Foxton's estate agency. That is when the trouble started, with SWA filing court papers to take the licence from Burke and Power as his manager. They 'threw the kitchen sink at us', as lawyers for these vast conglomerates do, says Power. In one hearing, a judge – though he ruled in favour of SWA – lambasted what he called its 'aggressive campaign and unreasonable stance to the Defendant from day one'.

Christmas 2015 was very weird at the KPH. Suddenly, two

minutes before the offices of the Royal Borough of Kensington and Chelsea closed for the weekend – gateway to any publican's most lucrative period – Vince Power lost his licence on a technicality: he kept the licence but lost the ability to operate it because his 'Designated Supervisory Officer' on the local authority – without whom a pub cannot legally function – was removed by the landlord.

On Tuesday 23 December, Power served his clientele without a licence. The following evening, Christmas Eve, with a jazz show sung by Loretta King scheduled, the beer taps were covered. Power, running at a loss, called the occasion 'a service to the regulars', who were allowed to bring their own drink, conditional upon having retained a receipt and proof of purchase elsewhere. A few ordered the coffee or soft drinks Power was allowed to sell. For Christmas lunchtime, a notice was pinned to the door: 'Private Party, Invitation Only.'

The authority which took away the licence was that which has overseen the transformation of Notting Hill: the Royal Borough of Kensington and Chelsea, which as recently as 2014 produced a 'core strategy' lamenting 'the continued loss of the borough's stock of public houses' that 'offer a source of identity and distinctiveness'.

Let's see, we thought: maybe there are people on the Kensington council who want to preserve what is left of our community. Who maybe are even *determined* to do so. Let's see who they are, whether they care a damn about anything other than the big money. If the KPH could survive, we'd have a reason to believe that there might still be some slim hope for the notion of community and democracy in London, some faint faith in the local authorities, we thought.

I asked SWA's director, Steven Archer, what his plans were. 'The bailiffs,' he said, 'are ready and I've instructed my managing agents to install a new manager and keep the pub open. We don't yet know what exactly we'll do with the property, but I'd like to see the pub remain as a pub.' That was late 2015, and it was true for a while: the KPH limped on, diminished, melancholic.

But in the event, goodbye it was. On St Patrick's Day 2016, of all days, Power lost his final appeal. People arrived at the pub that evening for Irish dancing and festivity, but it was bittersweet, laughter laden with doom. 'I've lost a fortune in my life,' said Power, looking out from his corner at the rain wrapping Ladbroke Grove, people passing by. 'And I've had to say goodbye to many people, many things. But no goodbye would be quite as hard as this one.'

A couple of weeks later, crowds converged for the wake – from what is left of the community and from among those whom the speculators had expelled elsewhere – for the last supper, the farewell as bitter as it was defiant. On the stroke of midnight, last orders were taken for the final time after 150 years. On came the lights and up went the volume: Edith Piaf's 'Non, Je Ne Regrette Rien', and Sinatra's 'My Way', sung from the heart and a hundred pairs of lungs. Next morning, a truck arrived and men to load the fridges, unfinished barrels, bar stools. It was a white truck, but it was Notting Hill's – London's – black hearse. Eighteen months later the pub is boarded up. People have sprayed the hoardings with bright colours, and written 'RIP' – as well they might, whether for the pub, Grenfell Tower or just the whole damned thing.

PEOPLE'S ART IN A TIME OF CRISIS

Nicolette Jones

2017 HAS BEEN a year of trauma in the UK, and not least in London: the Westminster Bridge attack, the London Bridge atrocities, the Grenfell Tower fire, the van attack at Finsbury Park, the bucket bomb at Parson's Green. Against a backdrop of austerity policies that have led to a widening social divide and dangerous cost-cutting in the area of health and safety; the perceived undermining of the National Health Service; and the rejection of the Dubs amendment, which offered safe haven to unaccompanied refugee children, Londoners have taken to the street. And we have not only protested; we have built shrines. Political outrage and personal grief have been widely processed through poetry and folk art.

I live in Finsbury Park, a diverse area which became, because of the Islamophobic attack by Darren Osborne, a beacon of the celebration of multiculturalism. With one voice, the neighbours of the Finsbury Park Mosque declared their horror at the terrorist hate crime on their doorstep, and their appreciation of their own melting-pot. A vigil, a demonstration against racism, a parade of non-Muslims giving roses to their Muslim fellow residents, and a communal street iftar, in which locals of every faith and ethnicity sat down together along the full length of the road outside the mosque, to break fast during Ramadan, were manifestations of this apparently unanimous emotion.

But it was not only through gatherings that the mood was communicated. Flowers and notes were left in their hundreds outside the mosque, beneath the bridge by Finsbury Park Tube station and in front of the Muslim Welfare Centre where the attack took place. As happened in Kensington after the Grenfell Tower fire, a huge blank sheet of paper was attached to the railings of the mosque with a box of crayons, inviting declarations of support, sympathy and warmth from passers-by. 'We are one community' and 'These are your streets', said the contributors. Most conspicuous was one which read: 'Love will reign.'

But such sentiments were not just passing words – they were inscribed in colour, personalised with handprints and rainbow fountains. Schools and classes collaged the work of individual children into posters, with recurrent motifs: the peace sign, hearts, doves and rainbows, all filled in with bright felt pen, and some depicting the Earth, clasped hands, families or London landmarks. They were the children's representations of global unity and friendship.

Many of those who left messages found decorative ways to embellish them. Among the artwork that appeared in the area was a – homemade? – red heart cutout with delicate fretwork, including a bird and butterflies, and interwoven with pieces of torn paper on which were written '#onelondon' and '#westandtogether'. It was more than a message; it was an ornament.

Some contributions went beyond words: small children had contributed a colourful row of paper dolls. And a wallful of white butterflies was stuck to the bricks under Finsbury Park railway bridge. This astonishing non-verbal installation was a communication, suggesting peace and gentleness. Perhaps the medium aimed to be universal, and to touch people who spoke any language.

This wordless creativity allowed everyone to take part. Adding an element of craft can involve more observers and more makers, including those too young to write. The offering that outlasted the clearance of all the dried-up flowers and plants and rain-soaked cards on the railings of the mosque was a large sheet on which the words 'You Are Loved' were spelt out in pompoms. These varied in size and colour, as if each might have been made by a different child in a class, choosing one or several colours of wool and cutting out bigger or smaller card circles; a craft activity was turned into a gesture of humanity.

Perhaps inclusivity, for creators or observers, is one reason people turn to making art in a crisis. Though it is clearly not the only reason. Partly it must be for the effect – because images have impact. The marches of 2017 – the women's marches that took place all over the world on the day after Donald Trump's inauguration, as well as those against the Muslim ban, in support of the NHS, to defend the environment, show solidarity with Europe, the Pride march and more – were evidence of the resurgence of the homemade placard, with all its power and distinctiveness.

Although signs were provided by interested organisations, the majority were handmade, for individual expression. The making became an intrinsic part of the protesting, just as the 'pussy-hats' of the women's marches made use of a traditionally female skill – knitting – to satirise Trump's misogyny and demonstrate unity. Every stitch bound people together.

Whether the art is verbal or visual, it has this characteristic: unlike most of the artistic creations in these genres that go public, the art of protest and grief is not curated. The poetry bypasses books or other edited publications, and performances programmed by selectors. Apart from open mic sessions, we rarely encounter unmediated poems. Meanwhile art, other than graffiti and Banksy-esque guerrilla murals, is for galleries, unless it is commercial art made by professionals. The folk art of resistance and trauma is truly of the people. We make it unselfconsciously, without fear of judgement of our skill. It is not to be marked, assessed or reviewed.

So when, for instance, the vicar of a church close to the Grenfell Tower, Father Alan Everett of St Clements, turned to poetry in the aftermath of the fire, his heartfelt utterance made the newspapers, when it would not have made it into anthologies on literary grounds alone. Although many of the products of anger and sorrow are things of beauty, no one minds about the level of skill, nor is anyone deterred by ineptness.

We are simply reminded that making things comes out of the depths of us, and fulfils a profound need. And that creative acts are crucial to channelling and managing emotion. Such reactions to what truly shakes us are proof that art is not peripheral to human experience. It is what we turn to when we are most moved. When the chips are down, it is clear it is necessary. And it can also be the best way of saying: 'You Are Loved.'

THE CIRCUS COMES TO TOWN

Tom Dyckhoff

AN AMUSING SERIES of Tweets did the rounds the day that Britain entered the second plunge of its double-dip recession, the first of its kind since the 1970s. 'London has a giant ferris wheel and a high-altitude cable car,' went one. 'And a clown for a mayor,' replied another, alluding to the self-conscious media buffoonery of its then mayor Boris Johnson. 'The Barnum Conspiracy?' questioned another Tweeter. 'London is being circusified.' Bread and circuses has long been a hackneyed metaphor for political attempts to quell the seething masses with treats and theatrics, ever since the tactic was used repeatedly by the emperors of ancient Rome. But London of late does seem to be taking it rather literally.

In order to see the circus, we must leave Old Street roundabout and get onto the Tube Northern Line to London Bridge again, then Jubilee Line to North Greenwich. The circus's big tent is easy to spot. What was once called the Millennium Dome is now the O2 Arena, after its sponsorship deal with the telecommunications giant. The Dome, and the exhibition built inside for the 2000 millennium celebrations, the Millennium Experience, its budget approaching £1 billion, was such a colossal, monumental, iconic failure that it haunted the then new, fresh and optimistic government of Tony Blair for years to come. However, since then, in private hands, it has become the most financially successful music and entertainment venue in the world. This icon, a failure in its first life, has been rehabilitated. The project is ongoing. The Dome's latest wheeze is Up at The O2, the most recent in a new breed of what might be called architectural extreme sports – such as climbing the Sydney Opera House – in which from the 'base camp' you can scale the heights of the Dome, and gaze, from the top, at the landscape all around.

What you can see from up here, the Greenwich Peninsula, was once dubbed the 'black hole of London', a marshy land of gas works and gravel extraction plants, some of which stubbornly refused to disappear to make way for the festival future planned for it for more than 20 years. This project is also ongoing. At night, the area around the Dome comes into its own, like a salaryman who lives for Friday nights. The landscape inside and out is transformed into lights fantastic, *son et lumière* and videoscreens all themed to the act performing onstage in the big tent. It is a landscape of hyperactivity, designed to get visitors in the mood. During the day, though, a sleepier air descends. It seems mostly populated by parties of school children and East Europeans from local building sites, both groups munching sandwiches on the vast shadeless plazas, though never the twain shall meet. Despite such thrills as Up at The O2, and the legion of superstars that perform within it, the Greenwich Peninsula has never yet quite escaped that forlorn air that clings to it, attractive only to lovers of melancholy, estuarine landscapes.

As if to compensate, the O2 has spawned a landscape of wide-eyed urgency, like an overdressed wallflower trying to catch the eye of dancers at a disco. Office blocks are plastered in gaudy walls. A gigantic prong of twisting metal, apropos of nothing, simply announces its own existence and place in the world. They are what town planners and developers call 'markers' or 'gateways', three-dimensional exclamation marks. The state continues to pour money into the Greenwich Peninsula to court private investment – cleaning up its contaminated past, building a Tube line, a model village, the world's most successful entertainment venue; there is no end to the largesse. They come, but – a little like those who came to the Millennium Experience – never quite in the numbers expected. Almost two decades on, the O2 is still mostly surrounded by hopes rather than buildings. Like much of the east of London, the retreat of industry in the 1960s and 1970s has left behind so much land there's not quite enough future-with-a-viable-business-plan-attached to fill it. Maybe the newest plan will do the trick. In 2012, the peninsula was bought by Hong Kong developer Knight Dragon for around £786m. 'The idea is to create a hi-tech village for arty, foodie, design-savvy Londoners,' the *Evening Standard* explains.

The latest addition to the circus is, with perfect economic symbolism, a high wire act. That high-altitude cable car is open for business. Though business is not quite booming. It is hard to know what to call the Emirates Air Line, as the cable car is called. Is it a piece of public transport? Or a theme-park ride? Or both? The (historically richer) half of the capital west of London Bridge has dozens of river crossings; the other (historically poorer) eastern half of London has just one bridge, two tunnels and a ferry, all the product of 19th- and 20th-century industry. This part of town needs river crossings. But it is not altogether clear that the Emirates Air Line is quite right for the job. The first new crossing over the River Thames since the millennium cost about £60m, more than half of it funded by the Dubai-owned airline, the rest by public funds. Such overt private sponsorship of public infrastructure has become commonplace in cities. Someone has to pay for the public life. Though there are strings attached.

In theory this cable car can transport 2,500 people an hour. If only they would use it. In July 2014, London radio station LBC found that just 44 people got on board during an average rush hour. To reach it from North Greenwich Tube station involves a dash of several hundred metres across sun-bleached or rain-soaked car parks. And maybe Emirates knows something I don't about the future prospects of this patch of London, because right now all this multimillion-pound chain of steel seems to link is one giant empty car park in a neighbourhood where very few people live to another giant empty car park in a neighbourhood where very few people live. Defending his creation, the then mayor Boris Johnson, as always, protested too much: 'On school holidays, later in the day it absolutely starts heaving. This thing already covers its cost. The cable car is still sensational value ... It is a howling success.'

If Emirates wanted to invest in London's transport network, I'm sure most Londoners could have suggested something more useful. Round here a bridge would come in handy, for instance. But that would be to mistake the actual point of the cable car. It exists not so much to be useful as to be talked about. There was some disquiet when the Emirates brand name appeared on the London Underground map, a design classic dating from 1931, a time when the state was stepping up its role in the management of public life after another period of speculative excess by the corporate world. The cable car itself, though, is branding in three dimensions, not two. This is not so much about getting from A to B quickly, the harried commuter's clear aim, as about branded thrill-seeking. It is a fairground attraction, a theme-park ride, thinly disguised as a piece of public transport. Very thinly disguised.

Around £9 pays for a return trip of fifteen minutes or so. Or, for £88, you can exclusively hire a whole cabin, for a (very brief) birthday celebration, perhaps. At the ticket office, you are greeted with a huge banner: 'See London like you've never seen it before.' Before you travel, you may visit the 'Aviation Experience', a flight simulator. The brand-aware illusion of airflight is rigorously enforced throughout. The stations at either end are called 'terminals', the tickets 'boarding passes'. Another billboard invites you to 'Share the view from your journey' on Twitter, using the hashtag #MyEmiratesView. As if to reinforce the point, each of the cabins is covered in Emirates advertising: 'Experience a new way to see Mumbai.'

The cable car itself is impressive: three thrilling towers of twisting metal, 295 feet high. The sights you can see from the top! I get on with a mother and two middle-aged daughters down in London for a day trip. They are very excited. 'If I start hyperventilating, grab me.' 'I hope it doesn't go upside-down.' The cabin rocks free of terra firma. 'Ooooo!' 'I'm a bit scared, actually.' 'At least there's no sharks in the Thames.' 'Oh my God, we're really dangling in thin air.' The cabin steadies. The phones come out, poses are struck. 'Could you get my slim side, please?' 'I don't much like the Millennium Dome, so I'm not taking a picture of that.' 'Me neither. Those sticky-out things look like they're made out of pipe cleaners.' We arrive, a little quicker than expected. 'Is that it?' 'I think I preferred the London Eye.' 'So where's this then?' A very good question. They stay for a coffee, gaze at the expensive apartment blocks, and briefly peer into the Crystal, another brand experience disguised as public service, in this case 'the world's largest exhibition about our urban future' courtesy of electronics firm Siemens, though our urban future seems pretty obvious from the landscape around. Then, with nothing else to tempt them, they get back on the cable car for the return journey.

THE LEAFLETS

Ferdous Sadat

I am carrying a big bag full of leaflets
for a Pakistani restaurant called Lahori
There are so many of them, maybe 600
and every one I have to put through a letter box

One huge building on Edgware Road is called Park West
Maybe 800 flats in this one place
So normally I am in there for two hours at least
I always go up in the lift to the very top, floor 8,
And then work my way back down

Today, on the third floor by the stairs
I find a £50 note. And I take it
And I finish the leaflets for the third floor,
and the second one
And the first

And then I stay there, at the main door
next to my bike, and I hold the £50 note in my hand
So that anybody walking by can see it
And I look for people with tension or stress,
who maybe have lost the money

And I watch many different people
From many different countries
Black, white, tall, short, man, boy, children,
two Arab ladies with a lot of shopping bags
Who I have to help through the door

And some people go one way and then come back the other
And I remember the first time I ever came to Edgware Road
When I lost my way as I tried to get to work
Four hours!
And every street, building, house all looking the same

And so today, when I have waited for a long time
maybe three hours
And nobody says that the money is theirs
I decide to give this £50 to charity
For poor people.

And I am happy. But when I get back to the shop
I still have some leaflets which I have not delivered
because I have been waiting all that time, watching people
       pass
And because I have to give the leaflets back I get paid less
But not so much. It is all OK

DOUBLE WHAMMY

Helen Simpson

LONDON

IT WAS A Monday towards the end of 2016, the dregs of that
shock-delivering year, and it was still dark: winter. I was driving
to City airport for the first plane to Zürich, my flight bag packed
with samples of powdered dulse plus a pair of fair-isle gloves for
Alina.

The roads still weren't too busy at that time of day. Somewhere round Leytonstone I drew up in the middle lane of three
at some lights, unsure which to take, then realised it should have
been the right-hand lane and flipped on my indicator. Since
there was a single car on my right and a clear lane to the left
I was surprised when a van drew up behind me. In the mirror
through the dim dawn I could see the baldhead driver in sil-
houette waving his arms around and banging them down on the
steering wheel.

I stayed expressionless, unresponsive, as the least provoca-
tive reaction. Or were you now supposed to be assertive back? I
couldn't remember what the current thinking was on this.

The lights must change soon. He seemed to be in a terrible
rage. Solo women drivers did sometimes have this effect of course.
The situation was not unprecedented.

My heart was beating fast and I had gone into automatic

cringe mode; I had to remind myself that there was no logical reason why he couldn't have taken the free left-hand lane.

That is what he did next. He drew up on the left alongside my car and I could see his face contorted by whatever it was he was screaming at me.

He wound down his window and leaned over. Then he punched out my wing mirror just as the lights started to change.

I stalled.

He roared off in a spume of exhaust.

'Where did that come from?' I asked myself as I started the car again. 'Am I *that* bad?'

I continued to drive, the left-side wing mirror dangling from a tangle of wires. There was nothing else to do, there was nowhere I could stop to check the damage anyway, so I kept on.

This was one way to shock-start the day, though by no means as shocking as the way it would shock-finish. But I'm getting ahead of myself.

LONDON CITY AIRPORT

By the time I had collected my boarding pass and quarantined my lipstick in a sealed plastic bag and reached the other side of security at City airport, my adrenalin levels were almost back to normal. I was in plenty of time, as I kept reminding myself, and I had not been hurt; in fact I'd been lucky really.

The trick was to stop thinking about it and change the subject.

How much longer would it be, I asked myself politely as I tucked my passport back into my handbag along with my lipstick, before we needed to apply for visas to visit Europe? Soon we would have to learn how to queue again.

I found myself repacking my flight bag beneath a sign which read:

Have you left anything behind?
N'avez vous rien oublié?
Hai lasciato nulla dietro?
Ha degrade nada atrás?

Well might they ask! Would the company survive? Since school days I had been cheered by the look of these languages, the sound of them, and the knowledge that everything was different just across the Channel. The dream of Europe. Would I still have a job next year?

At the departure gate I took one of the newspapers on offer. The US election results had hit earth like a meteorite two weeks before and the world was still reeling. This tabloid at least seemed pleased with the way things were going. Here was a piece on family values, aimed at Thanksgiving the following Thursday. We had crashed out overnight back in June; now America had followed suit. Thanksgiving!

7.00 FLIGHT: LONDON (LCY) – ZÜRICH (ZRH)

As we lifted over the Thames I felt advance grief for the damage sustained by my adopted city. London had been dealt a body blow in June. It knew this and it was in a state of dismay.

I skimmed a piece about what good holiday fun you could have walking Hadrian's Wall now that the pound had nose-dived against the euro. Nostalgia, formerly wistful, was these days downright belligerent. When I was growing up in the '70s certain beliefs were beginning to gain acceptance, which had felt like progress then: peace is better than war; nationalism is dangerous; women are people too. Now they wanted us to return to the past, to go back to where we came from, but it wasn't possible. Things had moved on!

'Lying should be made illegal,' I said to my neighbour, stabbing at the newspaper with my index finger.

'That cannot happen,' he said, smiling darkly.

'Truth!' I insisted, crumpling up the paper and treading it beneath my feet.

He was from Athens, he told me, the cradle of democracy. Did I know Greece, he asked; yes, and had loved it ever since I first went as a student, I told him.

'When were you there? Eighty-two? The best times!' he said. 'Before the ones came in who destroyed the country.'

He had just spent the weekend with his brother, who ran a taverna in Chiswick, and in a couple of hours would be back at work in the Zürich hotel where he was assistant manager. He had moved to Switzerland some 20 years ago and was married to a woman from Frauenfeld with whom he had a daughter who was away on a few months' work experience in Auckland before starting her ophthalmology degree in Nottingham.

My turn, and I told him a little about Daisy Whole Foods. As I am used to reciting, we're a one-off independent company supplying multiple outlets across the EU with the latest health ingredient or umami flavour from home and abroad. When I started out, muesli was exotic and brown bread was for eccentrics; now, I supplied three varieties of iodine-rich Scottish seaweed to delicatessens from Sussex to Berlin and nobody batted an eyelid.

We paused as the coffee trolley drew up beside us. I checked my handbag for the envelope of Swiss francs; last time I'd forgotten it and packed euros by mistake. Zürich was savagely expensive so this would be my last coffee for today, I remarked.

'It is good we keep our currency in Switzerland,' he said. 'An island surrounded by mountains!'

'We had that,' I said glumly. 'We'd hung on to sterling and we really *are* an island. But we still voted out.'

'You do not agree?'

'No!'

'Why?'

I thought for a moment.

'I think we will all be poorer.'

Whether Daisy Whole Foods would survive future customs duties was a real worry. We had always operated on slender margins and the businesses from which we ordered were mostly the same. So it would be the easiest thing in the world for any or all of us to go under if the market turned against us. And of course another way we would take a hit would be if our warehouse staff went back to Latvia and Poland.

He saw all that.

'Also, the dream of Europe,' I said.

'What is dream of Europe?' I thought again.

'Unity,' I said at last.

'*No* such thing!' he crowed. '*No* such thing! Look at Bavaria, Bavaria doesn't even want to be in Germany! All over this happens. This happens for *every* country.'

'Maybe the German prime minister will find a way,' I said. 'She's the best politician there's been for a while.'

'Now?' he said with a curl of his lip. 'Now? No! What she do *now*? She have let it fall like sand through her fingers.'

He rubbed his fingers in the air to illustrate his point.

'How do you mean?'

'Think. A stranger needs help. OK. This is life. In Greece, yes, old tradition of hospitality. I *know* this. I say to stranger, come to my house, I give you meal, I give you ten pounds, good luck to you my friend.'

He paused.

'*Not*, "Bring 50 friends!"' he added, with withering scorn.

'Oh,' I said.

At this he gave a curt little nod and turned to his phone screen. I found myself gazing out of the plane window at the sunlit uplands of the cumulus clouds beyond, and soon I had segued into that blessed state of inflight freedom: temporary immunity from the demands of the terrestrial world.

My neighbour's comments chimed with something I'd heard the week before. Scraps from different conversations floated around in a confused jumble. When was it that I'd recently heard an opinion like that? Wasn't it last Tuesday?

Yes, it was when I'd gone out to Palmer's Green to meet Attila, a young Hungarian who had recently launched an organic jam start-up using his grandmother's recipes. Attila's preserves were really something; almost 90 per cent fruit, barely any added sugar, jewel-coloured and runny and intensely flavoured. Once we had agreed on the order he'd offered coffee.

'So,' I said, 'your prime minister has been making speeches.'

'Yes.'

'What does he want?'

'He is in favour of family. Increase in family.'

'What, he wants no contraception like the man in Turkey?'

'No, no. Not that. But he says, with tax we help people, *our* people, have more children.'

'Oh.'

'I think he is right.'

'But *why*? Why do you want more people? I thought the problem was, too many people.'

'More our *own* people.'

'Oh.'

'It is different mentality,' he insisted. 'Here in UK you have sea all round. Us, look at history. First World War, after this 90 per cent of our land gone. We are invaded all the time. *Invaded.*'

'The Austro-Hungarian Empire. Yes.'

'You have visited Hungary?'

'No. I'd like to. I once visited some fruit farms in Romania; but not Hungary.'

'Romania.' He gave a curious tight-lipped smile. 'You visit Transylvania? Transylvania once part of Hungary. You visit, in all villages of Transylvania they are speaking Hungarian.'

'I remember hearing some brilliant gypsy musicians from Transylvania.'

'Gypsies: *they* are Romanian. But all others, Hungarian.'

'Oh.'

This exchange had lodged in me, and later in the week, Friday it had been, when out visiting my old friend Rayna in Turnpike Lane – her probiotic-packed Bulgarian-style yoghurt, thick, creamy and deliciously sour, is one of our bestselling lines – I had repeated it to her, the gist of it.

'Turks razed Hungary to the ground three times,' she'd nodded. '*Three!* Not a blade of grass. Turks invaded us, yes; Turks, then Communists; but not three times like with Hungary. That is why he says that.'

After that our talk had turned, as it generally did, to her daughter Sofija, her pride and joy, who was studying for a law degree in Cologne. The last time they'd Skyped, Sofia had described how she felt bad that some of her fellow-students would not shake hands with the female tutors or stay in the same room as them, how this made her want to say something, to object; except this would not go down well, Sofija had said, so she kept quiet, which also made her feel bad.

Was it wiser to keep quiet at times like these? I wondered, looking out over the cloudscape. Or, to be more specific, was it safer for women to keep quiet at times like these?

Anyway, these were the Londoners I knew, the ones I worked with; incontrovertibly metropolitan but by no means universally liberal. As for elite, that depended on what you meant by elite. If you meant, enviable for being in work, then yes; also, to use that passive-aggressive phrase, hard-working. Spit it out: London's heart pumped lifeblood round the rest of the country. This was not an ideal situation but it was hardly London's fault.

ZÜRICH

Standing close-packed in urban dislocation in the funnel-like train whisking us from air terminal to passport control, there was only the disembodied bleating of goats over the sound system and the occasional tinkle of cowbells to identify the country in which we had landed. This was the land of Heidi, it seemed, the little orphan girl packed off to her rustic grandfather in the Alps who had discovered her health and true nature by sleeping on a fragrant hay-stuffed mattress and drinking milk straight from the cow.

Following the Leytonstone incident earlier that morning, I was hoping for a relatively stress-free day in the money-insulated tram-gliding neutrality of this compact city. It was almost like I felt I was owed it. Funny, looking back.

Once through passport control, I paused by a wall of illuminated ads to work out where I was. Heidi, so recently introduced, was here conspicuous by her absence. A gigantic banker, surveying the world from his skyscraper eyrie, brooded over the quality of his parenting skills. 'Time is precious – waste it wisely,' read the solemn rubric beneath a jewelled watch. Nothing made sense any more.

It happened sometimes, you lost your bearings. Where was the old compass? The mariner's ability to steer by the stars? Having grown over-reliant on satnav we had turned off that part of our brains.

I found the tram-stop right away though it took another five minutes before I worked out which direction to take.

SPIEGELGASSE, ZÜRICH

Zürich's air was like crystal after London's diesel soup. The time had come round to meet Alina for lunch, and I felt hopeful and energised. It had been a good morning's work and I'd taken multiple orders, the peat-smoked salmon in demand as always but the new laverbread from Laugharne proving a hit too. Also, in a rare coals-to-Newcastle triumph, I had sold a big batch of the London Fields muesli to a vegan restaurant recently converted from an insolvent auto repair shop out in Zuriwest.

As usual, the Bahnhofstrasse appointments had not taken very long. The more interesting food stores and specialist muesli shops were across the Limat on the left bank, tucked in among the Guild houses, in the compact cobbled medieval part of the city. This was where I had arranged to meet my old friend Alina, on Spiegelgasse, for a sandwich.

It was good to see her smiling face.

'Everything has changed in the world since we last met,' I said as we embraced.

'Not us!' she said.

'The last six months have put years on me,' I said, producing the fair-isle gloves from my bag. 'Here, I saw these on a trip to Lewis and Harris and I had to get them for you. And this tweed purse for Jana.'

We had been friends since even before I met Bruno. When I married him 23 years ago they had come over for our wedding, which was a bigger deal in those days than it is now. He was losing sleep, I told her now as she held up her woollen-patterned hands to admire them; he was having nightmares that he'd be forced to go back and live with his angry old mother in Genoa. No, he had never applied for British citizenship; why would he when we were part of Europe? But since June of course everything had been uncertain. Nobody knew where they belonged any more.

'He says he thinks of himself as a Londoner,' I said. 'In which case we're both Londoners. We grew up with each other in London. We grew into it.'

'That is what I feel about Zürich and Jana,' said Alina, firing up. 'A city gives freedom!'

Alina was one of nine sisters, and had grown up in the Berner Oberland, high in the Swiss Alps. Her parents kept cows and made cheese, as their parents had done before them, and also a little herd of nine donkeys named after their daughters. Every Christmas there was a group photograph where each girl was made to stand beside her long-eared namesake, until Alina one year refused and broke the pattern.

'Terrible,' she said, shaking her head.

Jana was over near Chur visiting her own parents, trying to untangle some problem with the broadband provider. Meanwhile their idea of a good day out in their late 70s (said Alina, laughing), was to drive across the border into Austria to one of the butchers which had set up shop there for Swiss customers like them. Everything was very expensive in Switzerland, particularly if you had retired; meat, for example, cost a fortune. You had to be careful to get whatever you bought weighed with great exactitude; even a little over and the Swiss customs officials who weighed the meat on the way back would slap on a massive fine. That had once happened to a friend of theirs, a joint of beef 13 grams over the limit had turned out to be the most expensive meat they'd ever eaten.

'The world has gone a little bit Dada,' said Alina.

'Dada, eh? I saw a poster for some Dada thing at the station.'

'It started here in Zürich a hundred years ago, that's why there are celebrations.'

'Some sort of protest art, was it? Why "Dada"?'

'That word Dada is a baby word: regression. They shouted "Dada!" at tavern doors then they ran away.'

'Why not Mama?'

'Dada, Mama,' Alina said, shrugging. The Dadaists had gone in for masks and mooing and hiccuping, trances and sound poems and playing invisible violins. If I spotted someone standing on a street corner spouting nonsense or miming some random action, she added, it would likely be the last of the year's centennial celebrations.

'Funny you should say that,' I said, and told her about the random wing-mirror performance which had started my day. 'Dada or what?'

'Disgusting,' said Alina, her face wiped clear of amusement.

'You can see I'm fine though. You don't need to worry about me.'

'Not funny,' she said, shaking her head. 'No, not funny at all.'

Soon after that it was time for us both to get back to work.

'Stay safe,' we said as we hugged. 'Stay in touch.'

17.46 TRAIN: ZÜRICH HB - ZÜRICH FLUGHAFEN

Later that afternoon, my remaining appointments concluded, I'd had time to dawdle en route to the station past shop windows full of sparkle and chocolate gnomes and silver roses. Trundling my flight bag across the cobbles I had paused at some Christkindli market stalls, professional eye caught by the homemade gingerbread bears and the vacuum-packed hunks of locally-smoked ham and cheese on sale from a group of women who were laughing with each other and stamping their feet against the cold. I'd also looked at a stall hung with Moroccan fretted lanterns and then at another where painted wooden dolls and eggs were stacked high against a display of black T-shirts emblazoned with the Russian president's face in sunglasses; but in the end I'd gone back and bought some Appenzeller from the women I had first noticed.

Now safely on the train for the airport I examined the cheese label for contact details in case they might be useful in the future, and remembered the laughing women. Imagine actually coming from somewhere, I thought; imagine having roots.

My father had been self-expelled from the north and my mother's childhood marked by rent-dodging flits from county to county. Dada, Mama. Dad had voted out. It's not that I don't get it. I come from there, I come from the other side. I grew up in the steady seethe of money-resentment at those who were 'rolling in it'. Back into my mind returned a phone call I had had with him in June.

As neutrally as I could, I had asked him what he thought of the result.

'I'm not surprised actually. These people who seem so devastated – are these the people with lots of investments? Rolling in it, lots of them, absolutely rolling in it. I'm eking out a very small pension, things are very tight. 1945, I'm reminded of 1945 when the whole country turfed out Churchill. Yesterday I went to a concert, they did a sort of mock-up of the last night of the Proms. There was a choir of 200 – "Land of Hope and Glory", sea shanties, tremendous patriotism. Marvellous! You could have cut the emotion with a knife.'

'So you think it was a lot of stuck-up rich people getting their comeuppance?'

'Yes that's about it. My own circumstances are very tight, I'm on a very small pension. I worry about the upkeep. My next-door neighbour is complaining about the lime tree at the front, he says it drops sticky leaves on his cars. Two cars! New cars! One's a BMW! Anyway, he wants me to cut down the tree.'

'Fine, if he pays.'

'That's an idea. Maybe I'll offer to pay half.'

'But I thought you said he was rolling in it?'

'Yes, he is. He's not a bad neighbour though. I don't want to get on the wrong side of him.'

Dad's lot were Newcastle but after a five-year apprenticeship at Doxford's he'd seen the way the wind was blowing and come down south.

'By the '60s we were viewed as lazy,' he once told me. 'Complacent. In the Hamburg shipyard I visited they were working round the clock, three eight-hour shifts, and the men were provided with clean overalls, washing spaces, cubicles for their home clothes. Back in England our men were still walking or cycling back home in their filth to a tin bath, there were no facilities provided as there were in Germany. Why? Now you're asking. It was what it was.'

ZÜRICH AIRPORT

I stood in the shiny area of shops and ticket offices and jewel-bright digital Arrival and Departure screens. There was my flight onscreen, ZRH – LCY 19.10. I was in good time, I saw, glancing at my watch: 18.02. No need quite yet to take the escalator up to security.

I spotted a co-op nearby and decided to buy some chocolate for the office. The other customers were in tracksuits rather than pinstripe, and this struck me as a place you might pick up some shopping if you worked at or near the airport and wanted to take something home for dinner.

A tall young man, his curly mop restrained by a plastic hairband, was joking with a couple of girls in pink aprons; he was the manager, I reckoned, so I paused to ask the whereabouts of the ready-grated rösti packets. It had been a good trip, successful meetings all day; I could afford to relax at last. Once I had located the chocolates and the rösti I joined the queue. It was quite a long queue and there was only one cashier, but even this I found relaxing rather than otherwise as I allowed myself to turn off at last.

From the next shopping aisle came some oddly disjointed sounds, a few grunts and gasps. Along with several others in the queue I craned my neck to peer round the corner in the direction of the noise.

Something was going on though it was unclear quite what.

In front of a frozen meats cabinet, three men with startled

expressions were sitting on somebody. A shoplifter? Had they just wrestled a shoplifter to the ground? Beside them the young shop manager with the plastic hairband stood wild-eyed, punching numbers into his mobile phone.

What was going on?

The queue shuffled forward, the cashier carried on bagging up and taking payment.

In the opposite aisle a young South Asian woman stood looking down at the floor in silent concentration as she leaned against a tower of boxed beer bottles. The fair-haired shop assistant in a pink apron beside her seemed to be half-supporting her, murmuring words of encouragement. Was she having contractions?

The queue was very slow. 18.23 – I should still be fine for my flight though I mustn't hang about. I was next in line for the cashier.

Not much was visible of the one being sat on; only his square hands, which were bunched into fists, and a slice of his expressionless face. He looked to be North African.

The cashier pushed the card machine towards me. As I punched in my PIN number there came a soft communal gasp from those standing behind me.

Turning round, I saw another pink-aproned shop assistant holding a long knife aloft for us to witness, as if she were in some sort of mime art revue. Her face was blank with shock.

A tribute performance of the sort Alina had warned me about? Some wacky cabaret sketch in the birthplace of Dada?

'*Scheisse*,' said the cashier.

The manager, still worriedly punching numbers into his mobile phone, started to shoo his customers from the shop. As we filed out I looked over towards the young woman leaning against the beer tower. In that same moment the fair girl at her side lifted the wad of kitchen roll she was holding against her and I saw scarlet on the white T-shirt.

The knife. The man. The man had stabbed her with the knife.

Why hadn't she screamed? Why was nobody shouting for a doctor?

This silence and her grim stoicism were awful.

The shop's glass doors slid closed behind us. In the distance I saw some flaxen-haired youngsters in police uniform approaching. Glancing at my watch again I saw it was 18.29. I wanted to shout 'Hurry up! Something terrible is happening here!' as they strolled towards us, but was struck dumb.

Two of the policemen were let into the shop while one was left on guard outside.

Surely now they would realise the urgency of the situation, I thought, as I watched them questioning the manager. If they did though they were certainly not overreacting.

Through the glass I saw the wounded woman sink to the ground and slide down out of sight behind the boxes of beer.

Didn't she matter?

'Doctor?' I said to the young policeman on guard. I pointed at the window.

He ignored me. Maybe he didn't speak English.

Unfortunately my German vocabulary was limited to the subjects of food and commerce.

I tapped 'doctor' into Google Translate, then tried again.

'Arzt?' I said feebly.

Unsmilingly he raised his hand to block further talk, and made it clear that I should go away.

19.10 FLIGHT: ZÜRICH (ZRH) – LONDON (LCY)

I reached the gate just as my flight was boarding.

During the preparations for takeoff the bad-dream feeling persisted. It felt wrong, morally wrong, to be lifting away physically from what had just happened.

We were up in the air, the last flight of the evening. It wasn't packed. On my right in the window-seat was a young woman in her 20s. Her hair was tidy and sleek, her clothes formal, and she had some sort of business report in her hand. I took out my own set of orders from the day but found I couldn't concentrate on them.

I closed my eyes and the events of the last hour replayed themselves in disjointed tableaux: the shocked face of the young manager framed by his plastic hairband; the knife held aloft; the grim silence of the woman who had been stabbed in the back; the blood.

I tried sorting my orders again, but couldn't settle.

When the drinks trolley paused at our row my neighbour ordered a coffee. She smiled politely as it was passed across me.

I thought, no I mustn't; and then I did.

'Such a weird thing happened just now at the airport,' I said, 'I saw something shocking. I wonder if you'd tell me if I'm overreacting? But I've got to tell someone.'

Her smile of assent was lukewarm and who could blame her, but I was old enough to be her mother so I ploughed on. I told her the story as far as I knew it, including the cashier's '*scheisse*' and the scarlet against the white T-shirt and the surreal torpor of the police.

'That is shocking,' she agreed. 'You're right. For the emergency services to be so slow, and in an airport too.'

This security angle was the element which seemed to interest her, but I felt she was missing the point.

'I think she might have been trafficked,' I said. 'It looked like that somehow.'

'Unless she was his wife,' said my neighbour. 'He could have gotten mad at her. Like, totally lost it.'

'The most basic human right of all, your right over the body you were born into, unbelievably that seems to be called into question again,' I burst out. 'You're young, you're young enough to be my daughter so I hope you make sure you fight for your body's rights!'

There was a pause.

'I'm also thinking of those shoppers in the co-op on their way home after work and the way they tackled him. So brave! And you know, looking round at the men on this plane, men in suits, I'm afraid I'm finding it hard to imagine them risking themselves in the same way to tackle that thug and his knife.'

I cast my gaze over the spry young passengers in the seats around us.

'Maybe they would have,' she said.

This shamed me from my prejudice, temporarily.

It was time to change the subject. I didn't want her thinking I was a madwoman. Of course it meant less to her, she hadn't seen it at first hand. To her it was no more shocking than something viewed online.

'You're from Australia, right?' I said.

'My accent, yeah. From Melbourne.'

'I'm a Londoner.'

'I love London. London's great!'

Was, I thought: *was* great. I did not say this out loud, however; I had ranted enough at the poor girl.

It turned out she was a financial analyst, working in Canary Wharf and living in Turnham Green.

'Some commute!'

'Yeah, it's a bit of a schlep but I'm with some good guys in this shared house.'

'And are you going home for Christmas?'

'Yes,' she said with a wince.

'A long way,' I said. 'Expensive too, at Christmas.'

'Tell me about it,' she said. 'My mother would be fine, why don't I come out for her birthday in April instead, she said. But it's a big deal for my sister.'

'Families,' I said.

'She made me promise to be there every Christmas. She wants me to have a close relationship with her three children. I want that too of course.'

'Yes, but your circumstances are different. She's at home with toddlers while here you are jetting round the world.'

'Kind of. But she's pleased for me too. I don't know if I'll stay. Or if London's where I'll have a job in future anyway.'

Quite. Again I managed to keep my lip buttoned.

'Yes. Meanwhile the money, what you earn, is that …'

She gave a tiny embarrassed nod.

'I do work long hours,' she said. 'I mean, tonight I hoped to get a soak in a hot bath, I was up at five this morning, but an email arrived from my boss just as we were boarding. He needs me to get on to something, he wants this report for a meeting in a few hours' time. I don't think I'll be getting to bed any time soon.'

'So where was he emailing from, your boss?'

'Shanghai.'

'Right. Not as far as Australia but it's still a long way.'

She shrugged.

'The time difference. Yeah. I love it though. I'd have gone mad stuck away back home.'

'Yes.'

'I love that feeling I can work anywhere in the world,' she said with a sudden radiant smile.

At this point we were interrupted by a seatbelt announcement warning of turbulence ahead, and I let her get back to her paperwork at last.

LONDON CITY AIRPORT

Once through passport control, I decided I'd need something

to eat before the drive home and that another shot of caffeine wouldn't be a bad idea either.

In the ground floor café beside the escalator I went over it all once again. None of it made any sense. Nobody had known what was going on. None of them seemed to understand what had happened, or what to do next.

As I munched a crayfish-and-rocket sandwich I checked my phone. A text from Bruno; I texted back. Maybe I'd have a muesli bar as well, I was still hungry.

The woman who had been stabbed, why didn't she matter?

But I was in another country now, I had been airlifted out. I was 500 miles away and it wasn't even the same time over here.

Was she still alive?

Come on! I would never know.

There was a good hour's drive ahead and I was tired. Gathering up the crumbs and paper cup for the bin, I struggled into my coat at last.

It wasn't a good idea to shout at armed policemen in airports, particularly if you didn't speak their language: that was common knowledge.

Outside in the cold and the dark I started to wheel my flight bag through the parking lot. It had been a long day. I would be glad to get home, and the drive should be easy enough at this time of night.

There was the car; and there was the left-side wing mirror, hanging by a thread. Unsafe. A tangled mess. *Scheisse*, as they would say in Zürich. I'd forgotten about that.

THE CITY AS A WARZONE

Penny Woolcock and Stephen Griffith

PENNY: I LIVE in the top half of a shabby Georgian house in Barnsbury, an affluent area of Islington in north London. Opposite there's a pretty little park with massive horse chestnut trees and 50 yards on the left a beautiful larger park. We have three gastro pubs nearby, it's a five-minute walk to the Almeida Theatre and just up the road from the Screen on the Green where we can sink into a sofa and sip a cocktail while watching the latest cinema release. Pet dogs trot around amiably day and night but our pavements are spotless because well-behaved owners always scoop up the poop. It's an oasis of calm, occasionally disturbed by a motorist and a cyclist yelling at each other at the narrow chicane on the corner of Thornhill Road. This is the Angel, Islington, and it's no longer one of the most undesirable properties on the Monopoly board.

I'm halfway between Upper Street with its snooty estate agents, boutique shops and dozens of expensive bars and restaurants and the Caledonian Road – the Cally – still shabby but sprinkled with the telltale signs of gentrification. Apart from remnants of the white working class and Asian market traders on Chapel Market, it's uniformly posh and very safe.

Or is it?

Look carefully and you might notice a uniformed security

guard outside McDonald's on Chapel Market, a sign that there is a parallel world right here. There are teenagers for whom this tranquil area is a deadly battlefield, laced with landmines and traps and this particular McDonald's is one of its most hotly contested territories. These same streets have doppelgangers, not elsewhere in the universe but under our noses. In his novel *The City and the City*, China Miéville describes two tightly crosshatched cities occupying the same geographical space, whose inhabitants are forbidden to acknowledge each other's existence and have to unsee each other instantly. In London we literally don't see the young people dying right under our noses, their bloodstains just seem to evaporate. My eyes were opened after making two films about gang life in inner-city Birmingham, leaving me no longer able to conveniently unsee this parallel world.

Two summers ago at the Copenhagen Youth Project, my friend Steve (who is a senior youth worker there) and I were talking to a group of teenagers about the recent murder of a young rapper they knew in south London. Nobody seemed shocked or upset and Armani, one of the boys, showed me a stream of ugly comments on Instagram that started like this:

Mdot was one ugly shit he dead now ☺☺☺☺☺☺☺☺
☺☺☺☺☺☺☺☺☺☺☺☺☺☺☺☺☺☺☺☺☺☺☺☺☺
his mum rape him in morg
yh tryna get him hard one last time
no more shit come out of his mouth

Myron Yarde's mum had recently died of cancer.

This callousness towards murdered peers is normal, we could reproduce pages of this stuff. But before you snap into labelling them as the Other, a different species of heartless young people, think about the degree of toxic self-hatred expressed in this attitude and turn the judgement on yourself. On Us.

Steve: We had a discussion about what goes through a young man's mind when he leaves his house armed, on a mission to harm one of his rivals. So many teenagers on the streets wear grey North Face or hooded tracksuits that one realistic hazard is stabbing the wrong person. But the boys were more concerned about the danger of leaving their immediate area at all.

O J said, 'Say I need to go Angel now, it's only a short walk. Maybe I catch the 274 and maybe that's safe. But it's a warm evening so say I decide to walk, well I could be caught *slipping* and something happens.' Sadly, a year later O J was in intensive care after a stabbing. It seemed he had been caught *slipping*. O J was one of the lucky 1,000 London stab victims every month who survive. Over a single fortnight this May, 11 young people were stabbed to death. This is not Chicago but we're on our way.

Penny: Half an hour later I walk home to Angel not thinking about losing my life.

As I cross the Cally Road I think about turning left to buy a pack of deliciously salty olives at the little Turkish shop next to the Co-op, and I walk as far as the Tarmon on the corner of Richmond Avenue. This pub's a remnant of the old Cally; a woman with carved wrinkles, dyed black hair and a voice she's smoked hard for marches in past two tattooed men staring morosely into their pints. I see the polished black sphinxes and obelisks outside the houses on Richmond Avenue up the road and I remember my friend James telling me they commemorate the Battle of the Nile in 1798 when Nelson destroyed Napoleon's navy. Apparently members of the famous criminal Adams family live in one of them. I decide I can't be bothered to buy the olives and turn back to stroll up Copenhagen, go left at Matilda and turn up Everilda Street with the dog park on one side and a row of tiny houses on the other. I watch a Dalmatian lolloping around the dog park in a foolish daze, instantly unable to remember where a stick was thrown, unlike the sharp little mongrel dashing to fetch it each time. It reminds me of the owner of Cally Pets telling me that royal pythons are the 'Dalmatians of the snake world, pretty but stupid'. I was looking after my friend Jake's python at the time and we liked to imagine that Hex was an intellectual because he slept comfortably on copies of the *London Review of Books*.

I hope to see the fat white man on the corner who feeds a couple of foxes every evening but he's not there. I enjoy thinking about how we relate to wild things. My friend Nick's brother collapsed in his garden one freezing winter night and before he died he said that foxes had licked him to keep him alive. Then I wonder why the Barnard adventure playground, which looks like a Phyllida Barlow sculpture, is always closed. I swing around and cross Cloudesley Road where some posh kids are playing cricket against a metal gate. I suspect they live in that gated community, which annoys me – why can't they have a front door on the street like everyone else?

Some evenings a group of Cally boys gather outside Angel Stores on bikes and mopeds and it can feel dodgy. I've had a couple of narrow escapes on that corner. One time I kept my wits and made eye contact, nodded and smiled at a boy who was swooping down to snatch my phone from my right hand with his three friends hovering on my left. He was disconcerted and backed away – his friends hooted and called him a pussy but I had briefly become more than a phone to him and it put him off. A street robber once explained that the story running through your head when you pounce is that you will make money and you can show off about it, the person you are robbing doesn't figure at all. You're not thinking about them being in pain or traumatised or the effect on people who love them. Your internal narrative is entirely positive. That's how it works.

Today it's calm. I remember the previous owner of Angel Stores, a Turkish left-wing atheist who changed my life by introducing me to feta cheese and salty olives for breakfast. I smile at the pigeon lady with her long grey hair but she ignores me, and make my way through the Sainsbury's car park where an Asian homeless man with big hair slept next to the trollies for a while, past the owner of the weird secondhand shop with her ratty leopard skin coat and erratically applied lipstick and into Chapel Market. A few stallholders are clearing up and a stooped old lady with white hair is foraging for squashed peaches in empty wooden boxes. I pass McDonald's and now I can see the gleaming silver angel wings outside the N1 shopping centre designed by my friend Tinker's son-in-law.

Steve: For the young people I work with the same journey goes something like this: Is it a walk up to Angel or shall we jump on the bus? The bus brings back memories of a stabbing on the platform of Caledonian and Barnsbury Station last summer. The perpetrator, an EC1 boy – more about this later – ran out of the station and jumped on the 17 bus only to be confronted by a group of Cally boys unaware that he had just stabbed one of their boys on the station. They beat up the EC1 boy and left him in a bit of a mess, but who knows what would have happened if they had been aware of the damage he had just caused to one of their own.

Once on the bus they're pretty much trapped and often the question is where to look if another youth boards the bus; to look away could seem disrespectful or weak and to look towards could be seen a challenge. Guess we're walking, but we still have to watch the eye contact and be mindful of who's about, so the best bet is to be looking around everywhere with a focus on escape routes should anything kick off.

The Cally Road shouldn't be a problem, it's fairly open with many known faces. However, two years ago Alan Cartwright, a boy from our youth club, was fatally stabbed by an EC1 boy as he was innocently riding his bike up the Cally. Now Cally boys feel vulnerable even in the heart of their own territory. Across the Cally Road and through the Barnsbury estate, where there is a lot of cover, is probably the best route. But EC1 boys now maraud around our area without fear, looking for Cally boys. So whilst there is cover, it might be safer to stick to Copenhagen Street because there are more random people about. But on the other hand there's more chance of being caught if the EC1 are on bikes or in a car. So better stick to going through the estate up to Chapel Market, where it becomes seriously dangerous for anyone involved in this life. Lots of people, lots of hustle and bustle as you walk through the market, but there are strange faces from different ends, so the Cally boys say it's *too bait*. And if we're trying to go that extra 200 metres from Chapel to Angel it really is walking through a minefield.

This lifestyle is a vacuum that never turns off, and young people who are sucked into it accept it as the norm. People on the other side of the street don't see the detail of it and therefore will never understand we can't just turn off a switch to make the vacuum stop sucking. There are some young people who have an extraordinary talent that could offer a way out, but more often than not the force of the vacuum puts an end to any dreams. People like Lewis Johnson, a boy from CYP, who was signed by Crystal Palace, a good scholar on a fast track to becoming a professional player. At Crystal Palace, he was the model academy boy, but during holidays and off-season his involvement in criminal and gang activity grew and grew until at 15, after four hard years at Crystal Palace, he turned his back on football for life on 'the Road'. The club offered him everything – a career, accommodation and private education – but he turned it all down to be free on the roads with cash, drugs, girls and exciting risks. He served two prison sentences in three years and was well and truly submerged in this life. I met him again at the funeral of one of his friends, Henry Hicks, who died after crashing his moped on Wheelwright Street while being chased by the police.

I had worked with Lewis since he was eight and thought I could help him again. At the funeral, he was clearly on edge, looking over his shoulder after every few words and, after a hug and a brief conversation, he told me it was too dodgy for him and he needed to leave. The next I heard was that he had been killed while being chased by police. He arrived at a junction where he couldn't go straight because the police were gaining on him, couldn't turn left into a council estate because people were after him there, so he turned right into oncoming traffic and was killed instantly. Two weeks earlier another young man, Stefan Appleton, had been stabbed to death in Nightingale Park after being mistaken for this Crystal Palace prodigy.

I take the young people I work with into other worlds – to theatres, to restaurants, to Sadler's Wells, the English National Opera, to the Roundhouse to give them experiences outside the vacuum, to broaden their map of the world. Out of their environment a lot of the swagger vanishes, heads go down and insecurity emerges. But there is one place where this never happens. They walk into any McDonald's and they're in familiar territory, whatever geographical space it occupies. In McDonald's they have a licence to behave however they wish, which often includes abusing the staff, leaving a mess, disputing the bill, claiming the order is wrong and returning food. As far as they're concerned, if you work in McDonald's and are not one of their boys your only option is to hand out free food. Otherwise you're an easy target because you're all the same, just like the fast food chain itself, where you are guaranteed to get the same food anywhere in the world.

Penny: Street robberies sporadically provide brief but meaningful encounters between our two cities but, much of the time, most of us float around in our own bubbles, blissfully unaware. If you're a north Londoner you've probably hung out in Exmouth Market in Clerkenwell where the Islington postcode changes from N1 to

EC1. It's a short strip of hipster paradise, where you can pop into Caravan at one end selling 'seasonally inspired sharing-plates with worldwide influences' or squeeze into Moro's and eat tiny tapas at tiny tables at whopping prices or drop into its sister Morito or any of the other 20 bars and restaurants squashed next to the hair-dressers, gift shops, flower, jewellery and leather boutiques. While your bike is fixed at the cool bike shop, you can browse for books and cards in Bookends or drink Prosecco on tap at the local pub.

Steve: This area is home to the EC1, also known as Easy Cash because of the ease with which they accumulate money through criminal activities. Shoreditch and Dalston provide not only a booming hipster market for recreational drugs but also lots of dozy punters with expensive phones ripe for the picking. Easy Cash have been at war with Cally for about 15 years following the death of a Cally boy. The war subsided for a while but recently younger even more reckless groups have reignited the feud. These boys feel they have nothing to lose: they are usually in the criminal justice system, excluded from school and able to roll a joint before they have even considered what work they might do. The top boys are often those who are the most intelligent; they can call on backup to implement their violent talk and usually have little or no parenting and there-fore no foundation. They are surrounded by negativity, which they accept as the norm. In my experience, without one adult who really cares about you, it is almost impossible to escape this life.

Nobody remembers the original reason for the feud and it no longer matters as it's now about who has the most cash in their rucksack and who is perceived as the most violent. Last summer, Easy Cash were using Periscope to advertise how far they were advancing into Cally territory, into the same parks that other peo-ple use to walk their dogs, lie in the sun and play with their chil-dren on the swings. These incursions into Cally are known as a vi-olation. And when you're violated you have to retaliate, otherwise you're seen as soft. Walking the streets is genuinely terrifying so you carry a knife to defend yourself.

After a period of breaking up into smaller factions we are now seeing a new pattern of gangs merging to become bigger: Red Pitch, London Fields, Zero Tolerance, Hoxton, Cally Boys and EC1 have struck deals to make their groups bigger, stronger, more violent and richer.

Penny: This whole city is carved up into little bits of turf and the rest of us blithely cross invisible front lines every day. Where I live is one of these front lines and they are all over the city.

A couple of years ago I went for a walk through Camden, just west of Islington, with Hassan, a young man who grew up on the Queen's Crescent council estate just behind the grand houses on Queen's Crescent. Camden Lock, a mecca for tourists and teenagers, was a business opportunity for QC boys, perfect for selling weed or, if you're broke, picking a clump of grass from the pavement, wrapping it in cling film and pretending it is weed. Hassan felt sorry for young people from poorer areas like Tottenham without easy access to crowds of mugs. We walked from the Lock to the south side of Hampstead Heath, a favourite location for romantic comedies, a vast green space where the middle- and upper-middle classes birdwatch or walk their dogs, swim in the various ponds and the Lido, picnic, play tennis, hike and fly kites. I asked him whether he and his friends ever visited the Heath. Hassan flashed his lovely smile and snorted, 'Hampstead Heath is ours.' Hassan didn't mean that the middle classes at play were trespassing on QC territory – they mean nothing to him. In his parallel world he would only see boys from rival gangs committing a violation by venturing into his green space.

Steve: Walking around with a knife is the same as carrying a mobile phone – for many of these young people it's part of the kit. If you're carrying a knife you're going to have to use it or lose face, and in this world losing face can't happen. Young people can be stabbed or shot or sprayed with acid over territory, or drugs, or criminal activities, over a stolen bike, over social media, over a girl, over being disrespected. If you're an uneducated young man with no prospects, having a gun or a knife makes you someone, and too many times I've heard the words, 'we have nothing to lose'.

Penny: Early this summer I walked past a large group of teenage boys standing with their hoods up in broad daylight by Tottenham Green on the Seven Sisters Road a few miles north of Islington. I felt something was about to kick off, but 15 minutes later I heard that a 16-year-old boy was already lying dead in the bushes. Osman Sharif had been stabbed in the chest with a kitchen knife by another 16-year-old, over a Snapchat argument.

Osman's life is over. The boy who killed him will be swept into the prison system where he will be trapped in the bubble, the matrix where all everyone talks about is their next move. And like many soldiers they are traumatised and desensitised to the horror of it, and trauma leads to constant, deadly repetition. They clean up their own mess as efficiently as the dog owners, wiping each other out. Three more have been killed in Islington since I started writing this chapter six weeks ago.

Steve: The Caledonian and Barnsbury area, sandwiched between the King's Cross Development with its expensive restaurants and fountains on one side and the leafy streets of Barnsbury on the other, contains six pockets of poverty known as Super Output Areas. These pockets are among the 20 per cent most deprived areas nationally. It's like a third world country on the doorstep of the richest, complete with its own language (incomprehensible to anybody else) and its own rules.

People live in cramped accommodation, side by side and on

top of each other, in little boxes with no space to breathe. If you walk along the balconies of these estates looking into windows, in the first you'll see a family preparing food, in the next they're eating, next door music is blaring and next to that there's a party. Arguments are frequent between people living in these conditions and they quickly involve everyone. Everyone in the flats above and below can feel and hear the aggression, the swearing and the violent talk; they are trapped, whether they stay at home or go out, and finding alternative accommodation is impossible. So the boys I work with choose a lifestyle that seems to offer easy access to what other people have.

Penny: In the hood there are more words for money than the Inuit have for snow. We have taught them well. They worship money and they'll stop at nothing to get what they want. But the eight richest men in the world are as wealthy as half of humanity and we are fighting seven covert wars in the Middle East right now. Is there a connection between grotesque inequality and petty criminal activity, between state-sanctioned violence and small turf wars? I believe there is. What I do know is that if white middle-class kids were killing each other on the streets of London, we would see them very clearly.

Some Street Slang

Addict – nitty, fiend
Ammunition – live corn
A person over 45 – big person
A person a couple of years older – elder
A person a year or two younger – younger
Asking for trouble – bait
Bad or dangerous – peak
Beaten up – boxed

Car – drive, whip, wheels

Doing your own violence – putting in the work, getting stripes, doing dirt

Drugs – food, the fire, snow line; heroin and cocaine: dark and light, champagne and brandy

Enemy – pagan

Fake gangsters – Netflix bad boys, internet gangsters

Friends – fam, famalan, G, cuz, cuzzie, homie

Ghetto – gully, greezy

Going well – popping, taking off

Gun – ting, shooter, strap, burner (also a phone with no GPS), gat, skeng

Home – crib, yard, ends

Insulting – merking, dissing, violating

Joint – blunt, zoot

Knife – shank, blade

Killing – drop, clap, duppy, pop, ghost off, gone, slap, drill, gweng

Losers – wastemen

Money – p's, papers, dons, scrilla, a bag (£1,000), a bill (£100), stacks, milli, cake, source, swag, mula, guak, gwop, racks, fetti, etc., etc.

Money (is making, or has a load …) – up or caked

Needing drugs – clucking

No mask – bare faced

Pretty girl – peng ting

Real men – G's, OG's, certi, mandem

Robbing – jacking, jumping, taxing

Selling drugs – trapping, shotting, flipping a box, being a trap star, grinding, hustling

Sex – piping, mashing

Sex (a girl who is available for …) – ski, sket

Shoes – kicks, creps

Shooting – plugging, busting or bussing, bun, banging,
    drilling
Skunk – cheese, lemon, ammi, cush, AK
Slipping - being too casual, caught off guard, caught
    unawares.
Stabbing – prepsing, wetting up, dipping
Stop – bun it
Swag – has source
Threatening – flexing
Violent disagreement or war – beef

A STORY IN THREE LANGUAGES

Memed Aksoy

WHO IS IT that can tell me who I am? – King Lear

In the beginning there was the story, so let's begin there. There is a distinct possibility you will not know all of the languages of this story, but don't worry. Even if you did, you still might not comprehend this story, because languages can be muddling. The other complication however is that I myself don't know one of these tongues, at least not well enough to spin a tale. So how does one tell a story in a language one does not know?

Imagine a small, dark classroom. Imagine rain pattering slowly against the thin windowpane and onto the desks. Imagine a seven-year-old boy being held up by his ear, tears gathering in his eyes. Imagine a class of 50 children hunched over one another, boys and girls all dressed identically as if in a military barracks, watching the seven-year-old boy being held up by his ear. Imagine the teacher, glassy-eyed, frothing at the mouth as he says to the boy, you will never again tell a story in that language, you will never again tell a story, you will never again in that language tell a story, tell a story never again in that language, language again never tell a story you will. Imagine the boy nodding frantically. Imagine him swallowing his tongue.

Slowly. Swallowing his tongue.

He lost his tongue. He wasn't born without a tongue. It was taken away. I ask you, where might he find that tongue – a mouth, teeth, and gums? How might he make a sound, sentences and paragraphs? And without words, how might he ever have a way of naming what he sees and feels? A bird, a flower a mountain a country, himself, anything.

I'll tell you a little bit about him. About where he doesn't come from, about what he doesn't believe in, about whom he's not related to, about what he doesn't do. I'll tell you about the books he doesn't read, the films he doesn't watch and the music he doesn't listen to. What I can't tell you is more important than what I can, so let me tell you about that.

I can tell you that he thinks about murdering those closest to him: the local Tamilese shopkeeper proudly wearing his national costume behind the counter, the Irish woman who sleeps outside the station with a placard written in Gaelic, the singing, skipping deaf kid who goes to school past his window every morning. I can tell you about the nightmares he has of his father, who was murdered in prison for refusing to recite the colonising state-nation's national anthem, about the hatred he has for his mother who never told him a bedtime story in her tongue and about the kleptomania that grips him in his home, the need to take back what is his own.

I don't know if I'm telling this story right. I can sing a song in a foreign language and you will feel it, but I cannot tell a story.

Does a language belong to a person, a people or the world; or does a person, a people, the world, belong to a language?

Why do I fear that you will not understand this story then? I believe it's because this story is my own and I am telling it to you in a language that is not its own. But …

Imagine that boy again swallowing his tongue. Imagine all 50 children swallowing their tongues. Imagine a whole nation swallowing their tongue. Imagine a nation of silent people not being able to tell bedtime stories to their children. Imagine a nation of people not being.

Imagine a land whose name is banned. Imagine.

I can tell you a story in two languages but I don't want to. One, Turkish, is the language that I was raped with, the other, English, is the shroud I lie in.

Did you know the word hate does not exist in the Kurdish language?

CRIME WAVES

Duncan Campbell

HE WAS NAMED after the king of Italy but better known by his boyhood nickname of 'Battles'. This was Umberto 'Battles' Rossi, who died at the age of 94 in the summer of 2017, just a few days before the publication of his memoirs, entitled *Britain's Oldest Gangland Boss*. In many ways, Rossi was the 'Little Big Man' of the British underworld. His links went all the way back to the 1920s when his Clerkenwell patch of east London was known as Little Italy and its godfather was the dashing Darby Sabini, a former boxer and the person to whom, as Rossi recalled, 'we all touched our caps'.

The Sabinis were an Italian immigrant family who had settled in that wily part of London where Dickens had placed Oliver Twist and Jack Dawkins, the Artful Dodger. The five Sabini brothers made their criminal mark almost literally by the ferocious way in which they would deal with anyone who crossed them; their profitable business was to offer protection to bookies on the race-courses of southern England in those long ago days before betting shops became as much a part of a London street as a newsagent or a dry-cleaners.

'Darby Sabini and his thugs used to stand sideways on to let the bookmakers see the hammer inside their pockets,' recalled Edward Greeno, the Flying Squad detective who pursued them and who described them as having a 'name like a mineral water'. But they were admired by all the young boys in the neighbourhood and young Rossi was to follow their example, delivering very rough justice to people who crossed him in a long criminal career.

The Sabinis's great rivals were another Italian immigrant family, the Cortesis, and their enmity came to a head in 1922 in a bloody battle at the Frattellanza Club in Clerkenwell in which a number of the Sabinis were wounded. At the subsequent trial, the judge, Mr Justice Darling, told the Cortesis: 'I do not think there is much to choose between you but the Sabinis are within the king's peace while in England and people must not be allowed to shoot them.'

These gangs were role models for 'Battles' Rossi, who got his nickname because his mother, with a thick Italian accent, would shout 'Berto, Berto' from her window and his little English chums thought she was calling him 'Battles'. He spent time behind bars for cutting up another of London's best-known gangsters, Jack 'Spot' Comer, in 1956 and over the years he was questioned by detectives about nearly a dozen murders but never convicted. It was in St Peter's Italian Church in Clerkenwell that descendants of Little Italy – and a few old gangsters – paid a final farewell to Rossi in July 2017, but that rough and raucous area had long since been gentrified far beyond the dreams of the Artful Dodger or Darby and his boys.

The Italians were just the latest in a long line of immigrants to be regarded as the generators of crime in the capital. A decade or so before the Sabinis's pomp, in 1911, wanted posters appeared around London with a £500 reward offered for information about a gang of ruthless villains: 'Peter Piatkok, a native of Russia, an Anarchist … complexion sallow; Joe Levi … foreign appearance, speaking fairly good English, thickish lips, erect carriage … A woman aged 26-27, fairly full breasts, sallow complexion, face somewhat drawn … Foreign appearance.' The wanted crew were anarchists and radicals engaged in an argument with the tsar of Russia and in need of funds.

Some of their comrades had already carried out a fatal robbery in Tottenham in 1909, prompting a headline in *The Times* which warned that 'Alien Robbers Run Amok.' On that occasion, two Latvians had ambushed a car delivering the payroll to a rubber factory in Tottenham, run off with £80 and commandeered a tram as part of their escape route before being cornered. Both robbers and two others died in the mayhem.

Then in late 1910, another botched robbery of a jewellers in Houndsditch in east London led to the famous siege of 100 Sidney Street in Stepney where the home secretary, Winston Churchill, directed operations in a top hat. The perpetrators of the Houndsditch heist, another two Latvian gunmen, were traced two weeks after the robbery, on 2 January 1911, to Sidney Street. The house where they hid was then surrounded by police and soldiers from the Scots Guards. When the house caught fire, with some of the fugitives still inside, Churchill prevented the fire brigade from extinguishing it: 'I thought it better to let the house burn down rather than spend good British lives in rescuing those ferocious rascals.'

Churchill had been made more than aware of the attitude of some Londoners to the presence of these foreign rascals. When he arrived in Stepney he was greeted with cries of 'who let 'em in? ... he's a cool one'. The *Manchester Guardian*'s reporter noted that 'a youth of the neighbourhood chuckled in unholy exultation. "They'll be fried like rats in an oven," he said.'

The police regarded many of the immigrants of the time as well beyond the pale. Writing in his memoirs of this period, the former head of the Flying Squad, Fred 'Nutty' Sharpe, noted that 'flocks of aliens, mostly Russians, were arriving at Irongate Wharf at the foot of Tower Bridge and were being housed in the docks area'. He described the new arrivals as 'Russians in top-boots, leather leggings and fur hats, wild-looking people from the most

outlandish parts of that great uncivilised land; a lot were despera-
does and went in for crime straight away'. Editorials in the press
called for tighter restrictions on immigration from Eastern Europe in much the same language as would be used a century later after any crime in London involving an Albanian, Romanian,
Latvian or Pole.

Meanwhile, a new form of crime was making itself felt in
London in the docklands area of Limehouse and in the West
End. Its most notorious protagonist was Chan Nan, better known
in the press as 'the Brilliant Chang', who ran one of the capital's
earliest Chinese restaurants in Regent Street. There, according to
a report in the *World Pictorial News*, he 'dispensed Chinese deli-
cacies and the drugs and vices of the Orient'. His 'obsession' with
white women led to him demanding, the paper claimed, that he
be paid in kind. Some women, readers were reassured, retained
'sufficient decency and pride of race' to turn him down.

But the *Empire News* advised that 'mothers would be well advised to keep their daughters as far away as they can from Chinese
laundries and other places where the yellow men congregate'. And
the *Daily Express* took its readers to a 'dancing den' where the
clientele were 'the same old sickening crowd of under-sized aliens, blue about the chin and greasy, the same predominating type
of girl, young, thin, underdressed perpetually seized of hysteri-
cal laughter, ogling, foolish'. The evil dealer, readers learned, 'was
not the Chink of popular fiction, a cringing yellow man hiding
his clasped hands in the wide sleeves of his embroidered gown'.
When Chan Nan was finally arrested, the *Daily Express* celebrated his demise: 'the yellow king of the "dope runners" has been
caught at last in the web of British justice'. Arthur Tietjen of the
Daily Mail commented: 'Chang possesses a strangely macabre –
some said hypnotic – power to persuade women to sniff cocaine. It
may well have been that he did so as a member of the yellow race
to degrade white women.'

It was always those damned foreigners responsible for corrupting poor, vulnerable Londoners. Decades later in the 1950s and 1960s, a different crew of purveyors of drugs in London were identified. Soho and the West End had taken over from Limehouse and the docklands as the place to head for dope. 'Coloured men who peddle reefers can meet susceptible teenagers at jazz clubs', wrote Chapman Pincher in the *Daily Express*. 'Reefers and rhythm seem to be directly connected with the minute electric "waves" continually generated by the brain surface ... Dope may help the brain "tune in" to the rhythm more sharply, thereby heightening the ecstasy of the dance.'

In the 1950s, too, another new group of immigrants to London were being portrayed as a threat to the nation. They were the 'Epsom Salts', rhyming slang for 'Malts' or the Maltese. They came in the shape of the Messina brothers, who had been expelled from Egypt after the authorities had become concerned about the extent of their brothel activities. Soho and the West End soon became their fiefdom and they imported young women from what was then 'the continent' to work in their brothels in Shepherd Market and New Bond Street. They were hardly discreet: Eugenio – 'Gino' – drove a yellow Rolls-Royce and Marthe Watts, one of the hundreds of prostitutes who worked for him and remained loyal, had '*Gino le Maltais, homme de ma vie*' tattooed on her left breast. Comeuppance arrived for the brothers when their network was exposed by Duncan Webb, the flamboyant crime correspondent of the *People*, who named the 'four debased men with an empire of vice which is a disgrace to London'. Prosecutions and jail followed and the brothers moved their operations to France.

Different parts of London where immigrants settled have traditionally been identified in the press or by politicians as the centres of vice or crime. It was Limehouse when the Chinese were the 'yellow peril' in the 1920s, Clerkenwell with the Italians in the '30s, Soho and the West End for vice in the '40s and '50s, Gerrard

Street and Chinatown for heroin trafficking in the '60s, Notting Hill and Brixton when West Indians (most of them, in reality, working in the National Health Service and for London Transport) were portrayed as the importers of marijuana and, later, guns and violence, and Green Lanes and Haringey when Turks were accused of using their kebab houses for money-laundering drugs profits.

When Eastern European nations were admitted into the European Union in large numbers in 2004, a small battalion of artful dodgers from some of the new nations saw London in particular as a very tempting honeypot. It would be easy to hide in plain sight in the most diverse city in the world. So it was in 2006, in Acton, west London, that attention was drawn to a new little world of miscreants. Around midnight on the morning of 14 October 2006, shots were fired in an Albanian/Kosovan club in Park Royal, northwest London. One man, Prel Marku, died from a fatal injury to his brain and two others were wounded. The shooting was the result of a feud between two gangs over who had the right to rob the parking meters of the West End.

The man who fired the fatal shots was Herland Bilali, who worked as a disco doorman, had a reputation for violence and was part of one of the gangs. He was jailed in 2008 with a minimum tariff of 34 years. It transpired that the murder was the result of a turf war over which Albanian gang was entitled to steal from the parking meters of Westminster using skeleton keys, a racket soon to become outdated as parking payments went cyber. But at that time, stealing from the meters was quite lucrative – more than £1m a year from Westminster alone – and had two advantages: heavy-duty criminals were not interested as the pickings were small and the work tedious, carting round all those heavy one pound coins. But for the newly-arrived teams of Kosovars, Montenegrins and Albanians it had the advantage of being relatively simple, and the coinage was untraceable, unlike stolen banknotes.

A couple of years earlier, Luan Plakici, an Albanian 'immigration expert', as he described himself unblushingly, was jailed for 23 years for running a massive sex-trafficking network. He had smuggled around 50 Eastern European women, mainly from Moldova and Romania, into London for prostitution. He entered the country as an asylum seeker in 1999 and worked for law firms as an interpreter. His trial at Wood Green Crown Court was a rarity. Usually, the witnesses were too frightened of what might happen to their relatives at home to appear. This time, some brave young women gave evidence against him.

I spoke to an Albanian journalist, Muhamed Veliu, about these cases at the time and he felt that his countrymen, in particular, had had a bum rap. 'Only a small minority are involved in organised crime but the tabloids have created a stereotype of Albanians as the new gangsters,' he said. 'In the past 12 years in Britain, I have read only one positive story about an Albanian – a barrister, in *Time Out* – but there are Albanian doctors in the NHS, Albanian LSE lecturers, Albanians in the restaurant business. The success stories are never reported.' The same was true of the other new arrivals: while a Latvian murderer or a brutal Polish robber understandably attracted press coverage, the countless others who had seen London as a place to start a new, hard-working life, tended to be ignored.

In fact, the major crimes involving foreign nationals come in a very different form. In 2015, the National Crime Agency concluded that foreign criminals were using the London housing market to launder billions of pounds. Donald Toon, the director of economic crime at the NCA, was speaking after it emerged that expensive houses were being bought by companies, trusts and investment funds rather than individuals. Often this would be done by people wanting to hide assets from their own countries' tax authorities. Said Toon: 'Prices are being artificially driven up by overseas criminals who want to sequester their assets here in the

UK.' Indeed, it would be fair to say that London became, in the early 21st century, the global capital of money laundering. Foreign criminals no longer had to bother about threatening bookies, corrupting innocent English womanhood or breaking into parking meters in order to secure their loot.

But the reality was that 'the underworld' was always a home-grown business, however much new arrivals were blamed for importing criminality. Groups of migrants in every country in the world commit crimes. They do so either because they are excluded by language, lack of contacts or prejudice from regular forms of moneymaking, or because they just prefer crime as a career. Since the police are unfamiliar with their mugshots or their fingerprints and probably don't speak their language, they have a little window through which they can operate for a few years. Often, once the crimes have served their purpose, the same chaps – and they are almost all chaps – move into respectable society, send their children to the best schools, and let another new wave of migrants from a different part of the world take the heat. So it has been in London.

Every great city – New York, Paris, Shanghai, Mumbai – has an underworld that consists of both home-grown villains and those who arrive unbeknown to the police and carve out a little illicit niche for themselves before, in the words of the late Mandy Rice-Davies, who came to prominence during the 1960s Profumo scandal in London involving call girls, they enter 'a slow descent into respectability'. And of course London has exported its own little criminal network. Most famously to Spain, where from the late 1970s into the 1980s during a breakdown in extradition arrangements between the United Kingdom and Spain, the 'Costa del Crime' established a very lucrative network importing drugs from Morocco, occasionally killing each other in turf battles.

London meanwhile will always provide a home for professional criminals, whether homegrown or imported and whether they wear leather leggings, embroidered gowns or a suit, shirt and tie.

I LIKE TO CLOSE MY EYES WHEN I'M TALKING SERIOUS THINGS

The Akwaaba Writing Group

AKWAABA IS A social centre for migrants in Dalston.

Juliana: The environment has made me to be strong and stand firm. You may ask me how.

*

Hadil: I was sleeping. As usual in my niece's room. I still remember the room. Literally, I remember all the corners of the house. I was sleeping in a pink bed, in this wooden house, and I was thinking about the 14 years I spent in my home town.

I was thinking about the last days I spent with my auntie. I remembered the last Ramadan and celebrating Eid. I was remembering all this and listening to 'Photograph', that song by Ed Sheeran.

So ya, my niece wakes me up. I wake up in this wooden room and see the shines of the sun coming into the window. I wash my face. It's my last breakfast with her for I don't know how long. This is my great day. The worst and the best day.

We eat breakfast. When we've finished I say to myself, Ya Hadil, no tears, you have to be strong, you'll see her again. Inshallah.

I was wearing grey jeans, a white dress with the Big Ben on it, a black jacket and a white scarf. I remember my trainers because they were my nephew's trainers. They didn't fit him any more so he gave them to me.

I came downstairs and everyone was getting ready, helping to put my luggage in the car. I was taking selfies with my nephews. The sun was shining and we were taking selfies outside in the garden.

We got in the car. Looking out the window of the car. It was like Tunisia was saying goodbye to me, saying hopefully we will see you soon, Hadil.

I was listening to everything carefully. I said to myself, Hadil, this is your time to prove you are able to take responsibility, to be strong, to be a good person. Yeah, Hadil, this is your chance.

No one can feel the pain of staying away from your mom, only those who try it.

*

Remmie: One of my mother's friends in the village took me in and started looking after me. She didn't have much either but she really tried. Her friend, a posh woman from Kampala, came to visit her. She saw me almost dying and she brought me to Kampala. That was the beginning of my success.

*

Warda: When they got the visa and called me, I was out of my mind. I was shouting and shouting and jumping. I fainted with happiness. I had never imagined this happiness. When my children were born, when my daughter got her university degree, those were all happy moments. But this moment cannot be explained. All my body went white, and numb. I could not breathe and I fainted.

The girls who lived with me could not understand and kept asking me: are you OK? They had never seen me overacting as I am always calm. I was by myself then, I had nobody with me, so I was always quiet. That day I was like a monkey: nobody knew what was going on. I felt like a newborn.

*

Hadil: I went inside the airport and put our luggage in and stayed with my sister and her daughter. It was still too early to go inside into the waiting area, through this door when I pass through, lots of things are gonna change.

I looked around to my niece playing around me, speaking with my sister, I do remember that she told me: I want you to support our mummy and never forget where you belong and don't forget that we love you.

How I'll never forget that, that will stay in my mind. Especially that my family loves me, that's something you cannot forget.

Now is the moment to say goodbye to my sister. Our tears just fell without our permission.

Now I'm in the plane. Sitting in the last place in the airplane, my brother on my right-hand side. Sitting in a red and grey chair. The plane moves but it is still on the ground. But now not any more: I'm in the sky like a bird, watching from the window how much my country is beautiful.

*

Warda: That day, I wore bright white colours. I wore my headscarf pink so that everybody could see it. I never wear pink. I remember the bright rose edge of the scarf falling on my beige dress. After that day, people that see me tell me that there is a new brightness about me.

I was at the airport from 12 o'clock, although they were only arriving at five. I was standing in front of the metal barriers at the gate, to get first position. Inside me, I did not believe it. I thought – they might be stopped at customs. I was shaking with fear. And then … it was like in the movies. I saw all the passengers from Tunis Air. I even met somebody I knew. I asked them if everybody had landed. Can you imagine?

After an hour everybody had arrived and they were not there yet! I thought the Home Office must have denied them entry because of my visa situation.

When I saw them, I was just mad. I crawled under the fence to meet them. I wish somebody had been there with a camera, because … their faces and my face … it is like I had them for the first time. It was like giving birth for the first time.

*

Remmie: My flight landed at 6am.

The escalator surprised me. I had never seen one before and I did not know how to get on. It took me an hour of admiring the white people jumping on it without fear. Today I am happy that the escalator is no longer a problem for me.

Furthermore, what has made me successful is having learnt how to eat English and European food. When I first came to the UK I grew very skinny. I did not know how to eat pizza or use a spoon and fork.

One of my friends took me to an Italian restaurant. They bought me a pizza but I could not eat it. I thought it was a plastic plate.

I always envied cats and dogs. They have a place to stay. They are well cared for and they hold British passports. Today I am so happy that I do not need to envy them any more.

*

Olu: The happiest moment has fear attached to it. When the council gave me the house, I was homeless. I was happy. And when they gave me money I was happy. But there was fear attached to it. The fear attached to it was this. Is there a limited time? Are they going to evict me. Because the first council evicted me. So I was scared. I said to myself, Oh, they gave me a house, they gave the children money. But it is for a limited time. Maybe one month, like the other council did. Will they come again and say, You will have to leave? They gave me cash because there was a problem with the accounting sector.

*

Kenny: They gave me a phone number and an address. That same day I went there. The agent called me and he told me, I'm outside Iceland. You see me?

He was a young guy with a black scarf on his head done like a turban but flat. He had glasses and a moustache. He looked trendy, this cool guy. He explained about the heating. Then he handed me the keys.

After he left I went around and looked again. The walls smelled of new paint. The washing machine – new. The fridge – new. It's on the ground floor and quiet, part of a house. There's a garden! I went in the garden. I thought: Hmm, this is a nice place for children to play.

There's this big tree and at the back of the garden is a canal. Sometimes you see the swan.

*

Olu: The lady I was staying with – she ordered some food for her own child. Cerelac. It's Nestlé who make that food. When the food arrived it was for the wrong age. It was food for a six-month-old baby. But she'd ordered six kilos of it.

The lady was so upset. She was going to send it back. I didn't say anything, I was silent. But I was praying in my heart to God.

Then she said, You can have the food then! I told her that when I had the money I'd pay her back, but she said it was OK. If you could see inside me! Inside me I was like, Oh! I still remember that thing.

*

Ola: The animal is a cat. The name of the cat is Whiskey. The owner of Whiskey is Carol Harris, my friend. Whiskey was white in colour. Whiskey grew up in Carol's house. Whiskey ate Carol's leftover food. She liked to hang around Carol's visitors. I am petrified of, and allergic to, cats and dogs. So Carol always locked Whiskey away whenever I visited. Carol always looked after me whenever I visited. Unfortunately Whiskey passed away three years before Carol. May her soul rest in perfect peace. Amen.

*

Olu: I went straight to the shop. I bought food. I bought fruit. The children, they didn't have underwear, so I bought underwear. I bought winter hats, scarves. I nearly finished the money that same day. Because I had to buy a lot of things, because there were some things I had had to throw away when we were homeless. Toys. We kept some things. But most we had to get rid of. When we were living in different places I had one bag for the whole family. So I had to get all these things back.

*

Anthony: The office was a bit hard to find. I was thinking of a big nice office but it was rather a small office on a quiet road.

I pressed the doorbell and heard a click. I pushed the door. Two office desks in the room and a man behind one of the desks. He was wearing this expensive suit. Most black Africans when they know they are in a higher level than you, they want to show off, so you have to give them that respect. They ask you straight questions and they expect you to answer in a straight way. They do not want you to joke around.

I told myself: OK. And I told him my story. I relaxed a bit, and he gave me the different options.

He said I can marry somebody from the EU.

I can just get somebody pregnant.

Or maybe just go back home and reapply with somebody who got a British passport.

Going back home was out of the question. And I was not having a girlfriend at the moment, so the option to get somebody pregnant on the street was out.

The option left was to do a fake marriage. He asked if I had anybody in mind. I said no, so he said he would try and help me. Because that's what they do.

So he gave me a form to fill and he told me that I have to pay a hundred pounds, which means I am a registered member. In other words it means he is now my lawyer.

I left the office a bit happy, but still I was thinking: is this the right thing?

*

Ola: I can't say we slept well. We were four, sometimes five in the bed. We slept head to toe. Me and my two children, my girl, and my baby boy. Her and her baby. Five of us in one bed! And her baby moved all over the bed. That's why Jude, until now when he sleeps, he sleeps in one place, he never moves. My youngest son, he manoeuvres everywhere. My daughter too. But when Jude is sleeping he is absolutely still. If you want to enjoy your sleep, let Jude sleep with you.

*

Lola: When I first moved in, the flat was empty. I slept on the floor with my children. At night it was very cold, my daughter was feverish with the cold. I had to take her in my arms and sit with my back at the wall until daybreak.

A few days later, a black woman, fat (a little bit), light in complexion with short gold hair and a cool voice knocked on the door. I thought, Who is this?

She wanted to know if I was the person who had been there before. I said I just moved in.

We started from there. I call her Big Mommy because she's older than me, 50-something. Anytime she needs help I'm there, anytime I need help, she's there. She eats out of my pot, I eat out of her pot.

Big Mommy loves Jollof Rice. She teaches me how to cook it. It's got rice, pepper, curry, thyme, butter, Maggi cube or Maggi chicken. She makes it tender, so it smells like lily flower, bright orange!

*

Kenny: We sang the birthday song to David. Usually, he goes HIP, HIP and we go HOORAY! But this time we did it the other way. We go HIP, HIP and he goes HOORAY!

*

Olu: So that morning I said to my children, Do you believe we won't be moving around and around again. They said they believed. I told them we were going somewhere nice. They said, Yes Mummy. I said, Do you believe we are not going to move around any more. They said, Well, we believe Mummy. The boys said it like, Yes we believe, we believe. But my daughter, she's older, and she said, Mmmm, I believe, I believe.

I asked them what they wanted to eat. One wanted pizza, the others wanted chicken and chips. So I bought both pizza and chicken and chips to take away.

I put the food on the table. It was a new table. The agency had put it there. We took the plates. The pizza was cut into four pieces, and we are four.

We put a slice of pizza on each plate. We shared the chicken and chips. We put out the condiments, ketchup, mayonnaise, barbecue sauce.

We also had drinks. Robinsons juice. We slept well that night. Oh my god. The kids slept in their own room.

*

Lola: I had my daughter premature. She was 26 weeks and four days when I had her. She was 900 grams – small like a lizard in your palm.

Three weeks after, I had a lot of pain. Before I left in the morning, I put out red bream for dinner. Then I went to the hospital. I told them I had pain in my stomach.

The midwife said: Don't worry, you'll be fine. You just had a baby, it's normal to have pain. You'll be OK.

So I came home. I was going to cook the red bream and rice. I went to the toilet and Oh My God. Instead of the pee the blood was just coming out. It was rushing! Rushing! Rushing out! Oh My God.

I get a blanket to cover myself. I open the door outside to shout for help. I saw a man on a bicycle – don't ask me what he looked like, I was at the point of death! – I just need him to go upstairs and call Big Mommy.

He saw me, he was shocked, he thought maybe I stabbed myself. He run up stairs – and Big Mommy with her gold hair come downstairs with no clothes on her! Just a wrap, no shoes, nothing.

When Big Mommy call the ambulance, they say: where's the blood? How much blood? When did the blood come? What colour is the blood?

Big Mommy say, She is dying! If she die, I'm going to SUE YOU!

When the ambulance arrived, Big Mommy stayed with my children. She cleaned my house. She cleaned the toilet with the blood on the floor. She took my children to her flat. She locked the door.

*

Juliana: The day I cried a lot was the second day when the stitches were trying to heal. I moved my leg and the pain was so much. The nurse told me I need to walk around. I tried. I picked up courage and moved. I moved three steps. Then the pain came! And I shouted for my mother. MAMA, OH, and I cried.

Then I thought, no one's going to help me but I can do it. I have to move on to do what I have to do. Then I continued walking, walking.

When I went home and I needed to wake up in the night to give the child breast, I needed to do it even with the pain. Later, as the child was growing, no one helped me as well. I'd change the child, bathe the child. All alone.

I'm not complaining but I have to do everything on my own. This is the life here. I have no one helping me. I do everything on my own. I'm always smiling – if you like me, you can smile back and we'll chat. That's my life, that's my story and the life continues.

ROSALIND

Arifa Akbar

I HEARD ABOUT Rosalind Hibbins before I met her. I was buying an attic flat on top of a converted period house on Lady Margaret Road, a tree-lined backstreet that runs from Kentish Town to Tufnell Park, and I had just exchanged contracts with its former owner, Holly, when she mentioned the woman who lived downstairs. She spoke of Rosalind with such strained diplomacy that it seemed as if she were revealing furtive knowledge of a faulty boiler or leaky roof that she'd kept hidden until too late. 'She's a character!' Holly said with a nervous laugh. 'Every street's got one.'

I was moving from a large 1930s block on Camden Road where my neighbours had been too many and too fluid to get to know beyond the briefest of helloes in the lift. It suited me that way; I had grown up on a housing estate in Primrose Hill after my parents returned to London from Pakistan, and as the only non-white family in our council block, we tried to live as quietly as we could amid the curiosity, and occasional hostility. As the postwar generation died off, our neighbours became far more unknown and indifferent to us, and we to them.

Rosalind introduced herself to me the day I arrived. She was a strapping woman with tidy red hair cut short, and a way of speaking that quickly travelled the scale from genial to spiky. The furniture was still being hauled up when she emerged at the top of my stairs with a box of organic tea, and looked at me with wonder. 'I'm so pleased to finally meet you,' she said. 'I looked up your name. I didn't know if you'd come veiled.'

Oh god, I thought, but she was full of neighbourly spirit after that. She asked me what else I needed, and when I spoke of a housewarming party, she saw my bare living room and said she'd lend me her corner tables so I'd have some flat surfaces to serve food on to my guests.

I found out more about her as time went on. She was in her early 60s, with no husband or children, and estranged from her sisters, apparently. Despite her age, she had a ruddy strength about her. She had grown up in the country and her hiking boots, which she kept under the settle by the stairs, were always muddy. She had been a librarian at the British Library but found, after retirement, that her true passion was stone-carving.

I also discovered that she had a knack for friendship, but for fall-outs too. She received floods of birthday cards and had friends forever doing her favours. Yet the other two flat-owners in the house spoke of her in the same nervous way as Holly when they took me out to the Pineapple, a pub on the adjacent street where we discussed all communal house matters after that. A few drinks in, they spoke in plainer language: she had fallen out with them dramatically over the years. She had differences in opinion with the Catholic church on our road too and had stopped going to Sunday service there. Even the owner of the local newsagent who had once been known for carrying her shopping home for her now pursed his lips at her name.

She took an interest in me from the first but I suspected it was because she needed an ally in the house. She told me she'd read newspaper articles I'd written on my father's dementia, and another on Terry Pratchett's death. 'Congratulations on writing without sentimentality,' she said in an email.

She called on me for small tasks at first – watering her plants while she was away, buying milk, hoovering the hallway. Then, a distressed phone call when I was in the office. The builder we had enlisted to lay our porch paving was threatening to take up every last stone and abandon the job in anger. Could I come home and talk him down? I did, begrudgingly, and found out afterwards that she had managed to alienate every builder who had worked on the house.

I got more phone calls in the office after that, some with Rosalind in tears, asking me to fix this or that. Stranger things too: she stopped me along the hallway in a panic, saying that there was a mouse in her kitchen and could I watch over it while she called pest control; another time, she ran up the stairs wild-eyed to ask if I could investigate a possible gas leak in her flat. With each episode, I felt what really disturbed her wasn't the problem she presented but fear or maybe even acute moments of loneliness beneath it. But alongside her vulnerability, she was difficult, demanding, and increasingly, I became confrontational back.

Then, one day, she caught me on the stairs when I was in a troubled mood about work and over tea she listened in such a way that I felt the possibility of a solution, though she hadn't given any outright advice. I came away feeling that I was no longer pressed up against my problem but could breathe easier alongside it.

There were other moments like that which crept up on me over the next eight years, when we'd bump into each other on the stairs and talk about life over tea – her joy at finally renting a studio in Bethnal Green and becoming a bona fide artist 'at my age!', my slow but steady progress with a book idea, her dislike of the new pope and, ultimately, of all organised religion. I felt I understood her better after hearing her ferocious attacks on parts of the church, only because she held equally outspoken views on Islam which she had volubly expressed to me in the past, knowing I was a Muslim. Now I figured it was nothing personal.

She'd point at objects in her flat as we talked – the stone-carvings propped up against the fireplace, the leather case which contained the love letters that her father had written her mother before marriage, which she claimed never to have read (I told her I'd never be able to resist). She cried each time she pointed to the photograph of her father, taken at 90-something, and told me again how it devastated her when he died.

She caught me exhausted one time and craving escape from the city. 'It's still bluebell season,' she said, 'you should go and see the bluebells', and gave me a map to a copse at the top of a golf course on the outskirts of London. As a British Asian urbanite, I hadn't even known bluebell season existed. I was curious, and so I trekked there with a flask and a packed lunch and the bobbing sea of flowers was so joyful that it breathed new life into me.

It became a friendship, of sorts, with its confidences, rows and appeasements. Or perhaps a kinship in which she saw something of herself in me and I, for my part, recognised my inability to compromise in her and I imagined it leading me to the same future – a woman without family, alone in older age. Yet her life offered reassurance too because it showed me how I could live fruitfully this way. She had warded off loneliness, for the most part, and kept a hold of her passions.

I never felt sorry for her because she emanated great strength of will. So, when she sent us a house email three years ago to announce that she had ovarian cancer, she made it clear she'd be fighting it all the way. She got herself on a drugs trial and the medicine seemed to work. Her cancer was contained and a year later she was just as alive, just as solid-looking, even though she wore scarves now where her hair had been.

Other emails came, but the starkest one arrived early last spring, over a year after her diagnosis. It was short and to the point. The drugs had stopped working. She was at Stage Four and they had given her 'a few weeks, maybe more.'

The woman who lived below her rang me. We should go to

see her, she said, but I wasn't sure I could. A few weeks earlier, my sister had died suddenly and it had left me poleaxed. Now, here was death again on my doorstep. It took all my strength to go two floors down, and then I was uncontrollably tearful at how vulnerable Rosalind looked. It was as if knowledge of her impending death had transformed her instantly; her hair had grown back in tufts of white and she had lost so much weight that she looked frail, all signs of the former battle-axe disappeared. She moved slowly and gasped for breath. We sat as a group in awkward silence until she looked around the room in shock and said 'what will happen to all my things?'

I saw her on Lady Margaret Road only one more time after that, just outside the house, with a cluster of women around her who must have helped her down the stairs. She was leaning on her walking frame and she told me in a whispering voice that she was going to visit her studio, and what struck me was how free and happy she looked in that moment. I knew it was because she loved the studio and the things she had made with her own hands inside it.

We heard that she'd been taken to a hospice in July. I wanted to say goodbye but felt too shy to call and too reluctant to visit. Facing death, I had observed through my sister, was such an intimate thing and I didn't want to intrude on hers. I was a neighbour who had known her only in passing. So I texted her, saying I would remember our conversations, particularly the first one when I had been thinking of finding an alternative career though I had no idea what else I might enjoy doing other than writing. She had talked about learning to navigate two things, and conjured an image of the woman who rides two horses at the circus. She has learned to slip from one horse to another, and she is in control of the manoeuvre so that it is not frightening for her, she had said, suggesting I might try at being her, metaphorically. The image had stayed with me, and I spoke of the woman, perhaps because I saw

Rosalind was poised for the ultimate transition from life to death, and I wanted to remind her of the sliding manoeuvre.

I got a voicemail back and it was so hard to hear her because Rosalind barely had a voice left and she struggled to finish her sentences before breathlessness got the better of her. She was saying she would love to see me again and inviting me to visit her at the hospice in Belsize Park, just around the corner from where I grew up, and where my mother still lived.

I was with her for a few hours. She had a big, bright room, with one wall covered with cards. She sat on a chair by the window and, every now and again, she looked down to the manicured garden and suggested we go down to sit in the sun, in a little while, when she felt stronger.

She asked after my sister, the details of how she died, and how I felt about it. 'Don't hold on to her too tightly. She'll come back to you, in other people you meet,' she said, which wasn't exactly a comfort but like the circus lady on two horses, it stayed with me as a possibility.

'Did she die alone?' Rosalind asked quietly, and when I said yes, she grew grave. She was not afraid of death in itself, she said, but she *was* afraid of dying alone. The hospice didn't have enough staff to allocate her a nurse overnight. What would happen if she found herself heading towards the end in the dark with no one beside her?

I knew the answer to that. My father's care home in Kentish Town had plenty of nurses who I knew would do extra night shifts if Rosalind wanted it. I asked my father's favourite nurse, Bobby, to stay with her over several nights. She was comforted by his presence and they had interesting conversations, he told me afterwards, but he had booked a trip to visit his family in the Philippines and when he went, I couldn't find another replacement that Rosalind liked. One nurse snored too loudly, another didn't look strong enough in the event of an emergency, and finally, she left me a message to say that friends were staying with her overnight in rotation so I shouldn't worry.

Her sister emailed the house in early September to tell us Rosalind had died and invited us to the funeral. I knew I couldn't go. One funeral that summer had been enough.

In the months afterwards, a certain hardness grew in me, or perhaps it was grief disguised as disappointment. She hadn't properly thanked me for the jobs I had done for her, I said petulantly to my mother, who didn't indulge me for a minute, and reminded me to give, and then to forget about it. That was too Buddhist for me, I told her. I was always giving but the world never noticed. It took givers for granted.

In fact, Rosalind *had* said thank you. A number of times, she'd said she wanted to get me a bottle of wine or invite me down for Sunday roast. 'But you don't drink and you're a vegetarian,' she'd sighed, as if these were terrible failings. She'd thanked me in emails too but in her usual, no-nonsense way and I now wanted something more as a validation of our friendship.

A year passed and a young art historian moved into Rosalind's flat who redecorated it completely. I went to the Pineapple with the new complement of neighbours. We talked about Rosalind and I told them how, a few days ago, I had passed a woman who seemed so much like an older, happier version of her, shuffling up the corner of Lady Margaret Road from the future on a walking frame. When I spotted her, she stopped me in my tracks and I thought *this* is what Rosalind would be like if she were alive many years from now. In her parallel earthly paradise.

Later that week, I got a letter from her solicitors. Inside was Rosalind's death certificate, her will, and a list of legal charges. They must have accidentally sent me these documents, I thought at first. I re-read the covering letter, absorbing lines that I had skipped over. Rosalind's estate was being settled and her flat had sold for not much short of a million pounds. And I was entitled to a percentage, because Rosalind had put me in her will. I read the letter again in disbelief. I put it back in its envelope and later, when I was on the Tube, I unfolded it and read it, as if for the first time. I did that several times until I made myself stop. Rosalind, I thought: a neighbour who lived two floors beneath me. A cancer sufferer whose medicine I collected from Boot's. An adversary with whom I occasionally butted heads. A friend who gave me solace, and whose grave I still hadn't sat beside.

A month before dying, she had considered my future and perhaps worried about it, knowing that I'd lost my sister and that a job of 15 years had also come to an end. And then she had put me in her will, and a year later – on a day when I felt especially grumpy – she had reminded me of the cups of tea and the bluebells. This wasn't the thank-you that I had so craved. It was a show of love.

THE MINISTRY OF COMPLIMENTS

Andrew O'Hagan

I THINK I'M living for the values of a vanished age. Maybe it's the London of Patrick Hamilton, the lonely bedsits, *Miss Dior*, and Camden gin. I admire those girls for all the wrong reasons, those literary girls of the 1940s, with their ugly boyfriends and small magazines, the tears before bedtime, the opinions that burnished the chandeliers. Walking across Russell Square of an evening, it's not prose and poetry I'm thinking about but T S Eliot taking Valerie to dinner at the Savoy. London above all is a city of events, as Pepys knew, as Boswell knew, and all my life I've liked the sort of people who never say no if they can help it.

I was at Scott's last night with an old friend and was glad to find him a prince among the decadents. He sleeps with everyone, has too many jobs and spends too much time with his shrink. I told him I was delighted to see he was now living for all of us. From the scholarly point of view, that's how it seems nowadays, when you spend time with the likes of Jack. He agreed it wasn't perfect but said the whole spectacle of his success left him feeling quite empty. 'London's like that, old duck,' he said. 'You come here with nothing and you end up with everything, yet you've still got nothing and someone else has the one you want.'

No one gets it right, of course, but there was something vital about Jack Eddington-Gage at the centre of his mistakes. He was very much a London person. He believed in the sprightly truth that character is something one goes out and chooses for oneself, and he cursed the bones of lives that are known and set out in advance. 'More often than not,' he said, 'happiness is the accidental overdose of carelessness, and there's a lot to be said for giving yourself up to accidents.' True to say: there was precision in Jack's management of the suddenly alarming pickle. As time went on, we thought of him as the Josephine Baker of the artfully contorted life-crisis. He was always better off and worse off at the same time. 'Have a martini, you handsome pig,' he said, putting up his hand for the waiter.

I took my spectacles out of my briefcase. 'You won't need them,' he said. 'I know the menu off by heart.'

'I like having something to do with my eyes.'

He went on to order for both of us: lobster salad, then turbot, steamed spinach and a ridiculous bottle of Sancerre Rouge. He flicked a thumb on the screen of his iPhone before laughing at a text and placing the machine down on his side plate. He leaned back and looked at me. 'You're hopelessly reserved, Jamie,' he said, 'always have been. And that's probably an excellent precaution against getting into scrapes.' You had to snigger when Jack went into advice mode. At St Andrew's, it was always him giving the tutors advice, usually about weed or Thomas Hobbes, or Tanqueray versus Gordon's, and he always had a talent for sounding faintly plausible about things he knew nothing about. 'London is best taken sip by sip,' he said.

'Still king of the uncheckable assertion,' I said.

'*Naturellement.*'

We drank our martinis, we laughed, and he told me about a colourful offer that was made to him the night before in a dark alleyway. He had no trouble inhabiting his various moments, and now, at last, he had become a genius at spinning prosperity out of fear, never failing to find a little laughter at the cold edges of middle age. In the days when he liked girls, we had both been in love with the same one, not at the same time, but the same girl ten years apart, him first. We could never agree about which of us was the better boyfriend to her, but I always suspected he understood her and loved her more. In any event, we both survived her dark wonderfulness, and knew exactly where the bodies were buried.

I knew he pitied me. He must have done. It was part of his London charm to find people pitiable for not being more like him. He knew I'd spent too long in the English department and had lost my sense of fun. He always said a quantity of fun was essential to the maintenance of a good prose style. But most of all it was the people he disliked – 'darling, the talk, the people' – and especially the younger academics and their torpid ambition, which was Jack's idea of the most blazing hell on earth. 'Go to Oxford, dear, or even Bristol or for christ sake Durham, but please avoid those London universities, pullulating with mediocrity.'

'That's not true, Jack,' I said, venturing to make him spit the wine. 'There's a woman in my department who is a gift from God when it comes to George Eliot and real estate.'

'I have no doubt,' he said, chortling. 'But it's those ghastly young men who want to be reviewers. Or want to be novelists once they've spent a few years making their names rubbishing novelists. So depressing. They don't know how to behave, those people. No style. Absolutely none. Look at how they've been with you. Bleed you for everything, use your name, don't know the first thing about how to be a good friend, never write a note of thanks, never invite anyone anywhere, want praise but can't give it, terrible writers, boring teachers who complain about the smallest tasks, they add nothing to the life of dear London. How can you stand them?'

Jack had ventured with some accuracy to describe the kind of academic who had robbed me for ten years. I had chaperoned them into print and introduced them everywhere and none of them was worth it. 'Plus,' he said, 'you wouldn't fuck any of them with a stone dick.'

I loved my dinners with Jack. He was supposed to be older than me but was younger in the ways that matter. We would always spend a part of the evening interrogating the bad behaviour of the family we had in common before shelving the whole thing under Fun. 'Let's move on,' he'd say. 'They know not what they do.' He was then talking about the summer holidays and what a riot it was going to be, how many beauties were attending, that sort of thing, and I thought I'd start the disco behaviour early by ordering more wine. He gave me such a loving look.

'You know something, Jack,' I said, 'the great difference is that you have energy and I have patience.'

'You mean dignity,' he said. 'You have dignity.'

'You have that, too.'

'Not really,' he said. 'The truth is I've never cared about it. Dignity is overrated.'

'False,' I said. 'Dignity is everything.'

'You are headed for a sad old age.'

'Harsh,' I said.

'Only kidding. You were always headed for a life of privacy. Did *our* wife ever tell you? At Cambridge we called you the handsome monk with the sacred spunk. You kept it dark. You were either heading for Holy Orders or were just a secretive bastard.'

'I was just quiet.'

'And some people are loud with quietness. You are loud with quietness, Jamie.'

'Not everybody...'

'Come on, man. You've got to raise your voice.'

'You're just a show-off,' I said.

'The show is everything,' Jack said. And he touched my hand, as if a little of his coldness might remind me of events.

'Be quiet,' I said. 'Privacy is its own show.'

'Like I said.'

I paused.

'Are you pausing?'

'No.'

'I thought that was a pause.'

'Shut up.' And then I paused.

'That was a pause.'

Sylvia said that Jack's distinction was to make life nicer – and not just nicer but nicer than it actually was. It didn't make him reliable but it made him wonderful. At St Andrew's he was in charge of the Ministry of Compliments, a small society of one, intended not merely to give people boosts, but dedicated to showing people, by generous example, how to live up to his compliments, and how to give them. Jack didn't just compliment a person, he complimented their good judgement in placing themselves in a position to be complimented by him. And he later understood that to be a very London distinction.

I asked him if he still read novels. 'God no.'

'How shallow.'

'I'm busy, Jamie. Nobody has time to deal with what passes for depth among those young novelists. I mean: all that "how strange it is to be me" bullshit, and how sad my daddy was. Fuck it.'

'I love all that.'

'You will die an ugly death, deranged with boredom.'

We discussed Henry James over crème brûlée, Jack tapping the burnt crust with a teaspoon whilst words caramelised in his mouth. 'Your young novelists are merely worrying about their profile or whether they have a sufficient number of followers on Instagram,' he said. 'It's all just fame-maintenance with those bores. But James knows the value as well as the price of everything and I'll die reading him.'

I looked for something helpless in Jack's eyes at that moment, but there was nothing of the sort, nothing gloomy, merely a mild acceptance, perhaps, of circumstances beyond the control of his imagination. I think he saw that I might feel sorry for him and he headed it off at the pass. 'It won't surprise you,' he said, 'that I love Mr Lambert Strether best of all. James gave him lines worth repeating to yourself every day.'

'You have to live. It's a mistake not to.'

'Precisely.'

In another era Jack would have been a popular guy at the Western Front, making ready for a terrible show. He would have been first with the nostalgic songs and a nip of brandy and an early death. But, as it was, he was heading instead to the Box nightclub, to a private booth full of monstrous narcissists and magnums of Grey Goose at 500 quid a pop. 'Remember me in your studies,' he said outside the restaurant, stepping into his mini-convertible after a kiss on each cheek. I stood on the pavement with my briefcase as he rolled down the window. 'Sure you won't come with?' he said. 'Come on, Sporty. There's no point going home to Jane Austen when there'a a club full of Jägerbombs waiting.'

I wanted to ask him how quickly it was spreading, and he saw it, I felt, with an eye for all the detail of our friendship, all the way back to those nights at St Andrew's when we would be up at the student paper polishing our put-downs. 'You know something, Jamie?' he said. 'I'm 50 years old and I've had a good time.'

'I suppose you think too much sacrifice makes a stone of the heart?'

'W B Yeats,' he said. 'I know my stuff.' He lit a cigarette and blew smoke into the dashboard. 'Now *there* was patience. She went off and married some gunman and Yeats didn't even get a shag out of it.'

'But he got the poems.'

'Fuck poems, Sporty. I've booked you into the house in Ibiza for the month of August. To hell with all those shy librarians you've been writing to. I'm talking Ibiza Town.'

'Agreed,' I said. 'Up to a point.'

'No limits,' he said. 'No limits. All the lunatic actors are coming. I'll send you the flight details.'

'See you there,' I said.

I knew I would never see him again. His teenage dimples were there like faint apostrophes on his weathered face as he blew smoke at me and buzzed the window down. 'Martin Garrix,' he said, holding his iPod aloft before speeding percussively into the darkness of Mayfair. I went to bed that night with a volume of poems from 1914. 'Pardon, old fathers, if you still remain/Somewhere in ear-shot for the story's end.' I read the poem as the lamps of Hampstead yellowed the trees and the city disowned itself. Before falling asleep I agreed that I must be at my desk in the morning, not opening my books and making notes as usual, but writing a cheque that would never be cashed to Jack Eddington-Gage, formerly John Gedge, to cover my room in Ibiza for the month of August. He had paid me the compliment of inviting me after all, and I knew I was lucky, and so did he.

THE CONVEYOR BELT

Ewa Winnicka

(Translated by Halina Boniszewska)

In Poland, Marcin was an advertising executive and drove an expensive car. But suddenly in 2008, he lost his position, and then another. Now aged 43, he took on a mind-numbing job in Dartford so he could provide for his family. When I hear Marcin talking, I have the impression that he's stared into the gaping jaws of hell.

Marcin: Our managers are Albanians. They're hard-nosed bastards. Some of them understand English. There are 90 Poles working two rubbish-sorting shifts, and a few Lithuanians as well.

Some of the Poles are on a special list, which means they're guaranteed work every day. The rest of them go up on a platform and wait for a decision, like in some sort of labour camp. The English employment agency which brings Poles over to our waste management sorting plant hired 500 people for our Dartford site, even though you can only have 90 people working any one shift. The agency couldn't care less. It gets paid through the nose for every employee on its list.

The Poles compete ferociously for work on the conveyor belt. So, for example, if you nick your mate's work gloves or safety helmet, he doesn't have anything to sort with, so he doesn't get any work. If you nick five pounds off another mate, he'll be so pissed off he'll go on a bender that night, knock back the cider, sleep in the next morning and miss the next shift. So *he* doesn't get any work either. If you don't actively mess things up for a workmate, by default you're helping him, which means you're doing yourself out of a job. If you help anyone, they say you're a faggot.

It's not so bad for the young women and their families. If one of the Albanians is sleeping with one of the conveyor belt women, then even a distant relative of hers from the back of beyond – from some hamlet in the Carpathian Mountains – working as a rubbish sorter in a different building, will get preferential treatment.

I'm in a privileged position because my brother has been working here for over a year. He's quite well-educated and can speak a bit of English – a bit of a know-it-all. He's just left conveyor-belt work and landed himself an office job; he's now working as a health and safety inspector in the factory. Apparently his office toilets are a bit cleaner than ours (which are beyond disgusting). He was supposed to get a pay rise, but they haven't given him one. My brother's not making a fuss though, because at least he now has a permanent contract in Dartford. So, he's in a better position than the rest of the pickers, who are agency staff, and who have virtually no right to any UK benefits. So, it's thanks to my brother that I don't have to go up on that wretched platform any more, waiting to see if the Albanian takes a liking to my mug on any particular day.

So we work on the conveyor belt. We have rubbish lorries coming from all over the country to our waste-management site. The rubbish gets tipped into a massive drum which has sharp spikes on the inside. The Poles sitting inside this drum have to remove all the large cardboard boxes. Cardboard is the most valuable recyclable waste material. You have to put the cardboard aside and fold it up neatly. Then the drum starts to turn and the large pieces of litter get stuck on the spikes. That's how the first sorting stage works.

It was funny last week because one of my colleagues hadn't put the safety lock on, and the drum began to rotate with the Poles still inside it. My colleague didn't know how to put the safety lock on because the Albanians were making savings by cutting back on health and safety training. The two Poles inside the drum were Wiesiek and Jarek, two alcoholic brothers who still hadn't made it to central London. The drum had made quite a few rotations before anyone realised what had happened. It crossed my mind that these two guys would now *never* see central London.

Somehow they survived. If they weren't such halfwits, they'd have sued the firm for millions. As soon as the Albanian noticed, he ran up to them and said: 'Shit, shit ... Look, nothing's happened! Let's just keep it quiet! You and me: Polish, Albanian – we're brothers, we are...' And the guys kept schtum. They were frightened of losing their jobs: six pounds fifty an hour, pre-tax.

Then the drum contents go to a massive hanger. You can smell the toxic fumes as you go in. This is where you have medical waste, food waste, broken glass, soiled sanitary towels, dirty nappies, surgical drains and plasma bags from people who are ill. Whoever takes the surgical drains and plasma bags out of the patient would do better to burn them, but I can imagine that people can't be bothered, which means that I end up having to deal with this crap; I have to transfer it to a small container, just as I have to do with every little piece of foil. The stench in the winter is unbearable; I can't imagine what it must be like in the summer. After an hour our rubber gloves are soaked through. The acid from the conveyor belt eats through the rubber.

I'm new here, so my colleagues don't speak to me much. They still don't trust me. I don't live with them, and I've never been out for a drink with any of them. I haven't told them that I used to be a director of a number of top advertising agencies – before I lashed out at my bosses, and then thought I should leave the country. I have a wife and children, and I want to get back to them.

This is how they talk to each other: 'All right dickhead! D'ya get any last night?'

'Fuck off, you wanker!'

'Do you do it on foil or aluminium?'

'Fuck off, you prick!'

'You fuck off, you wanker!'

And then peace returns because they've had a little banter.

Janek on the right here's 40, but he looks as if he's in his 50s. He's been working in the aluminium section for the last ten years. He may not realise it, but in working here he's digging himself an early grave. Or maybe he doesn't give a shit any more. Free radicals are vitamins compared to the stuff flying through the air above this conveyor belt. Anyway, I've no idea how Janek could ever get any action when there are so few women working here, and of those who are, the younger ones have been snatched up by the Albanians, whereas the older ones look like their own grandmothers. The guys aren't going to find any women in town either. The unattractiveness of Polish men is as widely known as *bigos* and Polish sausage – even in Dartford with its white-trash unemployed and its third generation of teenage mums on their third pregnancy, living off benefits.

Janek has been working for the last ten years. He's paid £650 a month. That's enough for fags, vodka and a room in a rented house that he shares with other pickers in this Dartford shithole. But it's not enough for a return ticket home. I don't know whether he gives it any thought; he was let out of prison ten years ago, and the truth is that he doesn't really have anything to go back to. He'll live out his days sorting rubbish. He'll eventually turn into a Polish Brit.

You can do a daytime or night-time sorting shift. The hourly rate's better on the night shift by 40p an hour. If you work nights, you age at five times the normal rate.

So, these bits of foil, these surgical drains, bottles, promotional leaflets and nappies that we throw into the left or right containers leave the waste-sorting plant in the form of huge bales. The recycled plastic is supposed to be pure, but it's not because we sort it quickly, so not very carefully. We follow the guidelines. The fines that the company gets for impure loads don't really make any difference to the bottom line. The plastic bales go off to China or Albania and they return three weeks later in the form of broken plastic handcuffs from a toy police set. You remove them from the conveyor belt and throw them into the appropriate container. You're just waiting for the little pink elephant with the waving trunk to come rolling up …

That's civilisation for you.

You can't think when you're picking out the rubbish. Not in that dreadful stench. You keep yourself entertained by trying to guess where the rubbish has come from. When you have new clothes on the conveyor belt, trousers with designer labels, or empty bottles of quality wine, you know that the rubbish has come in from the City. When the tatty trainers and empty cider bottles arrive, you know they've come in from somewhere like Dartford, Croydon or Slough. There are always plenty of empty handbags, bag-snatched off women.

Some of the workers eat off the conveyor belt when sealed food comes in from the better districts. If we're too embarrassed to eat a conveyor-belt sandwich in public, we might still pick up the occasional tin or jar of preserves. There's usually a harvest after Christmas, when we pick up unwanted presents – clothes that are virtually new. The rule is to always look in the pockets. One of the guys on night shift once found £800. The Albanian bosses turned a blind eye.

But they don't always turn a blind eye. About a month before that, a suitcase full of money came in on the conveyor belt. Fifteen thousand dollars in cash. Some drug deal gone awry; the guys on the run from the police threw the suitcase in a bin. That was rubbish from south London – maybe Elephant and Castle or Brixton, or somewhere like that. When my workmates opened up the suitcase, the Albanians stopped the conveyor belt, pushed the Poles aside and took all the contents.

I'm coming off the conveyor belt now. My mate, Marek, who dreams of being moved from foil to aluminium, hates the Albanians. He says they're dirty – worse than the Indians and Pakistanis – but he sucks up to them. He teases them – he makes out there's no toilet paper in the toilets because he's taken it home ... might even have stolen it ...

I read the *Guardian* every day. I recently read an article by some English university professor of ecology who was delighted with the successful enforcement of the stricter new rules for sorting rubbish. Were he ever to set foot in our factory, he would lose faith not only in rubbish sorting, but in humanity itself.

JONNY JUST COME

Yomi Sode

JONNY JUST COME. Hair nappy looking with dry
chalk like partings between his shaky fingers,

the west end wind wakes each follicle on his skin and says
welcome, your life is no longer what it used to be

Jonny has arrived, the only one in his family to do what
the others couldn't. A pressure so high it's as if from now on

he'll live each day on a tightrope and who would blame him,
last time he saw as many white people was the Brit Awards,

TOWIE, The Royle Family. In Nigeria, you see white people
and stare, you take selfies, test whether they can

pronounce words and laugh at their tongues' rebellion to
     pepper.
Jonny pinches himself to feel if it is real. Jonny, this is real.

He knows he is no safer and his family has him in prayers
Jonny greets everything that breathes, he is stunned.

People carrying plastic bags to scoop their dog's mess,
     wearing
T-shirts showing their chest hairs, wearing shorts

in weather that has him pleading with the Gods,
how can they do this he wonders, *their legs are like toothpicks,*

where is the meat for warmth? Jonny just come, holding a bag
filled with fruits, a map, African cuisine and £10,

the highest sum of money in his years of life.
In Naija, holding such a note would make him the man

so in London, he thinks this be Big money but
     unfortunately,
London is far from easy. The air tastes metallic,

the map smells like paint. Everything is confusing.
Little does he know, but Jonny will learn the culture

and swallow his mother tongue, his hair, once nappy, will
neaten at the edges, Jonny will have swag.

Tasting the strawberry gloss on female lips, his excitement
will heighten, *Oyinbo girl dey like me*

He will then truly arrive, but Jonny will grow and be more
aware of his blackness, he might get robbed couple times,

he might get called a Nigga, his blackness might attract
     attention
of gangs, his blackness will intimidate people

His blackness will make him question other people's
    blackness
so he'll wonder why he left Nigeria in the first place.

Behind closed doors, the police can be just as brutal
Bombs still go off in random places

Though not as bloody as home
Not as heart wrenching as 86 kids being burned alive

Or 200+ kids being kidnapped
maybe he'll buy a knife

But Jonny is not built for prison, nor to injure a man
he has a Mother that cares and the last thing she wants

is her only child to be made a stereotype
one of many words he will learn through his lifetime.

Jonny has arrived, and when he returns to Nigeria,
he may be taunted as being black, but not African,

then he'll find himself in a limbo. Jonny has arrived,
in this odd moment where being an African

in England is the 'in thing'.
White people speak of Dbanj and singalong to Wizkid.

Caribbeans shoki as if the dance is their own.
His culture is celebrated with every turn he takes.

But once in a while, he is reminded that this is not his home.
Whether his name is mispronounced/ he spots a clutched bag,

watches footage of his people being called immigrants.
Sees YouTube clips of Go Back to Where You Came From.

Inside, a part of him dies, inside
he felt like this was home, outside though.

NEW SYBARIS

Rowan Moore

IF AS CLICHÉ has it skyscrapers are penile then where am I now, in the express elevator of the Heron Tower, on the way to its rooftop bar?

Shooting past the corpus cavernosum, surging towards the urethral opening? And what am I, hurtling upwards, with others? It doesn't bear thinking about

At pavement level one passes the glass wall of a high reception area, with escalators and a truck-sized fish tank, before reaching a velvet rope and name-checks. Next a lobby as tight as the aquarium was ample and then the ascent, in an all-glass lift attached to the side of the tower, such that the streets of the City of London and then the rest of the capital unfurl around us. The rate of acceleration and degree of vertigo are just shy of nauseating, it being undesirable to spoil our appetite on the way to the rooftop restaurant. But there is still a mild test of nerve, appropriate to the risk-taking financial capital of the world.

On reaching the top we privileged homunculi pass through some tortuous corridors before entering a bar with a view of a terrace occupied by a tree aflame with an electric autumn of orange light. To the right stairs rise to two more levels past a glass wall; there are views of the Heron's companion towers, the Gherkin and Tower 42, Vegas-lit at their tips to announce that here too are pleasure zones. A community of cocktail drinkers is created 200 metres into the air, for which the rest of the city – the bars and clubs of Shoreditch to the north, the suburbs stretching east towards Essex – becomes atmosphere, a background lighting effect. Some drinkers occupy the stairs, like teenagers partying in their parents' house. At the top there is another rope, defining a more exclusive area.

If you don't turn right but continue straight on you reach the restaurant, a generous volume ceiled with a geodesic-looking lattice of thick curved bamboo. There are also hints of Oscar Niemeyer: as its name suggests, Sushisamba fuses culinary influences from Japan and Brazil, so the décor follows suit. A would-be enchanting space is formed by fragments of different sorts of nature – twigs, a crystal forest, the bamboo, the contents of plate and glass wherein slivers of flavour and texture have been sourced and combined from across the world to deliver tiny empires of experience, synaesthetic microsymphonies of look, taste, feel, scent and even, in the surprising crunches that detonate amid smoother sensations, sound. There are clouds. A sculptural object in the ceiling resembles crystallised vapour, lights gather in cumuli, and puffs of foam, elBulli-style, float over the food. A dish of opaque fluid invites you to fish in it, as in a delicate swamp.

This is a place where City people are rewarded for their hard hours of screen-based labour, for being in effect call-centre workers with high incomes, with affirmations of status and delights of the senses (albeit one that got middling praise from the restaurant critics) in these celestial spaces. I do, however, experience some disappointment that the place is not more flagrant, more strutting, more of a coke-and-hookers inferno in the sky. Rather there is a peaceable round table of large-wristwatched young Africans and Arabs; elsewhere are seated Caucasian diners, who if loaded are discreetly so. In the bar, City workers display the assertive nodding and wary bonhomie that passes for sociability when rivalrous business colleagues go out to drink and eat. There might be more overt excess beyond the rope at the top of the stairs and as the evening wears on the black skirts and heels arriving in the lift grow shorter and higher. But there is a well-behaved normality, relatively speaking, among most of the guests.

In London, as in other major cities, the arts of distraction have reached an unprecedented level of sophistication. If a cataclysm were to hit now, future generations would marvel – as we might over Petronius's descriptions of Roman excess – at our own time's range and ingenuity of food, drink, art, design and performance, of spas, bars, shops and clubs. Some are aimed at the rich, such as the 24K Cryogenic Diamond Mask facial (using diamond dust and real gold) offered by OROGOLD of Kensington High Street, Chelsea and Mayfair. Some are available to the reasonably well-off or to the large number of childless professionals with disposable income. Some, thanks to public art galleries and sponsored events, are free.

Not all these experiences will be to everyone's taste, but they are a sample of the diversity and invention with which London daily and nightly strives to de-jade the appetites of its inhabitants. Some are built on the inheritance of past benefactions, some occupy spaces intended for other purposes. Some – the pungent meals – exemplify ways in which immigration has enriched London. Some are works of love, of cooks or artists who want to do their best with their media, others of calculation, some of both. There is both brilliance and pretension in the list.

Many of these diversions consume references, memories and ideas, intellectual and physical material, with greedy promiscuity.

Peter Rees, for 28 years the chief planner of the City of London, under whom projects like the Heron Tower were encouraged and approved, started late in his career to tell stories of his experiences visiting leather bars in east London. On one occasion he left a bar to find a group of Bengali teenagers fascinated with his street-parked Porsche. Some tension might be thought present in this situation – poor area, posh car, gay man, Muslim boys – but in Rees's telling he let the teenagers photograph themselves with the car and in the driving seat, which delighted them, before the parties went their separate ways. For Rees, this sort of encounter is the essence of London:

> It has always been a place where a minority could find succour; whether it was gay or religious or whatever it might be, you could come into the East End of London and the East End of London would tolerate almost anything, within a very limited set of local rules which were community-run. If you think of the way that has produced a London that is the world's best party – the railway arches from Battersea to Bermondsey are full of gay saunas, discos, bars, all sorts of weird and wonderful things going on in those railway arches because there are enough people of any particular persuasion or interest in London to take a marginal space and come together in it. That then attracts more people. Twenty-, thirty-somethings come for the party. They only get the job to pay for the party.

In this eroto-economic theory of town planning, pleasure is an end in itself, a source of personal identity and freedom and an engine of the city's prosperity. The theory combines social and economic liberalism, both individual choice and competitive exploitation, in a way that is not in the end so surprising from a planner who promoted the growth of the City of London's towers: that's how Shoreditch came about, that's how Vauxhall came about, that's how Soho existed for many years until the degree of control started to become oppressive. Or Shepherd Market in Mayfair. You can go right back in history. There are the centres of doing naughty things or doing things that aren't the family norm which are very much part of a great city and the degree of tolerance and provision for alternative lifestyles actually determine the degree of creativity and adaptability and futureproofing that a city will have.

So central, indeed, is the pursuit of pleasure to the city that Rees believes families with children should live away from the centre of London.

To know better the economic driver he describes I find myself in a pleasant garden in the area celebrated by the poet John Betjeman as Metro-land, the northwestern corridor of suburbia that grew up along what is now the Metropolitan Underground line. Close by are the steep, bucolic slopes of Gladstone Park (opened 1901) and Dollis Hill synagogue, all concrete, with Stars of David and menorahs abstracted into hexagons and inverted arches, a quirky work of 1936-38 by the engineer-architect Owen Williams (the black glass *Daily Express* building in Fleet Street; Empire Pool Wembley; Pioneer Health Centre in Peckham; some clunky bridges over an early motorway, the M1, phase one).

I am talking to Edward, a retired professional about to hit 70, a pillar of the local Jewish community, born in South Africa to Russian parents ('my father worked with Trotsky'). On Wednesdays and Sundays, he says, 'there are SBN nights. That's Stark Bollock Naked. They start at 2.30pm so it's very convenient if you don't want to stay up late on Sunday night.'

Edward and his fiancé like to go to the sex clubs that Rees was talking about, of which the best known are in Vauxhall. They are often in railway arches, because the space is large, cheap, windowless, anonymous and contains noise, and it doesn't matter when a train goes overhead. They also give the sense of 'going into the darker side of life'. The outside will be discreet although with a special enclosure to deal with the fact that the law requires smoking to take place outside, but the clubbers don't want to be seen from the street naked or nearly so. One club might have four arches: 'one for getting changed, one for drinking and chatting and two for sex'. There might in the low light be 'four hundred, five hundred guys all looking the same all dressing the same: well built, a bit of leather and beard, a harness or something. Fashions change'. Some clubs 'have lounge areas to change in. You can see what's there and what you fancy. People walk by with nothing on. You don't present yourself, you just walk in and go dancing ... You start eyeing one another up and start touching and kissing or they're already busy and you join in. You're part of a big society. If you see someone you know you might just walk past and give them a stroke. The music is too loud to talk. At my age I'm hard of hearing'.

Sometimes they have shows, 'naked, perhaps a bit of leather. One or two people. The innovation is to have orgasms on stage. Sometimes they have a hard time getting there, but usually people are enjoying themselves too much to notice ... People are celebrating whatever turns them on. It's nothing to be ashamed of. You do what you want. You don't have to do what you don't want. You can be experimental. You can build your self-esteem if nobody likes you ... you're enjoying yourself but there can be an undercurrent of desperation that comes from growing up gay and suffering for it ... You have sexual urges. You're open. That's the best thing of all'.

Edward says that gay sex clubs are more peaceful than the atmosphere that can grow up around straight clubs: 'Nobody's drunk, nobody fights, nobody has a cross word. It's safe as houses. There's no aggro. People are friendly. The only problem is overdoses. Clubs search you for GHB. The last thing they want is ambulances being called round.' He doesn't see much BDSM. There are other clubs for that, frequented by both gay and straight, 'multisexual', often coming in couples, for 'a little bit of torture and whipping'. There is, though, a corporal punishment night at one of the gay clubs, piss fun at another.

And, when the time comes to put clothes back on and go back into the outside world, they are 'Morris dancers to a man, or computer programmers, or bankers. It's a complete leveller – income level, social background don't matter ... although you might sometimes get a bit of attitude, when gorgeous people don't want to be touched by less gorgeous people'.

All this is nothing new, to a degree. He cites the molly houses of the 18th century, the effects of the wartime city filled with British and American servicemen, the places described by Joe Orton. But there wasn't the same array of sex clubs when Edward – married, in the closet, leading a double life – first explored the gay scene 'just before AIDS started'. There was Subway in Leicester Square – 'you heard that you go to this club and you can get something that kills you'. There were bars, but more discreet. There was the Royal Vauxhall Tavern, perhaps the most venerable of gay pubs, into which legend has it Princess Diana was once smuggled, dressed as a man, with the help of Freddie Mercury and Kenny Everett. There were public toilets and Hampstead Heath, in all weathers, including snow.

At some point, he's not sure when, official attitudes began to change. One night he met a policeman on the Heath whose job was not to deter the gay men, but to protect them from violence by others. Sex clubs started in 'out-of-the-way places – Peckham, Mile End, Southwark, Dalston – often in pubs taken over, with black paint on the windows. Quiet. You don't want the self-righteous-indignation crowd to notice too much'. Local authorities became more tolerant, some more than others.

Now, he says, the clubbing and bar scenes feed on one another. The more people come, the more attractive these places become. London is a world leader. 'People fly in from all over. Paris is less tolerant. Amsterdam doesn't have the critical mass. Rome has got the Pope in the Vatican. Los Angeles and San Francisco? America doesn't allow as much as the English do. They have their Bible Belt.' He sees it as part of the city's wider cultural and economic attractiveness and openness – fashion, art, food, investment – that come from a 'stable society and a free society'. 'London belongs to the foreigners,' he says. 'We the foreigners feel at home. It's our city, it's not yours.'

Edward, in short, is describing a world of deregulated international exchange much like London's banking and property sectors. In the gathering of delights from all nations and the striving for innovation in stimulation, a Vauxhall sex club is not unlike a Sushisamba cocktail. It is different in one respect, however, which is that it is 'not exploitative'. Someone must be making good money out of these clubs, but in Edward's telling more than Rees's they form an almost utopian republic where wealth and status fade, apart from the aristocracy of looks. A night, with a free drink, costs 15 pounds or ten pounds to members. It costs less than going to the movies or the pub, or a single cocktail.

Elsewhere in London's contemporary hedonism industry, commercial calculation is more apparent. In restaurants and bars beautifully conceived and executed, offering concoctions of sublime craft, and in plenty that do not reach these heights, you can taste the PowerPoint presentations that were made to the investors without whom such things cannot happen – defining the clientele, the differentiation from competitors, the slicing and layering of the world's cuisines into a seam rich enough for a new venture to mine, the communications strategy. 'I ate a concept last Thursday', wrote Aditya Chakrabortty in the *Guardian*, in 2014, 'not just any old abstraction, but a "heavily concepted restaurant trend", in publicist-speak. No kidding: at the new Lobster Kitchen, the name is the menu is the business model. Here you can have whatever you like so long as it's pink: lobster tails, lobster rolls, lobster with macaroni cheese ... Just like central London homes,' he observed, 'the capital's eateries are becoming a global asset class.' The Lobster Kitchen was co-founded by Abigail Tan, 'the twenty-nine-year-old heiress to one of the wealthiest real-estate dynasties in south-east Asia, IGB of Malaysia'.

The more heterosexual sex clubs have also become profession-alised businesses. The most publicised is Killing Kittens, founded in 2005. Dedicated to 'the relentless pursuit of female desire', it has been well explored by adventurous young feature writers – to whom I am grateful for sparing me this duty – whose copy usu-ally feels the need to mention that its founder, the 'sextrepreneur' Emma Sayle, is a friend of Kate Middleton, Duchess of Cam-bridge. (They briefly went to the same school and were once pho-tographed in the same dragon-boat crew.)

Much is made of the club's elite eliteness. 'We are very elit-ist, but that's what it's all about,' Sayle told *Time Out*. 'True, not everyone's a supermodel but all members are attractive, aspira-tional, successful professionals aged 20–45.' Its parties are held in 'smart venues. The rooms are candlelit, we play the right kind of music and it's black tie, so people are dressed-up. There's often a champagne and oyster reception too, rather than cheese straws ... It's the little things that make a difference.' Now Killing Kittens is going global, to 'New York penthouses, St Tropez super-yachts and über-exclusive luxury locations the world over'. Not a railway arch in Vauxhall, then, ten pounds to enter, with 500 heaving bod-ies. More like a Conran Shop for sex.

PETTICOAT LANE *AL FRESCO*

Alex Rhys-Taylor

FOR FOUR CENTURIES, Petticoat Lane Market acted as a membrane between the City of London and the East End. The granite heart of global capitalism on one side of cast iron bollards, the red-brick muscle of Empire's labourers on the other. Over the last 70 years, however, the gradual closure of the docks and the outsourcing of industry has caused London's muscle to atrophy. The City, along with its cognitive labour, has metastasised through the old inner-East End. You can smell the coffee roasters and sourdough pizzerias chasing the cement and emulsion-paint fumes up the road, from Whitechapel to Mile End.

It has smothered Petticoat Lane in towers of glass and wipe-clean cladding before slowly digesting it. Over the past 15 years, the new fashion for inner-city living has almost entirely broken down and ingested the old market, transforming greasy-spoon cafés, luggage retailers and kinky underwear wholesalers into cocktail bars, gourmet candy retailers and Chicago rib joints.

There are still a handful of wholesalers in its vicinity, who are dependent on drivers making the expensive trip into London's congestion charge zone to buy their imported batiks, patent leather heels, phone covers and bongs. Between the remaining threads of the rag-trade is Petticoat Lane's food court; an assemblage of plastic patio chairs, polystyrene containers, a café, a restaurant and five to eight food trucks. Each is open every day of the working week. For now, the tradition of eating *al fresco* on Petticoat Lane is alive.

How did the market come into being? Before the 16th century the area around Petticoat Lane was a cluster of fields for grazing swine that had been driven along the outer edge of the City wall. The path was called Hog Lane. John Norden's 1593 map of London sketches trees on either side of it, noted in other accounts as a mixture of elms and hedgerows. It is likely that these offered shelter to some of the earliest *al fresco* diners in the area – the farmers and pig drovers who lunched on hard bread, ale, and in times of plenty, perhaps also an egg, some bacon or cheese. As the food historian John Burnett points out, for a large part of British history agricultural labourers 'ate out' more than any other group.

It is no coincidence that the hog-driving track and the porcine miasma that arose from nearby fields were downwind of the seat of power in London's west. That the East End is the lee of the prevailing westerly winds would determine its fate for much of London's history. At the start of the 17th century, following a fourfold increase in its population in less than a century, it was downwind around Hog Lane that London burst most emphatically through its traditional boundaries.

After hardly more than a generation, the City's eastern pastures bristled with slums, workshops, furnaces, brickworks. Many London labourers were migrants from elsewhere in England, Scotland, Ireland and Wales, but also from Europe. Each brought their own ways of being, doing and expressing, creating an explosion in the richness and complexity of the City's language and culture.

Less than a quarter of a mile away, Shakespeare and his players thrived on the new mix. Among the industries blossoming in the area were the spinning, weaving, cutting and sewing of silk-trades helmed by French-speaking Protestant refugees fleeing the hostility augured by the Edict of Fontainebleau, which declared them heretics. While the new arrivals had little choice but to adapt to local customs and produce, they contributed to the City's culture, bringing words such as 'refugee' and 'ox-tail soup' into the lexicon, and salads and sauces into the kitchen (gravy was from the French *grané*).

When John Ogilby plotted his map of London in 1667 after the Great Fire, he noted the remarkable area of building that had filled in around Hog Lane during the unprecedented population growth of his century. *Not* depicted in his map, however, was the daily efflorescence of stalls and traders that had started to appear on and around the street. (To this day, despite their durability and importance to urban commerce, street markets are rarely depicted on maps.) The market hawked secondhand shirts, chemises, and skirts, then called 'petticoats', and its existence is detectable because Ogilby put its new nickname on the map: Hogge's Lane became 'Petticoat Lane'.

It is a truism of the last half millennium of migration in the East End that each new wave of arrivees moved directly into the businesses, cookhouses and places of worship of their predecessors. Petticoat Lane is no different. At its pinnacle in the late 19th century, the market flourished under the patronage of thousands of Jews fleeing the pogroms that were spreading between the Baltic and Black Seas. With the British Empire at its geographic peak, and industry running at full steam, the street market that newcomers encountered was the place captured in Henry Mayhew's *London Labour and the London Poor:* two crowded miles of stalls and vendors centred around Middlesex Street (the respectable, though brief, Victorian renaming of the Lane).

Among a clutter of whale-bone corsets, bristles, Havana cigars, Bengal cheroots and sealing wax, Mayhew also noted the 'costermongers', who were the City's itinerant barrow-wheeling, and fixed-pitch, sellers of fast food and ingredients. They peddled bread ('wheaten, standard wheaten and household'), 'hot currant puddings', 'pickled cucumbers' floating in barrels 'like huge fat caterpillars', cuts of 'pale, bloodless meat' certified by rabbis, and oysters, definitely uncertified by rabbis. For a few unsuccessful months in the mid-1860s, there was even one of London's earliest street vendors of ice cream. Behind the market stalls, Mayhew also records several 'cookshops' dedicated to an 'eatable' that 'the Israelites delight in': 'fried fish'. The Lane has a strong claim to be the place where fish met chips.

Eating out had long been a habit for London's labouring classes, if only because so few had kitchens of their own (many bakers and cookshops offered cooking space in their ovens for a small fee). Some cookshops had their own special dishes: frittered flanders, pies, boiled trotters and tripe. Some of Petticoat Lane's cookshops and costers were kosher, offering herring, salt beef and other north European Jewish staples. But this was not a mosaic city with disparate ethnic groups existing side by side in parallel worlds. It was a space in which Londoners' lives intermingled, and old identities folded in on themselves. Where and what you ate was important in establishing your place in the mix. Jewish anarchists such as Rudolf Rocker marched past synagogues around Petticoat Lane with ham sandwiches aloft. Mayhew wrote that those less committed to public performances of sacrilege might sometimes 'creep into a Christian cookshop, not being particular about eating *tryfe*'.

Showing equal disregard for Levitical qualms was the famous Petticoat Lane stall established in 1919 by the chubby Jewish Russian migrant, Itzko Brenner. Tubby Isaac's Seafood was renowned for its whelks, cockles, winkles and mussels (strictly prohibited in the Old Books), as well as the local speciality of jellied eels. By the 1960s, the then-owner – a nephew of the original Tubby – had made so many television appearances that he joined the actors' union Equity. The eels of Petticoat Lane had become part of the national mythology of the East End, along with plucky Blitz survivors, egalitarian gangsters and flirtatious starlets.

Eels had been part of everyday East End life for centuries. While the pre-Roman tribes of the southeast had eschewed the bounty of the sacred Thames and its estuary, the Mediterranean occupiers who arrived in AD 43 set a taste for all things piscine and molluscular. Eel, expertly farmed by Romans, accompanied herring, flounder and plaice in local diets for centuries, and were still an important source of protein more than one and a half millennia later. They were seldom fished locally, but were imported from the estuaries that feed into the North and Baltic Seas. After the Great Fire, Dutch eel fishermen were reported to have fed the City with catches brought across the North Sea. In later recognition of their efforts, King James II rewarded the Dutch fishermen with a special charter to sell direct to Londoners, bypassing the middlemen of Billingsgate.

Long-term, this meant that migrant entrepreneurs found a ready customer base in the industrial East End. The consumption of jellied eels in, and around, Petticoat Lane lasted far into the 20th century, surviving the loss of fishing vessels and shell-fish harvesters in the First World War. As European fascism loomed, Tubby Isaac emigrated to New York, but eels went on being guzzled *al fresco*; pulled from a porcelain bowl chilled by a damp morning, soused in vinegar and sprinkled with ribald conversation.

The seafood stand was ill-prepared for the radical demographic, economic and cultural shifts after the end of the Second World War. As old East Enders migrated to the suburbs and new towns, many seafood vendors moved with them, often further down the Thames estuary. More fatal for the trade, though, were the new suburban identities of the children of re-located East Enders, who developed culinary tastes opposed to those of their elders. Jellied eels were the first victim.

Rejection of the parent culture is rarely total, however, and the loyal surburbanite sons and daughters returned to see their old relatives. An outing to one of Tower Hamlet's verdant cemeteries would be followed by a drive to Petticoat Lane to indulge their elders with a bowl of Tubby's jellied eels. But even this trade dried up after the millennium. In June 2013, faced with the soaring price of overfished eels, a road layout prohibiting access to cab drivers and the exodus of its patrons into graves, Paul Simpson, a direct descendent of the original Tubby Isaac, closed the stand.

Paradoxically, less than a stone's throw away, business is booming. In nearly every one of the last five decades, the number of middle-class Londoners eating out during their lunch break has increased. Changes in the socio-economic distribution of 'non-residential eating' started in the 19th century, as cities developed suburban residential zones for the 'middling sort'. The relative distance between home and work meant the new suburbanites had to eat out, and in the late Victorian era the City's chop houses offered public dining to an even wealthier class of Londoners, hitherto inclined to dine in private clubs or at home. War canteens, followed by fast food joints, expanded the practice. Petticoat Lane's food court, open from 11am to 3pm, depends on this trend.

At a national level, according to government agencies, every year since 2001 has seen a steady *decrease* in eating out, which is partly attributable to a revolution in home cooking accelerated by a financial crisis that made both running and visiting a bricks-and-mortar restaurant more difficult. In the three months after the 2008 crash, as many who worked in the nearby financial quarter were made redundant or had their expenses accounts cut, food stalls at Petticoat Lane fell in number. But London's post-crisis middle classes are still 'eating out', with the banquettes and serviettes of the restaurant supplanted by the pavement and paper napkins of the food truck.

The food court now gets going every morning at around 9.30am with the arrival of the Tikka Truck, British Bengali-owned.

This is followed not long after by a large transit van containing Tomo's Katsu Wrap tent (a Kurdish-Japanese joint enterprise). Soon after that come the falafel guys (Lebanese), the dumpling stall (Chinese) and the Thai Food van (until recently there were two Thai outlets). At some point in the late morning, where once there were cookshops vending post-Huguenot *pommes frites* and kosher fried fish, a Greek-Cypriot-owned fish and chip shop slices its potatoes, heats up its oil, and prepares fillets for frittering. By lunchtime, a constellation of aromas provide a mouth-watering testament to half a millennium of everyday eating in London.

While the food court is popular with City suits, as well as media workers from nearby creative hubs, it also still attracts the East End's residual working-class residents who visit to buy cheap clothes, shoes and fabrics. How long will it continue? With no heavy industry left in the East End, and a state committed to stripping spatial capital from the City's poorest residents, the future of cheap and tasty calories in east London does not look bright.

All around the market, behemoths of high finance or luxury living are springing up. The displacement of the residual working-class is a threat to the viability of Petticoat Lane Market. More significantly, the 'market'-driven society enveloping the East End is antipathetic to actual living and breathing markets. The largest markets near the financial quarter – Spitalfields old fruit and veg market and Billingsgate Fish Market – closed soon after 1986's Big Bang, when deregulation enabled global financial markets to supplant all others in the national economy.

Recently, a food market that popped up in the City between its most deliciously named buildings, the Gherkin and the Cheese Grater, was forced to shut down and re-open with changes dictated by local 'place makers'. The unpredictable smells and noise of the market stall create friction in the otherwise smooth flow of capital into and out of the City's bloodless veins.

The City's squeamishness does not mean the end of *al fresco* dining around its perimeter, and Petticoat Lane's environs offer new opportunities to lunch on the lush roof garden of a refurbished pub or to dine under street-lamplight on the roped-off, pigeon-shit spattered, pavement outside a new high-end Greek restaurant at prices that would make a taverna-owner's moustache curl. In the one car park yet to be turned into a hotel, you can visit a cluster of food trucks and tents for Taiwanese dumplings, Korean chicken, Swedish barbecue and Aussie griddled prawns. All stand some chance of becoming the everyday dishes of tomorrow's London, but most of the new opportunities for gastronomy under the City's unreliable skies are the opposite of everyday. Dining *al fresco* on and around Petticoat Lane is becoming an exceptional, and exclusive, event.

The East End, of course, always changes, yet for a long time certain features endured to make those changes possible. A pragmatic amenability to difference was part of the local DNA, growing out of necessity for generations who lived at street level around the City's port. Huguenot weavers made space for Jewish tailors, who made room for Sylheti sailors. Eating outdoors, where the breeze brings materials, people and cultures into contact, was part of what made the community so resilient. Current shifts in the demography, culture and institutions of the East End, however, seem more permanent. Failing another economic catastrophe, there is no need for the East End's new residents ever to get along with each other, cordoned off as they are from the miasma, or elevated above it on their 34th floor balconies, sipping negronis behind the security of a concierge.

A HISTORY OF LONDON
IN TEN STREET FOODS

Sophie Baggott

Oysters, AD 43

WIDELY SCATTERED SHELLS found in excavations reveal that, from the Romans' arrival, Londinium's inhabitants relied heavily on shellfish for nutrition, particularly the oysters that thrived around England's shores. Drew Smith, author of *Oyster: A Gastronomic History*, believes that oysters were eaten in the Neolithic age, were 'there at the start of humanity'. Modern Leadenhall Market is now atop the market once at the heart of Londinium, and remains a culinary hub. Romans grabbed their takeaways from open-air bars called *cauponae*, dousing their food with a pungent condiment, *garum* (fermented fish sauce). A cleaned-up version of that taste remains; an 1817 recipe for 'Tomata Catsup' notes a quarter-pound of anchovies as a vital ingredient.

Hot Peascods and Codlings, 15th Century

The 15th century poem 'London Lickpenny' describes a Kentish man encountering the bellows of street-salesmen: "'Hot pescods!' one gan cry, "Strabery rype, and chery in the ryse!" ... Then come there one, and cried "Hot shepes fete!"' Peascod meant a pod of peas (later dried pea soup was the warm nourishment of the streets) and hot codlings were small baked apples. 'Not yet old enough for a man, nor young enough for a boy, as a squash is before 'tis a peascod, or a codling when 'tis almost an apple', says Malvolio of the disguised Viola in Shakespeare's *Twelfth Night*. Although oyster shells were the heftiest haul from archaeological digs below Shakespeare's Globe in the 1980s, there were also the pips and stones of grapes, figs, blackberries, raspberries, plums, nutshells and small animal bones.

Trotters, 1728

Georgian London resounded to hawkers' cries of 'sheep's trotters!' These hooves were best served fried in hog's lard, marking the words of *The Country Housewife and Lady's Director* (1728): 'Clean them very well from the Hair.' A fricassee of sheep's trotters should be slathered with 'a Sauce made of Gravey, some Claret and some Mushrooms'. Trotters could be bought hot or cold at Borough Market seven days a week; vendors bought them cheap from slaughterhouses, then skinned and parboiled them, and customers purchased them whole, to suck the sticky meat and fat off the bone.

Sausage and Chips, 1750–1850

Beef sausages became the fashion in the 1750s. A German pastor visiting London not long after warned, 'A foreigner will be surprised to see what flesh-eaters the English are' and in 1771 Tobias Smollett's *Humphry Clinker* was horrified by an overload of meat: 'skin-of-beef, tripe, cow-heel or sausages … turned my stomach.' The more usual Victorian banger was a pork-based, boiled or fried, bright pink saveloy sausage, rather like a hot dog. Once potato chips joined the popular street-bought diet at the end of the 19th century, they might accompany sausages.

Muffins, 1820–

'Do you know the muffin man ... who lives in Drury Lane?' was recorded in manuscript in 1820. Not a modern cupcake-style muffin, but a yeast-raised bread, sold fresh, along with crumpets, around teatime from trays carried on the head or round the neck around middling residential streets in the new inner suburbs, and announced by ringing a handbell. To be toasted before a coal fire, and lavishly buttered. Villainous Uncle Ralph in Dickens's *Nicholas Nickleby* gets involved in the 1830s in a scam scheme for the 'United Metropolitan Improved Hot Muffin and Crumpet Baking and Punctual Delivery Company, Capital, five millions, in five hundred thousand shares of ten pounds each'.

Baked Potatoes, 1830–

Baked potatoes were first sold in the 1830s and '40s, 'roasted as chestnuts' on a small scale, over charcoal: 'Hot hot all ot – mealy and floury, hot ot ot. Yere's yer reg'lar Hirish fruit, with plenty of butter and salt, all ot ot hot.' Henry Mayhew in *London Labour and the London Poor* (1851), took down a seller's words: 'Such a day as this, sir, when the fog's like a cloud come down, people looks very shy at my taties. They've been more suspicious since the taty rot' (the Irish famine of the 1840s, caused by blight). The sellers did bigger business when they had their tatties baked in batches in a bakery oven, and transferred them hot to their magnificent metal 'cans', with a fire-pot hung below a hot-water boiler, and a steam-vent; there were other compartments for butter, pepper and salt, and for fire-pot charcoal.

Sandwiches, 1850–

London's population boomed from under 865,000 in 1801 to more than three million in 1871, many of them clerks who needed cheap protein and carbohydrates at work but couldn't afford the time or money for chop houses. In 1850 at least 70 street vendors were selling ham sandwiches, which had replaced the older habit of keeping a portion of meat clean while portable inside the hollowed-out crust of a penny loaf (although that avoided staleness of bread far longer than any cut slice). The first sandwich bar opened only in 1933, Sandy's of Oxendon Street in Soho, and between then and the 1980s the norm across the working capital was a small family-run shop that made up each sandwich individually to order from bowls of very plain ingredients, wrapping it in a paper bag.

'Umble Pie, 1851–

Umble was from the French *nomble*, deer's innards, and was just one of the – cheaper – meats that filled small hot pies sold from cookshops, the (probably rather coarse rye flour) pastry crust acting as edible wrapping. Beef, pork and lamb pies, with, and later without, spices and the sweet fruity ingredients that were the equivalent of brown sauce and ketchup, remain on sale today, although there were always suspicions about the meat. Sam Weller in Dickens' *Pickwick Papers* recommends pies only 'when you know the lady as made it, and is quite sure it ain't kitten'; Mayhew was teased by a vendor that cats were *barely ever* used any more for all that passers-by called 'Meow! Meow!' The prime cut of urban legend was an 1846 novella, *The String of Pearls*, in which the murdered clients of demon barber Sweeney Todd were raw material for Mrs Lovett's meat pies.

Roasted Chestnuts, 19th Century Onwards

Henry Mayhew described counters in the streets holding 'large matting baskets, some piled up with dark-brown polished chestnuts – shining like a racer's neck'. He thought it was one of the oldest street foods, though it was strictly seasonal as part of the fruit-sellers' trade, and had been displaced as a hot comfort in a cold hand by the baked potato. The nuts were roasted on a pan over hot charcoal, and sold 16 for a penny. The tourist-zone vendors sell the smell rather than the goods; one of the last real sellers could be found with his hot coals on a barrow on Sundays at Bell Lane and Wentworth Street in Spitalfields; he inherited the business from his Maltese family, and ran it for 50 years.

Mad for Miso, 2017

The Roman's garum sauce was fermented; so were the vinegars that sharpened the last two centuries of street foods – and fermented foods have returned to the menu in 2017, especially miso seasoning, fermented soybeans mixed with fungus. Where the vinegar, chop sauce and ketchup used to stand on takeaway tables, miso is the staple of the street food scene among vogueish clean eaters and the vegan food festivals taking over the pavements. KERB, a crew of eight traders, hosted a sell-out series in the summer of 2017, Living on the Veg.

A BETTER MAN

Jacob Ross

SHE'D BEEN LOOKING forward to the two-bar electric fire in the living room to warm herself. She'd just walked out of a drizzle that had misted the world outside from the time she got up this morning – as if the night before had bled into the whole day.

Shehu had his elbows on the little dining table when she entered the flat, his face turned up towards the ceiling. A bulging laundry bag sat on the floor behind him.

He did not return her greeting and a familiar heaviness came over her. She crossed her feet, swallowed on the creeping dryness in her throat, leaned a shoulder against the wall of the narrow corridor, and waited.

She sensed another presence in the room before she noticed the woman seated sideways on the old sofa, one leg over the other, a silver-strapped sandal dangling from her foot. Her purple nails were busy on the keypad of her phone. The woman kept her head down, a pile of tinted braids making a curtain around her face – the Congolese girl who'd just taken up residence with six other women in the flat above.

'I need you to leave. Right now.' Shehu swung a long arm at the bag.

She said nothing for a while, her eyes shifting from the young woman's downturned head, to him. She felt brave enough to ask him why. The woman made a clucking sound, sucked her teeth and carried on with her finger-tapping.

'You're not contributing anything,' he said.

She knew that Shehu was not talking about money. He'd stared at her face, then along the rest of her, and everything he did not say was in that glazed look: two months in his bed and she still wouldn't let him touch her.

'I have nowhere to go.'

'What's new? It's Friday, you have the whole weekend to find a place.'

He swung himself to his feet, threw a withering sideways look at her. Without the frown, Shehu was good-looking and laid-back. Half-Fulani, he'd told her. And proud of it. The other half he never mentioned.

He was happy, he'd said, to give her time.

'Shehu …'

He grumbled something under his breath and strode towards the kitchen. The last word she caught was '… useless.'

It was this that hurt her most.

*

Her feet took her through the drizzle to the 349 bus stop. She thought of phoning Gabriela, the laughing, older Saint Lucian woman who shared her shift, and lived on Stamford Hill. She imagined Gabriela offering sympathetic words, then advising her to call 'one of her people'.

She pressed her back against the dripping railings of the playing field that ran parallel to the main road, the yellow laundry bag against her feet. The 349 arrived, hissed to a halt, then moved off. More came and as each one left she raised her head at the misted windows, reached for her phone, then changed her mind.

She watched the lights of the grocery store and small post

office across the road go off. Shortly after, the Indian man came out, locked the door and pulled down the shutters, his wife a couple of feet behind him, hands held palms down over her head to keep off the rain. She disliked this smiling sari-clad woman who made it a point of not touching her hand when she dropped the change in it. 'You Idi Amin people,' she'd said.

The traffic grew heavier; the heavy rush of air from passing trucks dragged at her clothing. In the thickening evening, the streetlamps had turned the pavement a simmering yellow.

She was brushing the water from her hair when she became aware of the man at the edge of her vision. Same height as Shehu, the same bony muscularity. And because he stood in the glow of the bus stop advertisement, she saw that he was blue-dark, like the men at home. Neat in his white shirt, black tie and dark jumper – a painted crest with white print across the front: LPS Security. He held a Tesco bag of shopping tautly from his hand. It was as if he were listening to the very air around her with his body. She felt the stirrings of an old defiance in her blood.

'Are you alright?' His English was slow and careful; his voice soft and resonant – the kind that made you turn your head towards it in a crowd.

She pretended she didn't hear him. The plastic bag rustled, and she saw that he'd moved his shopping to the other hand.

'*Habari gani? Nini tatizo?*' He'd switched to Swahili. There was a new certainty in his tone.

She did not return his greeting; and she certainly wouldn't tell him what the trouble was. She was aware of her own breathing now, and the dampness of her clothes. She couldn't tell how long he stood there, his free hand rubbing the drizzle into his close-cropped hair, the long, blue-black face quiet as dark water. She saw that he was quite young.

'Maybe I help? I am not a bad man. Maybe I help?'

Another bus rolled up behind him, the headlamps making

him into a flat black manshape. A woman stepped out of the vehicle, a tumble of children behind her. The bus heaved and wheezed and trundled off, lifting a wave of dirty water onto the pavement. The man looked down at his shoes, raised his face to the retreating vehicle, shook his head and began walking on.

She heard him sigh; the bag of shopping rustled as he turned to face her.

'Alans Road. After Farm Foods.' He pointed at the store ahead. 'Number five. Blue door. *Kwa heri.*'

He hoisted the plastic bag onto his shoulder and left her there.

She counted six more buses, then the traffic subsided. Now, there was just the occasional car racing to beat the lights at the junction ahead, and men's laughter in the cab station next door. A group of women from the Turkish hairdressers across the road stepped onto the pavement, a hum of words between them, their scarved heads turning every now and then in her direction. The fat-bellied man in the shop next door had left his kebab counter and now stood facing her, his shoulders filling up the doorway. Outside the cab station on her left, a huddle of smoking taxi drivers. She felt their frank assessing eyes.

She took up the yellow laundry bag. During all her time in London, she'd been living by the words of a woman who saved her, when the rest of her village left her for dead: *If the river can't climb a rock, it will make its way around it.* She headed up the street, the picture of a blue door in her head.

*

The ground floor flat was no different from Shehu's or any other she'd passed through: a small electric heater on the floor of the living room near the fireplace, a bare plastic table in the middle of it. At the back, the tiny kitchen with a row of MDF cupboards above a three-hob stove.

She dropped her bag by the door.

He handed her a towel. Light blue. Clean. She thanked him in Swahili. 'Only for tonight,' she said. Then she thought again. 'Maybe tomorrow too … I … I …'

His cheeks lifted in a quick smile. 'Ah – she can talk! You from Acholiland, no?'

She nodded.

'From the Camp, no?'

She nodded again.

'Family back there?'

She said nothing.

'I understand,' he said. 'We are like Christians when they die – no one knows if they went to heaven or hell because they don't return to tell anyone.'

'Only for tonight …'

'Up to you,' he said, flicking a quick wrist at the sofa. Again the careful English. 'You hungry? Spaghetti? With cheese?'

He walked into the kitchen and began busying himself over the stove.

She dried her hair, rested the limp towel on the back of a chair and scanned the room. 'You live on your own?'

Her question halted his hand over the pot. 'Better for me,' he replied, without turning.

He brought the plates to the table and pulled out a chair. Long dark fingers, confident hands, a deeply scarred thumb.

He asked her to sit. She told him, no. Ate standing while taking in the long head, the neatly barbered hair, the jawline that made her think of the delicacy of bird-wings.

'Tell me your story; I tell you mine.' He'd leaned back against the chair, the food barely touched. Charcoal eyes – a pinprick of light in each one.

She told him of her home in Pamin Yai in the north – a place of cattle, rocks and maize; her months in the Camp near Gulu Town, then here.

She could hardly offer more than that. Here in London, she'd let its strangeness suffocate her memories – the welcome racket of this new world, the cold which, even at the height of summer, still found its way into her bones; the daily wordless gathering of litter from between stiff indifferent feet at Liverpool Street train station.

Her treks from flat to flat had also helped with *not* remembering: the shared rooms in Northolt, Harlesden, Peckham, Elephant & Castle …; the bickering of her housemates when the electricity ran out, or when the rent was raised and they either paid and starved or packed their things and left.

She swayed on her legs and listened to him speak in that beautiful voice of his, always in Swahili. Coal-dark lips moving around words that left her with images of a boy running from a disembowelled place named Kivu, picking up the languages of the people in the places he passed through. And though she would never let him know this, she found herself liking the way he talked – this oddly familiar stranger, his calming voice turned inwards, sometimes hesitating, often over the awful things he said he'd seen and preferred not to speak of.

At the end of it, he'd rolled up the left leg of his trousers and shown her the hole gouged into his calf; then made a gesture which took in the living room, the dripping streets out there; the world.

'This Africa – they tell us it is cursed. They help us kill each other off, and when we're all dead, they'll have it for themselves. They will never leave us alone.' He held out a hand to her. 'I'm Kiki Kinkela.'

It came as a shock to her that, until then, they hadn't exchanged names.

'Miya,' she said and withheld her other names.

*

She woke to an empty flat, a faint memory of warring voices in her head; of things being broken and turned over. She rummaged in her bag, went to the shower, then dressed, avoiding her reflection in the mirror over the sink. She pushed a head into his bedroom. His bed was neat. A green blanket rolled up like a carpet across the light-blue sheet; a small lamp on the bedside table without a shade; the light socket in the ceiling empty.

She dialled Gabriela, counted to the fourteenth ring, then cut off, reminding herself that the woman had said that she hardly used 'the thing' and only carried it because her eldest daughter insisted.

*

When he returned from work, she'd cooked. She'd gone to the vegetable stall on Ponders End Road, bought green plantains and chicken and made her own version of *matoke*.

He'd knocked on his own door and she let him in; had eaten the food and thanked her and when he went to shower and change, she allowed her eyes to rove around the flat again, as she had done all day. She did not know what she was looking for. There was nothing on the walls to halt her eyes. Everyone she knew who came from somewhere else – all the people she'd shared rooms and mattresses with – brought something from home with them. Or if they didn't, they recreated it. Sometimes it was a picture, or the colours of the clothing they were drawn to; or, like her, the food they chose to cook, or simply the ingredients they brought to it. There was nothing in this flat to place this man who'd been living there for five years. Yet he'd told her who she was so quickly and with such ease that she felt exposed.

'Maybe you can stay, I mean, after the weekend? I'm not chasing you.' He'd come out and seated himself at the table.

She picked up the plates and cutlery and brought them to the sink.

'I'm not chasing you,' he said again.

She did not turn around or answer him, aware now of his eyes on her and the dreadful leadenness that had crept up her back and settled under her shoulder blades.

She didn't realise he'd left the chair until she felt his breath on her neck, his hands reaching down to untie the knot of her lesu. She closed her hand around the cloth, raising the fabric up to her throat. She turned to face him, her eyes on the curved neck of his T-shirt. '*Nedda,*' she muttered, '*Hapana!*' and slid her body sideways, her back against the counter.

She looked him in the eyes, because that had always worked, and said the same thing she'd told Shehu the first time he placed his hands on her that way: 'I can lay with you if you want; but I can't, I can't take ... have ...'

His reaction was not like Shehu's – the slow retreat in the eyes, the firming of the lips, the slight turning of the head away from her, the gradual easing back.

He followed her gaze to the laundry bag, still leaning against the wall beside the front door. He drew breath and swallowed, and she noticed for the first time the very fine scars on the skin of his throat.

'It's fine,' he said, lifting the plates from the sink and holding them under the running tap. 'I promised myself to be a better man. You still stay, I won't ...'

'I won't stay,' she said.

He shifted his head towards the window, staring through the flimsy curtains that misted the streetlights outside. 'The damage is here?' He pointed a finger at his head, 'Or ...'

'Does it matter?'

'Sorry,' he said and headed for his bedroom.

*

On the sofa, she drifted between wake and sleep. The spill of light from the street lamp outside, softened by the curtains, filled the room with a twilight glow. It reminded her of the time of day her mother called *lak nyango* – when the sun had just risen and had not begun to sting, casting long cool shadows across her father's fields.

The cotton plants and maize were shivering with rain. A time for trapping the sweet white flying *ngwen* that emerged from the anthills after a heavy downpour.

She was running after her elder sister, Payaa, through the dripping cassava and tobacco, the air above them shimmering with silver-winged insects. All she was thinking of was the *odii ngwen*, the delicious ant-paste that their mother mixed with honey and gave them, along with roasted cassava.

Then, to the left of them the maize shuddered and came alive. Eight men stepped into their path. She saw again Payaa turning back towards her, a scream twisting her sister's mouth; then the fast flash of silver before her sister's body hit the red earth.

They ordered her to sit down. She remembered the glint of their blades as the men threw them on the grass and began walking towards her; saw again their approaching shapes against the great Pamin Yai rock that stood above their homes. Remembered Payaa's last amputated cry and the roar of the Ayago river in the distance.

Nothing else.

*

She must have fallen asleep because the howling woke her up. She sprang off the sofa and stood in the gloom, her body leaning towards the noise of the thrashing bed. It could have been another woman, but the sound came only from him, guttural and gasping. She heard no pleasure in those sounds, just the thumping and the awful, gasping noise.

And words.

She pushed open the door, entered the room and switched on the bedside light. It did not wake him. He seemed to be in the grip of something terrible. Whatever disturbance he was living through made a flailing, throbbing thing of him. Spittle and words torn from his mouth like bloodied cloth, and those two words: 'Sit down ...'

He was an Acholi man. The language of his nightmare was the same as hers.

If he'd really crossed Rwanda on foot from south Sudan, drunk the piss of others to survive the desert, escaped the AK-47s and machetes of the children and men who burnt and killed so easily, his was an escape far different from hers.

A better man, she thought.

She lowered herself on the bed, felt his sweat-sheened body quieten under her hand, his eyelids fluttering like trapped moths. As he emerged from his dream, his face grew still, the dark lips settled once again over his bared teeth, until he became the watching, dark-eyed man who'd met her at the gate by the bus stop.

She watched him from under lidded eyes, asked, 'What is your name? Your real name.' He blinked at her, said nothing.

'*Nyingi anga?*' she insisted.

He was still heaving from the dream. She eased back, her hand still on his chest.

'I don't need to know your name. I know what you are: *olum* – one of those who left the bush. Mama Auma,' she said. She felt his body stiffen under her hand. 'You are worse when you call her name. Who was she?'

She didn't need to ask; she already knew.

A small change had come over him. She felt it in the swelling of his chest.

'I am not afraid of you,' she said. 'I died once; I have no more fear of dying.'

She pushed her weight off the bed and stood. 'Mama Auma – you killed your mother too. Her *cen* is strong in you. All those people … they have followed you here. They are alive in you.'

She left him in the room, went to her bag, dragged out some clothes, stood in the living room and dressed.

She heard the rumble of the first trains at Ponders End; the bang and trundle of the bin trucks down the street. And birds.

Her hand was on the handle of the door when he came out – a shadow in the gloom of the living room. That voice of his – so lovely to listen to – reached across the room to her.

'I was a child,' he said. *'Wan dano mere calo dano adana ni ya.'*

He was reaching out to her now in the language of their nightmares. *We are humans too*. Maybe if he hadn't camouflaged himself with lies at first – maybe …

'I saw what a Joseph Kony child could do with a machete and a gun,' she said.

She lifted the bag, stepped out of the flat and pulled the door behind her.

LONDON, TWO WAYS

Lynsey Hanley

WHEN I MOVED to London in 1994 to go to university, I already
knew it was scruffy. My mum's friends told her I'd get stabbed as
soon as I stepped off the coach, and although I didn't believe a
word of it – if London was so dangerous then why did all the pop
stars live there? – I'd seen enough of it from the TV to know that
the capital had more than one side. News reports in the late 1980s
described Tower Hamlets, in the East End, as enduring 'the highest levels of deprivation in Europe', and I remember feeling sorry
for the people who lived there, in grey-brown tower blocks strewn
with muck and walkways. What I didn't know then, of course, was
that, within a few years, I too would live in Tower Hamlets, at the
foot of one of those walkways and, curiously, not feeling sorry for
myself at all. It was part of London and, when looked at in the
whole, London was a living refutation of the kind of prejudice
that leads people to assume you'll get stabbed as soon as you step
off a coach. It was a place of variety and coexistence, where people
could mix things up and create new things from the mess.

That view is at once true to my experiences and highly romantic. In the 1990s Tower Hamlets was, indeed, a place where a majority experienced deep poverty, often in barely tolerable housing
conditions. I'd see young children in the part of Mile End where
I lived, still wearing flares and polyester shirts, handed down from

decades previously. The Tube station wasn't vastly busy because people couldn't afford to use it unless they could put together two quid for a sold-on travelcard, and then would likely have nothing to spend if they went up west. As Tube-using students, we were interlopers, and then, as young graduates, we were 'fackin' yuppies'. When they heard your voice minicab controllers would cackle, brand you and double the quote. The number 8 Routemaster bus from Bow Church to Mayfair was still a place where elderly cockney women might scream 'Oh my God!' and move if a Bangladeshi person sat on the seat next to them. In contrast, if you seemed a bit different but were white they would just look you up and down, and then sniff, sniffily. If you fell into conversation it often settled into a familiar groove: 'Course, it's all changed round here'; 'It used to be lovely round here, now look at it.' My heroes were my neighbours, born in Stepney, who thought the idea that the East End had once been 'lovely' the funniest thing they'd ever heard, while knowing and loving every inch of it.

By the turn of the century the East End was starting to change from being mostly poor and mostly 'white' (that category folded in, as it always does, people of Irish, Jewish, Spanish, Portuguese, and a variety of other immigrant backgrounds, as well as working-class migrants from all over Britain) to someplace resembling a boomtown. Having organised to get better housing and schools, business loans, and jobs and representation in local government, even the hitherto marginalised Bengali population of Tower Hamlets began a steady climb upward.

I met my husband Jamie while we were working in the Tower Hamlets schools' library service, a shared resource for the borough where harassed teachers would rush in during their lunch hour to chuck copies of Wibbly Pig in ten languages into a large green crate and take them back to their classrooms. Our job was to check the books out and stamp them just as you would in a public library. We came from everywhere. We were like a Zadie Smith novel; we were like London. Northern interlopers like Jamie and I lived in private house shares for £200 a month (we earned £800), spending a good bit of the rest of our money on beer and Turkish meat platters in Hackney, while our younger colleagues who joined straight from school still lived with their parents on nearby estates.

We stayed in the East End for much longer than many people we knew who weren't from the area, because it had everything we needed. I got to know the bus routes as though I had them tattooed on my arm, though I had an ambivalent relationship with the journeys themselves. Buses are often the only places in London where hard lives and easy lives rub up against each other. The endless and stressful S2 between Stratford and Clapton. The 25, known as 'the homeless express' because it was once a bendy bus, with self-service ticketing, so you could get on through the back doors and cop an hour's sleep between Ilford and the West End. The 8 to Roman Road and Brick Lane for veg and bagels, the 277 for Vietnamese and Turkish dinners.

I relied on these buses to get to work on time or move from one postcode to another without getting hurt. And they were frequently stressful in the sense that, when you are living a relatively comfortable life in London, able to pay your way and make the most of the city's cultural delights, you don't know what to do when someone begins acting up because their life is impossibly hard. I wasn't expecting to get stabbed, as my mum's friend predicted, but I often encountered situations of alarming unpredictability. Teenagers would flick their lighters repeatedly against the bus's seat fabric. The guy sitting behind would click his teeth, steadily, closely into your ear while your bus sat stuck behind a crawling lorry. Back then no one could film loud, obsessive racists and post the results online, but that didn't mean they didn't exist. I saw fights aplenty, with blood spilt in the aisle. Once, a slim kid climbed through the fire escape window at the rear of the lower deck. Buses can be madhouses on wheels. People who live in the endless unglamorous parts of any city know this but have to get on them anyway.

We lived in Tower Hamlets, in Poplar, Mile End and Bromley-by-Bow, for 13 years, until we went mildly crackers, having accumulated stress from numerous sources. There were the buses for one thing, but also the noise and pollution that accumulated under the flight path of City airport and a few yards from the A12. The 1930s council blocks opposite our flat on Bromley High Street faced directly onto the flyover and dual carriageway; anyone who lived on our estate would have to alight from the bus that ran to the centre of town beneath the flyover, on the far side of a roundabout, and somehow cross it without choking or getting run over. Many who did so were shift-workers returning after dark.

We were aware of our privileged position. We weren't council tenants, but rented an ex-council flat privately. We had the resources to get out if we felt the need. Many people we knew in the area were desperate to move and were on the waiting list for another flat. But so few were available that they were stuck. If you are one of a minority in your neighbourhood with the means to move out it's easy to feel your presence is taunting to those who are not so lucky. There was a constant anxiety about being resented, being fully aware of your status as an interloper but being too young and consumed by your own life to be able to see what to do about it.

We were also concerned about whether we were gentrifying the area in a way that would make it more difficult for those less fortunate than us to afford to live there. I had middle-class friends who had lived there as council tenants since graduating in the early 1980s, when the flats were so unpopular that people had to be actively encouraged to take tenancies. In the intervening period the borough's population had grown while, at the same time, the council had lost many of its homes through the right to buy. Cuts forced it to sell houses to tenants without having the powers or the resources to build replacements.

We were involved in the neighbourhood in the sense that we became leaseholders from the council when we bought a former right-to-buy flat on the same estate, and joined the residents' steering group when it was declared a 'regeneration zone'. Although we loved our flat, the estate as a whole was poorly designed and had been left to decline. It felt like a wasteland. A 'marketplace' in front of our block only attracted one stall, run by a lonely and permanently grumpy fruit-and-veg man who seemed to hate everyone, though for different reasons. The marketplace attracted alcoholics who would often trip and crash into his tarpaulin on the way to the off-licence. He evidently had little time for the breezy middle-class types from the other side of the main road who would cycle up and loudly – performatively try to be his mate by telling him how great it was that he was selling 'local' produce (i.e., pallid Dutch tomatoes). And he *really* hated awkward sods like me who only bought two bananas at a time.

The area seethed rather than breathed. The most common refrain I would hear drifting up from the square to our balcony was 'Yeeeew caaaaaant!' The garages directly beneath our flats were used for dumping rubbish, which every Friday night became fuel for a pyro display soundtracked by the local pub's weekly rave. Its landlords treated the pub as though it was in an abandoned area, with an accordant lack of consideration for anyone who lived nearby.

We had the resources to get out but it wasn't easy. There were few other places, north of the river at least, where we could afford to move. But eventually, in 2007, the decision was made for us. As leaseholders, we were offered compensation to leave our flat in preparation for demolition. (It still stands, but that's another story.) With ten years' hindsight I can see the estate had been subject to managed decline, and that the lack of noise-pollution enforcement and the failure to erect proper garage entries to prevent the area from being set on fire every week, was the preamble to a drawn-out project of demolition and rebuilding. At the time I was wholeheartedly in favour, which is why I played an active part in the consultation process.

The estate had only been built in 1981, and I blamed its apparent failure wholly on its design and not on a wicked combination of factors which in the end all come down to one thing: how we treat people who have less money than the average. I still maintain that it was poorly designed: shoehorned behind that Grade II-listed pub which had nevertheless been left to rot, stuck on stilts above a shopping parade which had had all life pedestrianised out of it, with flat roofs that collected rain until the whole lot tipped on your head as you left the house, in the manner of a childrens' TV gunge tank.

But that was only a sliver of the story, the main point of which was tenants' enforced isolation and poverty in one of the world's richest cities. They didn't ask to live next to a dual carriageway with the night bus stop on the wrong side of the flyover, or to be forced to eke out a meagre living from their Giro payments while living within ten minutes' ride of the gleaming business towers of Canary Wharf. That's why the area seethed. Meanwhile teenagers in Bow and Poplar were forming pirate radio stations and inventing the musical genre of grime. When Dizzee Rascal released his debut album, *Boy In Da Corner*, in 2003, he said he thought few people outside Bow would understand his music, as it sounded 'like the end of the world'. Well, that *is* what Bow sounded like.

There's a coda to this story, which perhaps illustrates what I knew tacitly about London when I first moved there as an 18-year-old. It may have been scruffy but it was good enough for pop stars. After a couple of unhappy years living elsewhere, we returned for a while in 2009, taking advantage of the offer of an eccentric lease that required us to leave our new flat for at least two months every summer so that our Canadian absentee landlords could have a holiday at their tenants' inconvenience. We took it for one reason: it was cheaper than Bow but it was in Hampstead. Just as I'd imagined as a sixth-former – until taken to one side to avoid embarrassment – that you were only allowed to go to Oxbridge if you'd been to private school, I'd always been convinced that only millionaires were allowed to live in Hampstead. Well, millionaires and Michael Foot. (Though perhaps he'd been a millionaire, too.)

I'm not going to pretend that I didn't love living there, but it's only possible to live somewhere like that in the long term if you are prepared to overlook – to accept and to ignore – the evidence of London's morally disfiguring inequality. I loved it because it was so bloody easy. I learned from living in Hampstead that the true advantage of having both money and status is to be able to exist without environmental stress. These privileges give you the ability to breeze around weightlessly, to sit on the top deck of the bus without a sense of paranoia, to get all your groceries on foot, to go to the post office without queueing for half an hour or witnessing a fight, to take your child to a park that smells only of breeze, to have your bins collected promptly, your streets swept without you even noticing, your verges planted, potholes filled, and everything in life laid on as if it were there just for you. It became clear why people in rich areas live 20 years longer than people in poor ones: their environment holds no fear.

Two years in Hampstead gave me the evidence, the visible and lived proof, of something I'd always suspected: it is possible to construct urban environments where people can live without avoidable impediments or threats. So why is this true for some and not others? Why are people's lives made so hard when they don't have to be? Why build flyovers next to flats? Why make people feel as though they are drowning in stress when it is possible to take that stress away? Perhaps the answer is that privileged people want the less well-off to be kept away. But if you build housing that keeps people apart according to how much money they have, and allow some areas and not others to become isolated, congested and polluted, you will have deep spatial inequality. If, as a government in a representative democracy, you do everything you can to reinforce an idea that people in 'nice' areas have 'earned the right' to live there while people in 'not-nice' areas 'deserve' to live where they do, you will end up with people voting to perpetuate that inequality while working constantly to stay in the 'nice' place or to get out of the 'not-nice' place.

I experienced London two ways, neither of which was nice enough.

SPOOKS

Richard Norton-Taylor

C's VIEW IS spectacular. Downriver are the Houses of Parliament. Upriver, conveniently close, the new US embassy is being built. Beyond it stands what estate agents call the 'iconic development' of Battersea Power Station. Tate Britain faces him across the river.

C, as he is officially known throughout Whitehall, is the Chief of Britain's Secret Intelligence Service, or MI6 as it is more commonly called. If he looks diagonally across the river from his suite in Vauxhall Cross, a concrete and glass juggernaut sometimes compared to a Babylonian palace, he can just about see a rather less ostentatious building.

This is Thames House, headquarters of the country's domestic Security Service, MI6's traditional rival. From an office high up in the corner of this more sombre edifice, MI5's head of counter terrorism can in turn peer at what mischievous observers revel in describing as the 'Islamic green' glass window shades that adorn Vauxhall Cross.

Both men are hoping that disputes between MI6 and MI5 are in the past. But they are not entirely sure and still need to spy on each other, one on the south bank of the river, one on the north.

Vauxhall Cross is well-known to watchers of James Bond films, in which it has been blown up more than once. This scenario has become so familiar that MI6 officers have reported that they would flinch whenever a low-flying helicopter passed on the way to and from the nearby Battersea heliport.

Behind those Islamic green shades, MI6 officers instruct their spies to carry out all sorts of dirty work far from Britain's shores. They are protected, by what is known as the 'James Bond clause' in the 1994 Intelligence Services Act, if they undertake activities abroad that would be unlawful in Britain.

MI5 officers spend their time following threats or potential threats to the safety of the public at home, on the streets, in cars, taking photographs, scanning computer screens. The ethos in Thames House is much more downbeat, as befitting their rather gloomy headquarters, a neoclassical Edwardian listed building on Millbank, of Portland stone and granite, which was once was the HQ of Imperial Chemical Industries (ICI).

Both organisations moved into their current homes in 1994 in operations that were shrouded in secrecy. As MI6 left a miserable tower block in Lambeth, MI5 was packing up its unostentatious headquarters at the intersection of Gower Street and Euston Road. I visited the building before it was pulled down. Telltale signs of its former occupants included a photograph of Arthur Scargill, the miners' leader and long-term MI5 target. At the same time MI5 also quit its vast registry in Curzon Street, Mayfair, where all its files and card indexes were kept.

MI5 works closely with the police in an alliance that is reflected in their geographical proximity. Along the north bank, eastwards from Thames House and beyond the Houses of Parliament, on Victoria Embankment, stands the new New Scotland Yard building, headquarters of the Metropolitan Police, including its Counter Terrorist Command. Close by is the Ministry of Defence 'main building', as it is called, the headquarters of the military on whom the police and MI5 can rely for reinforcements, if necessary. So anxious were senior MoD officials about enterprising spies that they warned staff not to open classified documents that might be seen through binoculars from pods on the London Eye across the river.

Both MI5 and MI6 have traditionally had male-dominated cultures, albeit with a very different ethos. MI5 officers might be recruited from the Civil Service, the police, or an Infantry regiment – and, on retirement, become advisers to a high street bank or commercial company. Eliza Manningham-Buller, MI5's director general, told me that when she was rising up the ranks in the 1980s she found herself in a peculiarly male world, with former members of the Colonial Service 'coming out of the sun worrying about the Communist party in Woking'.

Then MI5's culture changed dramatically. In 1992 Stella Rimington was appointed its first female head. She was also the first whose name was officially revealed. Manningham-Buller followed her into the post in 2002.

By then more than half of MI5's senior staff were women. The proportion fell a bit in the later years of the decade, partly, MI5 officers suggested, because female officers would be uncomfortable when so many of their targets, and those they wanted to recruit as informants, were Muslim men. Nevertheless in 2017, by which time the number of MI5 staff had increased significantly, as many as 40 per cent were female.

MI6, meanwhile, remained male-dominated, with officers who were predominantly white and educated at public school. Some were recruited from posh regiments – the Guards or the Cavalry. After they retired, MI6 officers were most likely to go on to a merchant bank or an upmarket private intelligence company.

In a desperate attempt to diversify its personnel, it took the unprecedented step, in 2017, of releasing a recruitment film to be shown in cinemas. Over a picture of a woman, a voice said the person the viewer was watching didn't work for MI6 'but she could'.

MI6 has never quite wanted to shake off the Bond connection. Alex Younger, the new C, told journalists at the end of 2016:

168 Richard Norton-Taylor

'I'm conflicted about Bond. He has created a powerful brand for [us] – as C, the real-life version of M, there are few people who will not come to lunch if I invite them. Many of our counterparts envy the sheer global recognition of our acronym. And, to be fair, there are a few aspects of the genre that do resonate in real life: fierce dedication to the defence of Britain, for example. The real-life Q would want me to say that we too enjoy (and indeed need) a deep grasp of gadgetry. But that's pretty much where the similarity ends.'

He then revealed that the present Q – played by Ben Whishaw in the two most recent Bond films *Skyfall* and *Spectre* – was in fact a woman.

MI6 started life in 1909 in the heart of Whitehall, where its first C, Sir Mansfield Cumming, is commemorated by an English Heritage blue plaque, unveiled in 2015. Its headquarters were subsequently moved to the Broadway, disguised as the 'Minimax Fire Extinguisher Company', close by St James's Park Tube station.

Since those early days, MI6 has preferred to keep its distance, on the south bank of the Thames – with one notable exception. In remarkable but largely ignored evidence to the Chilcot inquiry into the invasion of Iraq, Sir Mark Allen, head of counter-terrorism at MI6, said firmly: 'I believe in a Chief who stays south of the river and is not so easy to get hold of.'

Allen was referring to widespread criticism of Sir Richard Dearlove – C at the time – for becoming too close to Downing Street, too eager to please a prime minister who needed intelligence to show that Saddam Hussein was actively developing weapons of mass destruction. C's car was making too many transpontine trips.

While Dearlove desperately searched for ammunition to help Tony Blair make the case for war (despite the misgivings of many senior officers inside MI6), his opposite number across the river in MI5 was trying to stop him.

Eliza Manningham-Buller was frustrated and deeply

concerned. Ever since the 9/11 attacks on New York and Washington, she had been worried that the US would attack Iraq. There was no evidence that Saddam Hussein was linked to al-Qaida – far from it – and, she believed, an invasion would increase the threat of terrorism on British streets.

Asked by Chilcot whether, in her judgement, the effect of the invasion was 'to substantially increase the terrorist threat to the United Kingdom'. Manningham-Buller replied: 'I think because of evidence of the number of plots, the number of leads, the number of people identified, and statements of people as to why they were involved, the answer to your question [is] yes.'

She continued: 'We regarded the threat, the direct threat, from Iraq as low but we did not believe he [Saddam Hussein] had the capability to do anything much in the UK. That turned out to be the right judgement.' She added: 'To my mind Iraq – Saddam Hussein had nothing to do with 9/11 and I have never seen anything to make me change my mind.'

Asked how the invasion of Iraq was used by extremists and terrorists, Manningham-Buller replied: 'I think it is highly significant ... we were receiving an increasing number of leads to terrorist activity from within the UK and our involvement in Iraq radicalised, for want of a better word, a whole generation of young people – some British citizens – [who] saw our involvement in Iraq as being an attack on Islam.'

She continued: 'So although the media has suggested that in July 2005 – the attacks on 7/7 – that we were surprised these were British citizens, that is not the case because really there had been an increasing number of British-born individuals living and brought up in this country, some of them third generation, who were attracted to the ideology of Osama bin Laden and saw the West's activities in Iraq and Afghanistan as threatening their fellow religionists and the Muslim world. So it undoubtedly increased the threat.'

Sir Roderic Lyne, Chilcot's most forensic interrogator, asked Manningham-Buller whether there were other attacks or planned attacks in which she had evidence that Iraq was a motivating factor. 'Yes,' she replied. 'If you take the videos that were retrieved on various occasions after various plots, where terrorists who had expected to be dead explained why they had done what they did, it features. It is part of what we call the single narrative, which is the view of some that everything the West was doing was part of a fundamental hostility to Islam, which pre-dated 9/11, but it was enhanced by those events. Arguably we gave Osama bin laden his Iraqi jihad so that he was able to move into Iraq in a way that he wasn't before.'

The fundamental disagreement between MI5 and MI6 over the invasion of Iraq, with MI5 strongly opposed and MI6 a key player encouraging Blair to become involved, did not surface until years later – indeed, not until the Chilcot inquiry.

It was not the last serious dispute between MI5 and MI6.

Sir Mark Allen may have been reluctant to cross the Thames before the invasion of Iraq; however, not long afterwards he organised a dinner at the Travellers Club, MI6's favourite bolt hole on Pall Mall. The special guest that day, in late December 2003, was Moussa Koussa, the intelligence chief of Libyan president Muammar Gaddafi. Allen had helped to persuade Gaddafi to give up his Weapons of Mass Destruction programme after a cargo of banned components bound for Tripoli was seized off Italy.

MI6 was keen, on Blair's behalf, to cement a new friendship with the Libyan dictator with the prospect of huge oil-related contracts in what became known as the 'deal in the desert'. So keen that it enthusiastically colluded with the CIA in the abduction of two Libyan dissidents, leading members of the Libyan Islamic Fighting Group with loose links to al-Qaida, and their rendition to Tripoli where they were tortured.

MI6 sent information it had obtained from MI5 to Gaddafi's

secret police for use in the interrogation of the two Libyans – Abdel Hakim Belhaj and Sami Al-Saadi. Manningham-Buller was so furious that she wrote to Blair to complain, saying that the actions of MI6 had threatened Britain's intelligence gathering and may have compromised the security and safety of her own officers and their informants.

In protest, she threw out a group of MI6 officers who were working at Thames House at the time on secondment from Vauxhall Cross. 'There are clearly questions to be answered about the various relationships that developed afterwards and whether the UK supped with a sufficiently long spoon,' she said later.

Dearlove's response to the treatment of the two Libyans is not known. However, when Manningham-Buller took the opportunity of retirement to deliver a BBC Reith Lecture strongly opposing torture, a former MI6 officer told me privately: 'She is out of her depth.'

The war of words between the former C and the former head of MI5 extended to Brexit, with Manningham-Buller describing the Eurosceptics' claim that the UK would be safer outside the EU, as 'nonsensical and spurious', while Dearlove came out as a Brexiteer, saying the UK would be better off outside and that Britain provided more intelligence to Europe than it got back in return. To which Manningham-Buller responded: 'Richard is talking from 11 years ago. I don't think that is necessarily still the case.'

Though hostility is the normal state of affairs, the two organisations did collaborate when it suited them. In a conspiracy that was only uncovered by the National Audit Office years later, they worked together to cover up huge overspends on their respective new headquarters.

Thames House and Vauxhall Cross together cost £547m, more than double the original estimates. On top of this, MI5 spent more than £200m, four times the estimate, on refurbishing

Thames House. MI6 spent £75m, more than three times the expected amount, fitting up its new headquarters.

When ministers were eventually told about the overspends and began to question them, the two agencies claimed that their activities and the safety of their staff would have been put at risk without the extra cash. As the Audit Office made clear, secrecy surrounding the projects was used to cover up incompetence rather than genuine security needs.

The budgets of MI5 and MI6 remain official secrets. But while official secrecy can be necessary for legitimate reasons of national security, it also protects both agencies from embarrassment. It is one thing they have always had in common, and always will have.

They now have something else to confront together: the threat of terrorism. Despite the differences in their culture, ethos, personnel, and – in the case of Iraq – their politics, we are assured that MI5 and MI6 are sharing intelligence more than ever before. We can only hope this is true – that historic animosities can be set aside, enabling the channels of communication to run strong and clear between the north and south banks of the Thames.

SO FAR FROM HOME TO FIND HIS FAITH

Daljit Nagra

There was a man swallowing down in a man-hole
and none he knew were near him in the crowd,
he began to be plunged, then he held out his
heart and he wailed. Till the God-Word
shone from the foreign and flowed
him far above the world. Where
he lived upon the round
no longer mattered.

LONDON FIELDS

Jo Glanville

IT'S AUGUST, the busiest time of the year for London Fields Lido, and the pool is closed. When the lido shut down for major repairs and refurbishment in April, Hackney council announced that work was expected to be completed by the end of the summer. With no sign of an imminent opening, Josephine Bacon, who runs the user group, wrote to the council asking for their definition of late summer – did they mean the meteorological or astronomical season? (If meteorological, the date would be 31 August; if astronomical, the equinox is on 22 September.) She did not receive a reply.

The lido is a great success story for Hackney – a triumph for local campaigners and a magnet for visitors since it reopened in 2006. More than a quarter of a million swimmers visit each year, a figure that is 'unheard of' for an open air pool according to Better, the charitable social enterprise that manages it. Over the decade, the number of visitors in a year has increased by 140 per cent. When I first moved to the neighbourhood 20 years ago, the pool was derelict and the campaign to save it was already nine years old. Much to the annoyance of campaigners, who had just organised a clean-up so the site could be used for communal activities, in 1998 squatters moved in and began holding raves, at which revellers partied in the old pool tank.

But the campaign group did not give up, joining forces with local architects and the Environment Trust to develop a proposal for the lido. When they presented their plans for the pool to the community in 2003, interested residents were invited on a tour of the abandoned site. As locals were shown around, the squatters sat on the ground in front of the changing rooms, purple buddleia growing above the doors, and gazed mutely upwards at the visitors. Outside on London Fields, the developers displayed a model of the proposed new lido and answered questions. One woman enquired: did she have to swim if she wanted a coffee or could she have a coffee without paying for a swim? It was a surreal moment that captured the extremes of Hackney life – the young homeless squatters facing possible eviction and the affluent resident who saw a new opportunity for a latte.

It took 18 years of remarkable tenacity to resurrect the lido: Hackney council finally agreed to fund the renovation in 2004, but brought in another team to develop the site. If the council had had its way when the pool was first closed, the lido would have been demolished. Mike Martin, born and bred in the neighbourhood, remembers standing in front of the bulldozer at 7am one morning. He and his fellow campaigners had managed to halt the council's plans to knock the pool down and were then tipped off that the demolition team had somehow not got the message and had turned up to do the job anyway. The lido was saved in the nick of time.

Now, on a hot summer day (though sadly not this summer), the crowds queue round the block to get into the 50-metre heated pool. Floodlights were installed in 2015 after another campaign (lasting eight years), which means that people can swim from 6.30am until 9pm all year round. Staff think the regulars who swim in the snow and the rain are crazy. It's also a tough job for the lifeguards: sitting outside in all weathers puts most of them off swimming. But the rest of us owe the campaigners a great debt.

You could write an alternative history of Hackney in the first decades of this millennium through the story of its pools: the catastrophe of Clissold Leisure Centre, which cost £45m (nearly seven times the original budget) and closed in 2003 for four years following a flood, just 18 months after it had opened; the battle for Haggerston Baths, a Grade II-listed building which shut very suddenly in 2000, was the centre of a 16-year campaign and is now earmarked for development that will not include a pool; the furore over Britannia Leisure Centre, which is to be demolished amidst much protest to make way for major redevelopment that includes a sports centre with three swimming pools, a school and 480 new homes, 80 of which will be affordable, to help fund the scheme. Councillor Jon Burke, a member of the council cabinet with responsibility for energy, sustainability and community services, also has Clapton's Kings Hall Leisure Centre in his sights for development.

When public swimming pools are under threat, campaigners are impressively dogged in their pursuit of victory. It's not just about health, sport and leisure: swimming pools, like libraries, are central to community life – for everyone's use and part of our heritage. The closure of pools was also disastrous for Hackney schoolchildren: a feasibility study on Haggerston Baths in 2006 included a survey of primary and secondary schools' provision of swimming for their pupils. Four out of the five secondary schools surveyed did not provide curricular or extra-curricular swimming – either due to lack of funding or lack of facilities.

Mike Martin, now secretary to London Fields user group, remembers swimming in the old unheated London Fields Lido as a boy, but was a bigger fan of Victoria Park, once home to the largest modern lido in London, which was demolished in 1990 to make way for a car park. No one, unfortunately, turned out to stop the bulldozers that time.

The heyday for building lidos was in the 1930s (London

Fields opened in 1932). As Janet Smith reveals in her very enjoyable history of lidos, *Liquid Assets*, the boom was driven by an egalitarian ethos. When Morecambe's open air pool opened in 1936, Sir Josiah Stamp, a director of the Bank of England, declared: 'Bathing reduces rich and poor, high and low, to a common standard of enjoyment and health. When we get down to swimming, we get down to democracy.' London County Council (LCC) was particularly zealous in its lido building programme. Herbert Morrison, when leader of the LCC in the late '30s, wanted London to be a 'city of lidos', with every citizen within walking distance of an open air pool. It was ultimately Margaret Thatcher who spelt the end for the survival of the lido with her war on local government spending – lidos became a common casualty in the '80s as councils cut their budgets.

When I met Jon Burke for a brief tour of work in progress at London Fields in mid-August, a roof of scaffolding stretched across the pool, bubblewrap protected the lockers that edge the lido and the reception area was a shell. The pool had been retiled, but the late summer opening looked distinctly unlikely. Repairs became urgent when the tiles began to crack and come away from the walls of the pool, and it emerged that there was a major problem. The council first put the job out to tender last winter, but no one came forward – it was, as the councillor tells me, a risk at that time of year, since the tiles will not bond to the render below a temperature of ten degrees and the council was also asking for a very high level of indemnity insurance. So the summer closure became unavoidable and Hackney will have to compensate Better for the loss of business. Meanwhile, given the borough's unreliable aquatic history and the delay in starting the repairs, swimmers have understandably become nervous that the pool will remain shut indefinitely. Josephine Bacon remembers turning up at Haggerston Baths to find a notice saying it was closed till further notice – the pool never reopened.

Burke is a young councillor from Liverpool, who arrived in Hackney as the council was emerging from the near bankruptcy it faced at the beginning of the millennium. The borough has long been one of the most deprived in the country. While its ranking has improved relatively since 2010 (moving from second most deprived borough nationally to 11th), there are stark pockets of inequality, where some of the poorest in the UK live alongside the most affluent, particularly in Stoke Newington, Hoxton and Shoreditch. Twenty-eight per cent of children in the borough live in poverty. Over the millennium, the gap has grown more visible, as Hackney has become one of the hippest destinations in London, with its chic restaurants, boutiques and cafés. Its new appeal to visitors from outside the borough makes Burke distinctly uneasy – a sentiment shared by other longterm residents.

When the councillor buys us both a coffee from the kiosk at the lido, which has remained open through the building works (yes, you can have a coffee without swimming), he has a lengthy conversation with Caroline, who serves the customers freshly baked croissants and toasties at the café. Her flat overlooks the park and she complains about the impact of the crowds on London Fields – the shortage of toilets and the noise. On a hot summer weekend, there are so many people in the park that it looks as if there's a festival underway. Caroline has lived in the neighbourhood for 33 years. She tells me that she regrets the loss of community spirit and feels that, with rare exceptions, the incomers don't know how to be good neighbours. 'I think they're afraid, they don't want to mix. People walk past you as though you've got green wires coming out of your head.' For Burke, who speaks proudly of Hackney council's achievements in the face of severe cuts, the influx of visitors is symptomatic of a wider national trend.

'What does it say about the last 30-odd years of government in this country that people from other parts of the country are travelling down to London to spend the weekend in a park?

Where have we gone so badly wrong that Liverpool, Sheffield, Leeds, Newcastle, Hull, don't offer this standard of living to everybody?'

Burke himself came to London from Liverpool ten years ago, looking for work. He gave up the one-bedroom flat he shared with his girlfriend before they married – where the rent was £350 a month – and now lives in a flat in Clapton with his young family, paying close to £2,000 a month in rent.

'I suppose I occupy a bit of a crank's position on the left, which is that I don't believe we have a housing crisis,' he says. 'What we really have is a crisis of uneven economic geography. Liverpool has the highest rate of under-occupied private property in the country. There are streets of Victorian terraces that people would kill one another to live in, but there's no jobs there, so you have to have an industrial strategy that eases the pressure on somewhere like Hackney.'

The transformation that has taken place in the neighbourhood since the millennium was initially driven by campaigners seeking to regenerate the borough – not only at the lido, but also a few minutes away on Broadway Market, a street that was once a drovers' route into the city and which runs down to the canal from London Fields. It hosts a hugely successful Saturday market launched by local residents and traders in 2004, two years before the pool reopened. *Time Out* calls the street 'a promenade for the East End fashion set'.

For some of the campaigners who kickstarted the regeneration, there is a rueful recognition of the role they may have played in changing the character of the neighbourhood. Liz Veitch, a retired teacher, says that when she first moved to London Fields 25 years ago, she could almost see the tumbleweed blowing down Broadway Market, a street that had once been home to a popular East End market. Hackney council made a number of failed attempts to revive it, and it was only when local residents took on the challenge that the market succeeded. Her husband, journalist Andrew Veitch, who died last year, played an instrumental role in the market's success, setting up a community interest company that he ran for ten years. It was the catalyst that helped transform London Fields into a destination for hipsters, swiftly followed by the reopening of the lido.

'In the beginning it was local people trying to make what was a beaten-up area a bit more attractive,' says Veitch. 'People who moved in here like us felt they ought to do more in the community. I would say that the people buying into this area do not seem to share the same sense of community. The youngsters buying or renting these flats are too busy trying to live, but also there is an air of entitlement amongst some of the more affluent members of the next generation. Thatcher's children, if you like. They don't get involved here. When we were growing up, it was a mantra that was part of our upbringing – if you're in a community you join in and do what you can.'

When Hackney council began selling off properties in Broadway Market at the start of the millennium, resulting in the eviction of popular local independent businesses, there was a remarkable campaign that received national coverage to stop the demolition of a café. Gentrification became a very dirty word, as Hackney council was accused of betraying the locals and getting into bed with the property developers. At the time of writing, the council is in the process of attempting to take over the running of the market – a move that will be strongly resisted by the community that has managed it so successfully for 13 years.

When the market was first launched, with its stalls of organic fruit, vegetables, cheeses and meat, alongside fashion and jewellery, I did my own very unscientific poll of the longstanding neighbourhood shopkeepers to find out what they thought of the changes. Some were not too fussed (including the butcher, a family business that had been in the street for generations, and has since been replaced by a restaurant); some said that it was not serving the local community, a criticism that continues to be heard and is also made of the lido. It's not easy to make an accurate assessment: a survey by the market in 2015 revealed that 81 per cent of its visitors were from east London; they were predominantly white and under 40. The survey assessed a small sample and did not include the socio-economic background of the customers. Better, which runs the lido, only has data on its members (there are 2,000), so one has to rely on observation and anecdote.

'The lido does not reflect the demography of Hackney,' says Josephine Bacon. 'It's very white, it's very middle class, it's quite young. Hackney and Better's advertisements promote swimming for everyone, saying come and join in, and they have photographs of black people on their posters and banners. Of course there are some black people there, but hardly any. And probably not very many unemployed or low income swimmers either. And I'm not really sure why – whether because it's too expensive or because London Fields has become a chi-chi area. I don't know what can be done to make it more inclusive.'

When I put the problem to Councillor Burke, he tells me that the lido 'is not a country club for the affluent residents. It's important that this facility is able to be accessed by people irrespective of their socio-economic, ethnic, religious backgrounds.' He hopes that the refurbishment of the changing rooms, which includes the introduction of internal cubicles and internal lockers, will broaden its appeal, and may satisfy those who have previously been concerned about modesty or security, but it's unlikely to be enough to effect a significant change.

It's a problem that goes beyond Hackney – Swim England's most recent research in 2015 revealed that ethnic minorities are twice as less likely to know how to swim as white members of the population. The closure of Hackney's pools in the noughties (at one point there was only one pool with lanes serving a population of more than 200,000) may also have had an impact on the next generation of swimmers.

Meanwhile, swimmers come by London Fields Lido every day to ask at the café for news. 'I'm dying for a swim,' says one young man who stops for an update as he cycles past. A young mother who has recently moved into the neighbourhood tells me that she had been planning to spend the summer there with her partner and two-year-old. Both are young and white, more apparently typical of newcomers than longtime residents.

This may not be the classless vision of lido culture that its great political advocates imagined in the '30s when they built the pools in London and across the UK. It may not be the neighbourhood that the campaigners imagined either, when they fought to revive the lido and the local market. But it's now a fixture and a landmark for the borough, even if it may be a symbol of divide as much as transformation. In the last week of August, Josephine Bacon sent an email to the lido user group with the news that the pool would reopen on 30 September: so, she quipped, the council did mean an astronomical late summer after all.

After yet more delays the swimmers were finally allowed back into the water in January, closer to the solstice than the equinox.

A GOOD PLACE TO GET LOST

Jane Shilling

To BECOME LOST in a strange city is a romantic and desirable thing. Without responsibilities other than to walk and watch, you wander invisibly through the streets collecting vignettes – an old man in floating pierrot pyjamas doing slow, fluid t'ai chi under a plum tree in a park; a tortoiseshell cat asleep in a shaft of sunlight on a stone doorstep; a basil plant on the windowsill of an open window from which drifts a smell of cooking onions, the clattering of pans, a snatch of conversation in an unknown tongue. In your pocket, the clue that will guide you out of the labyrinth: the electronic blue dot that will lead you back to the safety of your Ramada or Hilton, your Airbnb, when you have seen enough.

But to be lost in your own city, where you have lived for almost 40 years – the place that, after so long, you have almost learned to call home – is an affront, and it happens to me all the time. I take precautions against it: writing out the route, marking my destination in the A-Z, keying the postcode into my phone. Sometimes it works. But just as often I find myself lost in places I thought I knew. The streets look familiar, but they seem no longer to connect in the way they once did. It is as if I have developed an urban version of prosopagnosia. The city's face has become strange to me.

I do not think I will get lost on the way to the fish stall, which

Tom in the wine shop has recommended for the excellence of its fish and the keen wit of the fishmongers. It is in Deptford, a little over a mile from Greenwich, where I have lived for 23 years. If I follow the river, I will get there. I am in no particular hurry. It is a high summer morning, warm and humid. The clouds over the river are low and billowy, gravid with the promise of rain. The light is lurid, the water a sullen verdigris. The air smells sweetly rank, of buddleia and municipal petunias. I walk past the Peter the Great statue; past the great empty hulks of new riverside apartments with their inexplicable public art (a stainless steel globe with a segment missing; a giant representation of a human cochlea in black and grey striped granite); past Phoenix House, once a ships' boilermakers, a paper wharf and an egg distributors' warehouse, now an unpeopled art gallery with pictures by Chinese school-children of big-eyed cats and spring blossom displayed in its plate-glass windows.

After a while the road turns away from the river, and at once I am lost. I walk past a building site, under a railway bridge and then I am in a sparse open space with pale granite benches and spindly trees and a children's playground of wooden ladders and walkways and little huts where no children play. On a monu-mental granite wall is carved in assertive capitals, CHARLOT-TENBURG PARK. A little further on is a row of white builders' hoardings on each of which someone has sprayed in tender green aerosol, Fuck Trump.

I have been lost in Charlottenburg before, but that was in Berlin. My phone says I am in Amersham Grove, SE14. Behind me is a tree-lined avenue. I walk up it and see ahead stalls, not of vegetables as I was expecting, but of bric-a-brac. It is Deptford Market. I have arrived at my destination. I look further up the road and see the Docklands Railway. It has taken me just un-der two hours to walk here. The train would take me home, if I wished, in a few minutes.

*

'There are some parts of London which are necessary and others which are contingent', says the narrator of Iris Murdoch's novel, *Under the Net*. When I first came to live in London in 1979, all parts of the city seemed equally contingent. My whole life until that moment had been spent in two places: the first 17 years in a small, dull market town, 50 miles east of London; the three years after that in a university city, 50 miles west of London. Of the capital itself I knew nothing, except that it was a place where the past might be shed like skin. Sometimes home is defined not by where we are, but where we are not.

At first I stayed with university friends in a house overlooking a canal. It had internal doors stained a heady 1970s deep purple and a tarpaper roof, accessible by a rickety ladder, where we sat stickily in summer, eating cherries and talking in a wistful prolongation of our student habits. There followed a trip to a flatshare agency and a brief period in a small, furniture-crammed room whose grimy window gave onto the gloomy internal courtyard of a blackened red-brick mansion flat in Earls Court Square. The peach nylon sheets made my hair crackle and were changed weekly by the haughty German landlady's elderly husband, a mute military figure who vacuumed angrily in cavalry twills and tweed jacket. After that, a quiet room in a shared house in Putney where the flowering cherry trees reminded me of the suburban streets of my childhood, and a few weeks in the box-room of a Blackheath basement where my new flatmate, a trainee barrister, chased me around the living room with a dead bird's skull before concluding that I was not girlfriend material.

In all these places it was evident that I was in transit, although with no notion of my onwards destination. At last I saw on my office noticeboard a handwritten advertisement for a studio room. It was in the basement of a house overlooking the Thames at

World's End. It had its own front door and the rent was exactly half my monthly salary. I took it.

The rise and fall of the tides, the shifting riverscape, the honk and shriek of waterfowl lent the World's End a rackety, impermanent air, as if its inhabitants were perpetually poised on the way to elsewhere. It was not a place into which you could be effortlessly ejected by the swift dark peristalsis of the Tube. It occupied one of the white lacunae that punctuate the orderly grid of the London Underground map: the nearest Tube stations were a stiff 15-minute walk away. But it lay at the convergence of three great bus routes: the 22, from Putney in the south, via Piccadilly and Shaftesbury Avenue to Homerton in the east; the 11, from Hammersmith in the west to Westminster, Trafalgar Square, Chancery Lane, St Paul's, and Liverpool Street; and the 31, whose route began a few yards from my door and ran northwards through Notting Hill, terminating a few minutes' walk from my best friend's flat in Chalk Farm. He was a mathematician; the fact that we were linked by a bus route with a prime number seemed apt. So from the top decks of London buses, among the smokers, the fare-dodgers and the roaring boys skipping school, I began to map the city and my place in it.

Vivienne Westwood's shop with its 13-hour clock whose hands spun backwards was at the World's End, but my budget ran to finery from the Oxfam shop next door: a 1950s hat like a coronet of shocking pink velvet bows; bracelets of Afghan silver, heavy as manacles. On the bus I heard a language of languorous diphthongs and jagged consonantal collisions and wondered from where its dark-eyed, olive-skinned speakers had come – until I found, at the base of the brutalist red-brick World's End council tower blocks, a Portuguese delicatessen, pungent with salt cod, coffee and hard little cylindrical cheeses, where the language clattered and sang above the hissing of the espresso machine.

A grocer's shop occupied the site where, in the 1960s, the

fashion boutique Granny Takes A Trip had half a car embedded in its shopfront. The grocer, John, used to give me punnets of raspberries past their best while hinting at a dodgy past. In the cramped kitchen of my dark basement I began to cook: ox kidneys with watercress, rabbit with turnips, tripe with bacon and tomatoes. Home, I began to think, might be a place where you made food for yourself and other people.

World's End was on the change. Upriver at Sand's End, where William de Morgan had his last pottery, a tower of luxury flats began to rise, capped with a toylike pagoda roof. My landlord doubled my rent. It was the market price, he said. My grandfather had left me enough for the deposit on a basement flat in Peckham. A long thin corridor ran the length of this flat; off it were a kitchen, a bathroom, a bedroom and a living room with a marble fireplace and wooden sash shutters. The kitchen door opened onto a long, thin garden which ended in a steep, buddleia-covered slope up to a railway embankment where foxes lived.

I had never had a garden before. I got two cats, a mother and a leggy adolescent son, and planted sweet peas. While watering the seedlings one summer evening I met my next-door neighbour, Judy, a thin nervous chain-smoker with a husband, a teenage son and daughter, and an extravagant talent for making plants bloom. It was good soil for plants. All summer long the bees rioted among her busy Lizzie and begonias and my sweet peas. I dug up a section of the coarse lawn to sow vegetables. Round the corner in Bellenden Road, not yet punctuated with the artistic street furniture of urban regeneration, a street market – not yet artisanal – sold Scotch bonnet peppers, pearly white aubergines the size of hens' eggs, bunches of coriander, parsley and dill, red snapper, sprats, cow heels and pigs' ears. From the junk shop at the end of the road I bought two heavy cast-iron frying pans and a wooden cupboard painted the singing cobalt blue of childhood poster paints.

When I got pregnant by mistake Judy was the only person, including me, not to think the news a disaster. Over the garden wall she began to pass, piece by piece, a lavish newborn's trousseau: little jumpers and cardigans, a hat and a lacy shawl, intricately handknitted in tactful, gender-neutral colours: turquoise, white, pale yellow. When the baby was born she took care of him in the daytime while I went back to work. Perhaps this was a home: a place where you raised plants, animals and a baby, and your neighbours cared for you as though you were family.

Or perhaps it was a place where you woke each night in the small hours to the sound of the baby crying and walked the floor with him, singing every song you knew – nursery rhymes, hymns, old pop songs – trying to get him to settle, until it was time to go to work again. And where you eventually ended up broken in the local psychiatric hospital, saying that you couldn't do it, not any more, and a kind young psychiatrist said that you were 'not quite psychotic'.

*

A short ride from Peckham on the 177 bus, at the end of a road in East Greenwich, is a house like a child's drawing: a hedge round a small front garden; a gate; a path leading to a front door with a ground-floor window on either side, three windows in a row above, and a pitched roof with a chimney-pot. Here we came to live when the baby was not quite two years old, and there have we lived for nearly 24 years, while he grew from a baby to a boy to a teenager to a man. Sometimes he, too, used to get lost. Once, on an early solo outing, he rang me, panicking because it was dark and he couldn't find his way back. Trying to get him to describe where he was, I heard a heavy familiar chime. 'Are you near a very big clock tower?' I asked. He was. The Jubilee line fetched him safely home from Westminster to North Greenwich.

It took me a long time to understand that he shared none of my ambivalence about the meaning of home. He was a lad, a south London geezer, a West Ham supporter, a person who knew the right answer to the question, 'What endz you from?' In short, a Londoner. Home was the house, the street, the endz, the urban village with its sharply defined boundaries, where he grew up. Long after he left London to study in Scotland, 500 miles away, I was surprised by his sudden fury when I speculated idly about going to live somewhere else, now that he had flown.

*

I find the Deptford market fish stall and buy my fish – a fine fat plaice, deftly filleted by the fishmonger, his tongue as sharp as his blade. The clouds are lifting, the threatened rain unfallen. Walking back through the market I linger at the bric-a-brac stalls, wanting a set of green-enamelled cast-iron saucepans, half a dozen curvy wicker chairs (but how would I get them home?) On the last stall something catches my eye: a small, glass-fronted box, wooden framed, perhaps nine inches by six, a couple of inches deep. Inside, a swarm of miniature objects arranged as though in a very cluttered room.

Looking more closely, I see a doll's-house grandfather clock, a pair of little boots with a shrimping net propped in one of them, an enamel saucepan, a bell the size of a hazelnut, a mousetrap no bigger than a fingernail, piles of books, a lamp, games boards. On the wall, a straw hat and several postage stamp-sized black-and-white photographs. One shows a solemn Victorian family of eight – moustachioed men, women with important hats and redoubtable corseted bosoms – grouped around a pair of small boys in stiff collars. A second photo, modern this time, shows a smiling man in a white shirt holding a dark-eyed baby. In a third, a pretty, dark-haired woman with a pixie haircut holds another (or is it the same?) baby, while an older woman and a bald man cut a cake. At the front of the box is a golden treasure casket from which spills a diminutive pirates' hoard: necklaces, brooches, gilt-laced bottles in faceted emerald and ruby. On top of the casket is a label, the tiny font just legible: 'Our Wedding Memorabilia 20.11.99.' On top of a pile of books is another label: 'Danny & John.'

It is impossible to tell how many stories are trapped in this box: Danny and John's, the dark-eyed baby's, the stern Victorian forbears' and who knows how many more. What became of them all? How did these enigmatic signifiers of memory come to be arranged with such meticulous care within the cramped confines of this wooden rectangle – every Thumbelina-sized object fraught with a meaning impossible to decode? And by what bleak turn of events has Danny and John's box, still forlornly radiating the vestiges of the love that inspired it, come to be abandoned on a market stall for a stranger to wonder about?

I find myself wanting quite urgently to rescue this box: to take it to a place of safety, to give its stories meaning and context once more.

'How much?' I ask the stallholder.

'Ten quid,' he says, pushing his luck.

He doesn't care whether he sells the box or not, but he can see that I want it too badly. You can't save lost stories, I tell myself. I put the box back where I found it, and turn for home.

DOWN WHITE HART LANE

John Crace

A WALL OF noise greeted the Spurs players as they walked out on to the Wembley pitch for their first home Premier League match of the season against Chelsea. I cheered too, but my heart wasn't really in it. Nor was I alone. I had caught the eye of several other Tottenham fans nearby in the crowd whom I had sat next to for years at White Hart Lane and they looked similarly out of place, out of time. The noise was real, but the emotion was somehow confected. Deep down, none of us really wanted to be there.

Not that we had a choice. This was Spurs, after all. Tottenham had signed a deal to play all their home games at Wembley while their new stadium was being completed at White Hart Lane and that was that. Where they went we would inevitably follow.

Tottenham had done their best to make Wembley feel like home. They had left a Spurs flag on every seat and intermittently the drum beat of familiar chants would play through the stadium's PA system. But no amount of tinkering around the edges could disguise the feelings of dislocation. Wembley might be a home, but it wasn't home.

The atmosphere even seemed to get to the players. Despite dominating the game for large periods, Spurs lacked the fluency and penetration to make their possession count. Having clawed their way back in to the game with a late equaliser courtesy of a

Chelsea own goal, they lost it in the dying minutes after a series of uncharacteristic errors. The team that had gone through the whole of the previous season undefeated at White Hart Lane had just been beaten at the first time of asking at their new temporary residence. As I left the stadium, I couldn't help feeling that the coming season was going to be a test of endurance.

*

I became Tottenham long before I even knew where Tottenham was. I was nine years old in the summer of 1966, living in Wiltshire and football-obsessed. What I was missing was a team to be passionate about. Neither of my parents were interested in football so there were no tribal loyalties to inherit. The field was completely clear: I could support anyone. But who? In May 1966, the sports pages were full of previews for the World Cup that was taking place in England over the summer. And one man and one face stood out: Jimmy Greaves. Brilliant striker, stylishly Brylcreemed hair: here was the epitome of cool and glamour. I wanted to be Jimmy. In my mind and in the garden, I was Jimmy. I became Spurs.

It should have been obvious from early on that this was going to be a love affair characterised largely by heartbreak. Greaves got injured in the group stages and was replaced by Geoff Hurst, who scored the winner in the quarter-final against Argentina. By the time Greaves was fit for the final, he had lost his place in the team. My dad and my sisters had gone out for the afternoon of the final, but I had made my mum stay behind to watch it on our poky black and white TV. I cried when Germany equalised with almost the last kick of normal time. I cried when England scored twice more in extra time. But I have a feeling I was one of the few boys whose tears were also for Greaves. Hurst had scored his hat-trick.

Looking back, it seems less improbable now that I chose

Spurs than it did then. Here was a side that had won the double only a few years before, a team that had followed that success by winning the FA Cup again the following season and by becoming the first English team to win a European trophy the year after that with a 5-1 demolition of Atlético Madrid. It was a club forever associated with free-flowing, attacking football. But I really didn't know any of that back then. I had as little idea where White Hart Lane was as I did about anywhere else in London. I'm not even sure if I'd ever been to London then. If I had, it can only have been for the day. London was a scary place: my parents seldom visited the capital and when they did my dad always felt the need to dress up in a jacket and tie. They certainly never dreamed of spending the night there.

But Spurs it was. I've often since wondered whether, in some cases, it's the club that chooses you rather than the other way round. It certainly seems we are the ideal psychological fit, though neither of us emerges with much credit from this. Spurs are a team with a sense of entitlement that generally exceeds their on-field successes; a team that lives off memories of past triumphs while all too often falling short in the present. Decades of under-achievement? Tick. An heroic sense of injustice? Tick. A pathological ability to rewrite failure as success? Tick. A seemingly infinite capacity for self-destruction? Tick. Selective memory? Tick. Yes, I'd say Spurs and I were made for one another.

But there's more, much more. There's also an undeniable sense of the absurd – a rich strand of comedy – written into the club's genetic make-up. Most of all, though, there's the fallibility. Good as it sounds in theory to be a Chelsea supporter, guaranteed to collect at least one piece of silverware per season, there doesn't seem to be much joy to be found there. One regulation win after another, with no one needing to break sweat. Least of all the supporters.

Nor do I have the stomach for life as a Fulham fan though I

have a sneaking admiration for those who do. I'm just too much of a thrill seeker, too much of an attention seeker. I couldn't hack the endless backs-to-the-walls, try-to-sneak-a-goal-on-the-break afternoons with avoiding relegation the only real aim. My fragile psyche needs at least the possibility of glory; though equally it needs the probability of disappointment. It needs to be tantalised with riches and rewarded with next to nothing. In short, I need an abusive relationship. And Spurs are the perfect partner.

With their occasional high points and their many, many low points, the Spurs team have played out my life on the pitch with uncanny accuracy. They are my mirror. I watch them and I see me. And the longer it's gone on, the deeper the narcissistic attraction has become. I know that each season is almost certain to end in some kind of disappointment – five decades of following the club have taught me that – but I still keep coming back for more. And I can't imagine it any other way. The last two seasons in which Spurs have posed genuine title threats have been as genuinely problematic for me as they have been wondrously enjoyable. Cognitive dissonance is all that has stood between me and a loss of sanity.

*

It wasn't easy for me to follow Spurs in the late '60s. For some reason, no doubt linked both to their lack of interest in football and a round trip of 200 miles up the old A4 – the M4 stopped at Maidenhead then – to a destination they were as hazy about as I was, my parents managed to fend off my intermittent demands to be taken to White Hart Lane. So my support had to be conducted as a long-distance affair: something which was a great deal harder than it is now.

Televised football was on a drip-feed. *Match of the Day* only featured one game per week – later increased to two – and was on at a time that required my mum to be in an exceptionally generous mood to allow me to stay up, while ITV's Sunday offering *The Big Match* also only featured one game. So the chances of Spurs appearing more than once every few months were slim. Mostly, then, my relationship with Spurs existed entirely in my imagination – a shimmy of emotional trickery I've been accused of many times since.

I did finally make it to White Hart Lane for a third-round FA Cup replay against Nottingham Forest in 1975. I went on my own as I didn't have anyone else to go with, and just followed the crowd leaving the station to the nearest turnstile, ending up behind the goal at the Park Lane end. Forest were in the second division and Spurs were expected to romp it; when they took the lead and the away fans started going mad, the bloke standing next to me said, 'Right, let's go and do the bastards.' With my unerring ability to be in the wrong place at the wrong time, I'd managed to position myself in the middle of the Spurs hardcore. 'Er, OK,' I said, having no intention of following the mini exodus across the terraces to where the Forest fans were grouped. A few minutes later there was a full-scale fight taking place between opposing fans and the police. The upside was that I had rather more elbow room for the rest of the match; the downside was that we still lost.

There weren't any fights in my next two games but we lost those too, and I'd begun to wonder if I would ever see the team win. It was fourth time lucky, but by then I had reconciled myself with only going to White Hart Lane once or twice a season. It was just too much like hard work getting there any more often, either from Exeter, where I went to university, or from south London, where I've lived ever since, what with unimpressed girlfriends, unfortunate lifestyle choices and, more latterly, having kids of my own. Yet even when stuck in south London part of my psyche has always been on secondment in N17. My tribe is Tottenham.

*

The excitement usually kicks in when I emerge from Seven Sisters Tube station. It's there I generally meet Matthew, who sits next to me, and it's there that the crowd starts to build up. It's also there that the pre-match rituals start. First the guessing game about who is going to be included in the starting XI and then the ticking off of familiar landmarks as we walk up the Seven Sisters Road. The police station on the right, the Baptist Church on the right and our favourite kebab shop just minutes from the ground. It's a good 20-minute walk to White Hart Lane but it's one that never palls. Everything is then still possible. It's also sometimes the most enjoyable part of the afternoon.

One of the joys of being a season ticket holder is that you get to sit next to the same people year in year out, week in week out. It's one of life's stranger relationships. People you barely know other than to exchange the odd hello or moan about the team's latest poor performance and yet with whom you share some of your most passionate moments. They get to witness you going wild with joy when Spurs score a late winner; they share your pain as the team limps to yet another tame defeat. In many ways the people I sit next to are more Tottenham than the players themselves. These days footballers are little more than hired mercenaries with no feeling for the club's traditions and history. They come for a few seasons and then move on; shooting stars in the night. We fans are there for the duration. We've been going to White Hart Lane since long before any of the current team were born and will continue to do so long after they have retired.

To people who don't get football, the game is a form of collective madness. Who would willingly put themselves through all the expense and hassle of going to a match on the off chance that you will get to see 20 seconds of brilliance in 90 minutes of play? If that. Believe me, I've been to games where I would have killed for just 20 seconds of worthwhile football. But for me it's also a relief from madness.

For a good 20 years now, I've had recurring bouts of depression. Not every year or even every two years, but regularly enough to know that another one is never far away. Then all hell breaks loose. Crippling panic attacks, prolonged periods of insomnia and an overwhelming sense of futility. Medication helps. As does therapy. But so too does football. Knowing that there are fixed landmarks ahead – that in three days' time Spurs will play a third-round League Cup tie and that I will be there – creates a structure and sense of purpose that can be hard to find when everything else seems so out of reach. When every minute feels like an hour.

The joy of being a football fan is that it requires nothing of me other than a willingness to show up. I can shout or stay quiet as I please and no one will judge me. Or notice. Even when I'm depressed I feel safe in a football crowd: over and beyond a sense of common purpose with everyone else, I feel as if I'm in a bubble where there's nothing getting in between me and the moment. All the other worries that are assaulting my psyche 24/7 dissolve for 90 minutes. There is no me; only football. It's the most perfect time off, time out from myself.

A still more surprising side-effect of my depressions are that they can inject a temporary note of sanity into my football-watching. Like every fan I want to believe that my being at a game somehow has an impact; that if I wasn't there something different would have happened. To an extent this is true: if I hadn't gone, then someone else would have got my place on the Tube. But what my attendance definitely can't do is alter the result. Any correlation between me wearing a lucky shirt or shouting at the referee to give a penalty is entirely coincidental. And yet part of the collective delusion of being a fan is the notion that your participation and involvement can make an incremental difference. By willing something enough, you can get what you want. Being depressed is a wonderful – if unwelcome – corrective. Good and bad things happen regardless of my mood. Any control is entirely illusory.

*

There are some games I never want to end. Being at White Hart Lane when Spurs and Gareth Bale took Inter Milan apart 3-1 was a feeling I will never forget, all the more so because I shared it with my son, Robbie. It was one of those rare nights when every player was at his best and the crowd of 36,000 was of one voice. Rather more normal are the games I would quite like to end after just 15 minutes when Spurs have taken a 1-0 lead. It's insane, of course: no one in their right mind would pay £40 for a game lasting just a quarter of an hour. But there are thousands of us who would happily do just that in return for a certain victory and lower blood pressure. I've been to countless games when the last half-hour has been a living hell as Spurs try to hold on to a winning lead or search for an unlikely equaliser, and yet I cannot leave. The bottom line is that I need the suffering to feel the pleasure.

And pleasures don't come greater than when Spurs beat another London club in a local derby. And they are all the sweeter when they are achieved in the other side's back yard. For all the collective experience of going to home games, it's the away games that are often the most fun. Just me and a couple of thousand Spurs fans up against 40,000 home fans. And sometimes – very occasionally – the underdogs get to have their day.

Spurs' biggest rivals are their north London neighbours Arsenal, and any game between the two has a visceral pull. However much I may dislike Chelsea and Manchester United on a day-to-day basis, no game brings out my feelings of resentment and sense of underachievement more than the local derby. There's no other game that shapes my identity as a fan quite so clearly. What I'm talking about here is fear. Where Man United and Chelsea stimulate surface layers of *schadenfreude*, Arsenal brings out a more primal sense of dread. I may detest losing to United, but I fear losing to Arsenal. There's more at stake: the all-too-frequent defeats are the stuff of nightmares rather than anger. A sense of personal diminution. The certainty of being patronised. Being at the Emirates in November 2010 to see Spurs beat Arsenal for the first time since they moved to their new ground remains one of the highlights of my life as a footballing fan.

*

Though not quite the highlight. That took place at the end of the final game Spurs played on their old White Hart Lane pitch in May 2017. As the players left the pitch, some of the crowd – me included   went on it. I had waited more than 50 years to step on the turf and I was determined to enjoy every second. I scooped up a bit of grass as a souvenir, and wandered down to the goal at the Paxton End before making my way back to the centre circle. There I lay down and closed my eyes. Everything was close to perfect. Spurs hadn't fluffed their lines and lost their last ever game at White Hart Lane and I was living the dream on the pitch. For once in my football life there really was nothing that could go wrong. Until the next season, of course.

AULD LANG SYNE

Lisa Smith

IN ALL HIS 52 years in England, Rufus Samuels had never once been in trouble with the law. Now here he was, under arrest. The handcuffs pinched at his wrists, but he sat upright in the back seat of the squad car. It was important to maintain dignity and composure. They couldn't keep him here. He'd demand a phone call – although he didn't know any lawyers. For a brief moment Rufus considered contacting Pearl, but quickly dismissed the idea. He didn't need her. He could sort it out. At the first opportunity, he would explain in a polite but firm manner that he hadn't done anything wrong. That this was all a misunderstanding, and he was another black man who was the victim of wrongful arrest.

Not many men his age could carry off a Prince of Wales check. Together with his favourite cardinal-red shirt and matching hand-kerchief, Rufus knew that he looked crisp. It was the outfit he'd worn at his wedding last May, and although his fourth wedding had been a low-key event, he'd seen no reason not to treat himself to some new threads. He'd felt as special in this three-piece suit as he had done in the charcoal-grey one he'd worn back in August 1963, when he married Daphne Thompson at Effra Road Baptist Chapel. That day he'd received almost as many compliments as his bride, so after that he got all his good suits tailored by Monty, the Bajan on Walworth Road. He didn't have a single one of those suits any more. His second wife, Esme, took her shears to them when she found out he'd slept with Brenda from the laundrette. He'd always thought that if she had shown as much passion in bed as she'd taken out on his wardrobe, then he never would have been tempted to stray in the first place.

Rufus inspected the other people the police had lined up in the custody suite's foyer. Surely everyone could see that a man like him shouldn't be in such a place. Connie was probably waiting for him at the New Year's Eve party. Ready to welcome him with a can of Red Stripe and a plate of curry goat and rice. He'd never believe that his good friend Rufus 'Big Man' Samuels was standing in a queue between a middle-aged man whose tummy bulged over his tracksuit bottoms and some yout' whose jeans crotch hung down to his knees.

They kept him waiting while a 'bail dodger', a 'drug dealer', and a 'drunk and disorderly' were processed and then taken down to the cells. Each time they'd been led over to a set of double doors which folded backwards at the press of a button. In the cells, a baritone was slurring his way through 'Auld Lang Syne'. His voice drifted into the foyer before the double doors sidled shut. The young police constable who'd brought Rufus to the station guided him into the yellow square, painted on the lino in front of the custody sergeant's desk. The handcuffs were removed and Rufus straightened his back, pulling himself up to his full height, five-foot ten. He estimated the police lady behind the desk was in her early-to-mid 40s. Her dark hair was scraped into a tight knot on the top of her head, making her face look pinched, severe. Rufus thought that with a little rouge on her cheeks she might be pretty, he'd dated a couple of white women back in the '70s. He smiled at the brunette. She didn't smile back.

'Name and time of arrest,' she asked the policeman at his side.

'This is Rufus Harold Samuels, time of arrest was 21.00 hours.'

'Circumstances, please.'

'My dear lady, me no want to waste any more of your time. There are no "circumstances". Everything has been blown up out of proportion. You see—'

The custody sergeant cut Rufus dead with a look. This was the sort of woman who didn't like being interrupted. Best to keep quiet, and bide his time. The young officer relayed the events in police language: formal, stilted. Rufus listened; he would have given a better account of what had occurred. It was clear this copper didn't grasp the complexity of his domestic situation. After all, he was just a boy.

'Mr Samuels, I'm going to authorise your detention so that we can act on the information my colleague has reported, and give you the opportunity to provide an explanation. Now, I'd like you to empty your pockets.'

'Me beg you no take.'

'Sorry?'

'Madam, me would like to keep me hat if it's all right with you. It's me lucky hat, and me nah want to catch a draught, and be sick come New Year's Day.'

They confiscated Rufus's mobile phone, his wallet, his watch, his tie and cuff links. They even took his shoelaces. He was allowed to keep his Homburg, after they'd checked the lining and the brim.

'Are you on any medication?' the custody sergeant asked in her monotone.

Rufus was 72, but believed he could still pass for 60. He had always taken pride in his physical appearance, and had been able to maintain his athletic build – his slender waist and barrel chest – until well into middle age. Then came a diagnosis of high blood pressure, then diabetes, and after that he started having the sort of trouble associated with an enlarged prostate. But all the men he played dominoes with at the Duke of Sussex had the same problems.

'You're as old as the woman you feel,' was Connie's philosophy. Cheryl was 36. Healthy and strong.

The bolt on the cell door echoed as it shot home. Rufus overheard the policemen conversing as they retreated along the corridor.

'What's Granddad in for?' asked the Asian custody officer. 'Wearing a loud suit in a built-up area?'

'Domestic,' his arresting officer replied.

'Blimey! Has he asked for a lawyer?'

'No. He does want a phone call though.'

Rufus padded carefully across the cell floor. Without the laces, his brogues were large and awkward. The blue plastic mattress, spread across a narrow cot, was thin and cold against his backside as he sat down. He inhaled, catching a whiff of sweat and booze. In a neighbouring cell, the baritone began slurring his way through 'Auld Lang Syne' again. A younger, gruffer male voice shouted: 'Shut the fuck up.' The singing continued. 'I said shut the fuck up,' Gruff-Voice repeated. The baritone stopped. '*You* shut the fuck up,' he shouted.

'No, *you* shut the fuck up.'

'Go fuck yourself!'

'No, you go fuck *yourself!*'

Their expletives echoed up and down the corridor for around five minutes. Then there was silence. Rufus took off his hat and allowed his head to rest against the concrete wall. His mind drifted back to this time last year, and the moment Cheryl arrived at the community centre dressed in that white strapless gown. It clung to her bosom, slipped over her hips, and hugged her broad backside, before cascading in folds with silver sequins down to the tiled floor. Cheryl and her girlfriend stood at the edge of the dance floor, with their Beyoncé-style weaves, clutching Bacardi Breezers. Being red-skinned, Rufus wasn't usually attracted to women of a darker complexion. Cheryl's smooth, blue-black skin had the lustre of a Nubian woodcarving. Expertly applied makeup accentuated her chiselled jawline and hollowed cheeks, features that he would normally call handsome, rather than beautiful. It was the assurance in her step and the swing of her waist that had truly mesmerised him. His eyes were drawn to her all night as she glided around the hall, the sequins on her frock leaving a trail from the buffet to the bar and all around the dance floor. At first he watched from a safe vantage point, but as if wound in by some invisible wire, Rufus found himself at her elbow when the clock struck midnight. She'd turned and raised an eyebrow.

'So mi watchdog dare fi approach at last!'

'Mi nah watchdog. Mi just like to look 'pon a beautiful woman.'

'And mi like man with moustache,' she said, a gold canine glinting as she smiled. She bowed her head to plant a waxy kiss on his mouth. 'Happy New Year,' she said.

'Fooor Auuld Laang Syyyne my dear, Fooor Auuld Laang Syyyne …'

The baritone along the corridor had resumed his carolling. Rufus shook his head. With it being New Year's Eve, the cells would soon begin to fill up. Might he end up having to share with some drunken ruffian? Did Cheryl realise what she was putting him through? Rufus heard the keys twist in the lock. The cell door opened, and a white policeman in his 50s was standing beside the custody officer.

'Mr Rufus Samuels? Come with me, please.'

*

There was a long, dull tone. Rufus shifted in the hard plastic seat, and waited for the note to end. At last, he could get this whole thing sorted out. The room he now sat in was almost as bare as the cell, except it had carpet, and a table where he sat across from the policeman. There was also a clock on the wall. It was 22.10. Connie's party would be well underway by now. He indulged himself in imagining that Connie was ringing his mobile at that very moment, or hurrying to his flat. Concerned, anxious to find out why Rufus hadn't made it to the party yet. They'd met in 1961 while on a double date with twins, Letitia and Denise Macintosh. The men hit it off with each other, more than they did with the sisters; their mutual love of rum, dominoes, gambling and women had made them firm friends. Over the years, they had loaned each other money and slept on each other's couches, and Connie had been Rufus's best man for three of his four weddings. Surely Connie would have noticed his absence by now.

The note ceased. Rufus sat up straight, and looked the policeman in the eye. 'For the benefit of the tape please state your full name.'

'Rufus Harold Samuels.'

'I am Sergeant Daniel Parsons of the prisoner handling unit. Mr Samuels, you've waived your right to have legal representation present during this interview, but should you change your mind you can request a lawyer at any time. Do you understand?'

'Yes.'

'Mr Samuels, you've been brought here under caution, following an incident at 12b Hercules Tower. Mrs Cheryl Marcia Samuels alleges that you assaulted her. Is that correct?'

'Well, Sergeant Parsons, Daniel, this whole situation just blow up from nothing. We were getting ready to go to my best friend's New Year's Eve party, it's a family-and-friends type of thing him been having for the past 30 years. Anyway, Cheryl come out of the bedroom in a short, tight-up frock – more of a nightclub type of outfit than a nice party dress. Now, I did tell her that she look nice, but I said that I thought it was a little revealing for Connie's party. After all, it's the community centre we ah go to, not a dance hall.'

'You took offence to what your wife was wearing.'

'Yes man! Me like her to dress nice, but at 36 she neither chick nor child, and no have no business going to a family party dressed like that. Are you married, Daniel?'

'It's Sergeant Parsons. Yes, I am happily married, and I don't tell my wife what to wear.'

'Good for you. I'm glad your wife's clothes no give you any cause for concern. But you understand that a husband should be able to offer him wife his opinion nuh?'

'Had you been drinking?'

'No. Me was saving meself for the party.'

'Would you say that you have a problem with your wife making up her own mind? Making her own decisions?'

'No-suh! I thought we would just have a discussion about her apparel.'

'Did you become angry, Mr Samuels?'

'Listen, Daniel, Sergeant Parsons, I am a reasonable man. When we first met, she did seem like a reasonable woman. Quick-tempered, but me like women with a bit of spirit, you know? Lately, me can't put a foot right with her, and tonight, she just went crazy 'pon me.'

'Your wife alleges that you assaulted her. That you held her by the wrists.'

'Well ah lie she ah tell. Ah no so it go.' Rufus paused, picturing the smirk on Cheryl's face as she prodded his chest with her index finger. He recalled the raspy tone of her voice.

'She say to me: *"what make you think mi 'ah go to Connie's party?"* She said: *"Yuh nah see you is an old man? You want to spend New Year with all you ol' friend and dem pickny, and dem grandpickny and call it a party. Cha! Ah true mi nuh young like spring chicken, but mi still have more life than you."* All me did was kiss me teeth, but then she raise her fists to thump me. Me say: *"Woman calm yourself nuh!"* Which was when me did grab her wrists.'

'So, Mr Samuels, you're saying that your wife was about to strike you?'

The officer leaned forward. He looked Rufus straight in the eye. His expression had been serious throughout the interview so far, but now Rufus thought he detected something else.

'Has your wife ever displayed violence towards you before, Mr Samuels?'

'What do you mean?'

'Has your wife ever struck you before?'

Rufus wondered if this was some sort of ploy. Get him to say he was riled, so lashed out against her. It was embarrassing enough to have to admit out loud – and to another man, that his wife had tried to hit him in the first place. He could imagine the mockery if it ever got out: 'Just look how Rufus let him young gyal rule him!' He'd never be able to show his face in the Duke again. None of the domino crowd would understand that he and Cheryl were still adjusting to married life.

Although Rufus kept his eyes pinned to the plastic spool turning in the tape machine, he could feel the sergeant's gaze.

'Mr Samuels, I appreciate this might be difficult to talk about, but I can assure you we take spousal abuse very seriously.'

Spousal abuse. The words churned over in Rufus's mind.

'All spousal abuse,' the detective added.

'No comment,' Rufus replied.

'All right, Mr Samuels,' said the policeman, closing his folder. 'I'm going to need a full statement from your wife in order to decide how to proceed.'

Rufus clutched the telephone receiver, pressing it to his ear. He could picture the cream-coloured phone on Pearl's hallway table, its ring echoing around her maisonette. It was 22.50. Pearl would already be at a Church of God of Prophecy's New Year's Eve service, sitting in a pew close to the choir. When he'd announced that he and Cheryl were getting married, several people raised an eyebrow, but said nothing. Only Pearl had been straight with him.

'Lord God, Rufus, you come here ah brag about how you gwaan go get married in three week, when you only know this woman three months!'

Pearl had reached for the kettle, then, changing her mind, had gone to the larder and taken a bottle of Wray & Nephew from the top shelf. She moved about the kitchen in a languid manner, dressed in the kaftan she thought concealed her big batty. Her face was moisturised, but otherwise not made-up. Rufus's marriage to Pearl had lasted six years, and although they divorced in 1987, he'd gravitate towards her whenever he needed to think aloud. He still thought his third wife was captivating. She had poured two large measures of white rum and nudged one of the glasses towards him.

'Well, if it wasn't for this thing with her papers, then me would have probably wait,' said Rufus. 'Have a proper church do, rather than a register office affair.'

'You know that's not what I mean. The woman live here six years already and nuh properly land yet? All she ah look for is a man with citizenship, a flat and a pension. You no remember that you already have daughters the same age as she? Time you ah spend running after women, you could ah spend with the children – and the grandchildren you barely know.'

'Dem nah want to know me. When last any of them come look for me? Dem out there, living dem life. Me maybe in me 70s but me have life to live too. Me no need to be alone.' He took a sip of the rum. 'Is it because you jealous that you say Cheryl just ah use me?'

Pearl had coughed down her rum before bursting into laughter. Rufus had always liked her deep, hearty laugh. It was the only time that creases ever appeared on her smooth, red-brown skin.

'If me did think there was a chance of we getting back together, then maybe me would think again about Cheryl.'

'Rufus, me always did love you sense of humour, but me too old for you and your foolishness.'

Rufus had kissed his teeth. 'You gwaan take me back one of these days you know, and I'll be waiting. Time longa than rope.'

'Nuh let your fiancée hear you say that. Me hear she have quite a temper.'

Now there was a click and the ringing tone was replaced with a long dull note. Rufus replaced the receiver; he rubbed the sweat from his hands on to his trouser leg.

'No answer?' said the custody officer. Rufus shook his head.

'It's that time of the evening. Everyone is out and about by now. I can't understand it myself, I'd rather stay indoors.'

'Can me make another call? Please?' The officer gave him a sympathetic smile.

'Go on then.'

Rufus dialled the only other number that he knew by heart. He held his breath during half a dozen rings, and then exhaled a deep sigh.

'You're through to the voicemail of Cornelius Benson. Me can't take your call now, but please leave me a message, after the tone. Thanks.'

'Connie, it's Rufus. Me deh a' Asylum Road Police Station. Cheryl have me arrest. Man, me no know where fi turn.'

Rufus was being taken back to the cells when his guard was informed that the duty medic had arrived. He was led down a new corridor, and stopped outside a room where the sign on the door said Forensic Physician. The custody officer tapped twice.

'Yes, come in,' said a woman's voice from inside.

Despite the ominous sign, the room looked just like a normal doctor's surgery, with a trolley bed covered in thin blue paper, metal thermometers, probes and a blood pressure machine. The room smelled reassuringly of disinfectant. The doctor rose from her desk, and shook his hand.

'Good evening, I'm Dr Kwarshie, and you are ... Mr Rufus Samuels?' Rufus nodded. 'OK. Thank you, officer.'

'I'll just be outside.' The policeman retreated from the room.

'Take a seat please, Mr Samuels.' Dr Kwarshie gestured to a grey plastic chair with thin green padding on the seat and back, placed to the side of the desk. While the lady doctor scanned some papers, Rufus mused on how much she resembled his daughter Sharon. Pearl had shown him photos of Sharon's wedding day that had been posted on an internet site: Facelink, MyPage, or something-or-other. She looked just like her mother, Pearl, on their wedding day. The same round face with dimpled cheeks, the same skin-tone, and almond-shaped eyes.

'Says here you're 70, I'd have had you down for at least ten years younger.'

'Well, you know that black don't crack,' he said.

Dr Kwarshie laughed, revealing a slight gap between her two front teeth. Rufus felt a little more relaxed in this room.

'You remind me of one of my daughters.'

'So you're a family man, Mr Samuels, that's nice. How many daughters do you have?'

'Eight. Me have four sons too, and six grandchildren already.'

'A big family. It must keep you busy.'

Rufus smiled faintly, but didn't reply.

'I see that you've been in here for almost three hours. Can I ask when you last took your blood-pressure medication?'

'This morning.'

'No headache or dizziness since you've been taken into custody?'

'No, young lady. The only reason me head ah spin is on account of the nonsense me wife say about me.'

'Well, I'm here to assess you're medically fit for detention, Mr Samuels.' She was still smiling, but her voice was firm. 'The investigating officers will deal with the charges. Can you raise your sleeve for me, I'd like to take a blood pressure reading.'

Rufus folded up the shirtsleeve on his right arm, in order to avoid creasing it too much. Dr Kwarshie leaned forward with the glove.

'Mr Samuels, may I ask – how long have you had these bruises on your arm?'

'Oh. It nah nothing, doctor. Me bump meself the other day, when me was getting out of the bath.'

'Well, I can see that might explain the bruise on your upper arm, but these marks here,' she said, her finger hovering above the dark patches from his wrist up to his elbow. 'These look like finger marks.'

Rufus looked at the woman. Despite the crease that had appeared in her forehead, she seemed even younger to him now.

'You know you're safe here, don't you? Is there anything you'd like to tell me?'

'It nuh nuttin', doctor. It nuh nuttin'.'

Rufus had lost track of time. He guessed it must be getting close to midnight, he could hear the place filling up. There were more drunks, but the baritone had finally stopped singing 'Auld Lang Syne'. The prospect of seeing in the New Year under lock and key was looming ever closer.

The cell door opened, and Sergeant Parsons entered. 'Mr Samuels, you're free to go.'

'What? You talk to Cheryl?'

'Yes, we have. Your wife has withdrawn her allegation against you. When our WPC arrived at your address your wife declined to make a full statement. She claimed that she still loves you, and she's prepared to forgive you, if you promise to behave. Then she left, as a minicab had arrived to take her to a party in Hackney. As it stands there's insufficient evidence to support that you attacked her, so we can't proceed. My colleague will escort you to the front desk, where you can collect your things.'

The custody officer accompanied Rufus up from the cells. He

was business-like and methodical in returning the confiscated possessions, and made polite chitchat. Rufus fastened the wristband of his watch and looked at the time. It was 23.55.

'Time flies,' said the policeman.

Rufus's smile was thin. He felt weary. 'Me was supposed to be at a party. Me nah go make it now. Not for midnight, anyhow.'

'Well, you could hang around here until the chimes if you like. One of my colleagues could make you a cup of tea. You could have a chat …'

Rufus looked at the officer. He realised that the look he had been getting from Sergeant Parsons, from Dr Kwarshie, and from his jailor was pity. He started for the door.

'Here, take this,' the sergeant handed him a leaflet. A helpline number ran across the bottom.

'Wha' gwaan, Big Man!' came a booming voice from behind. Rufus shoved the leaflet into a trouser pocket.

'Connie! What time you call this?'

'Me just get you message, it's me grandson Devlin drive me here, everyone else drunk already. Of all the caper you involve yuself in over the years, this one must beat all! What kind of foolishness is this Cheryl ah gwaan with?'

'It nuh nuttin'. It will all blow over. But, beg you let me come cotch on your sofa for a night or two. Give her time to cool off.'

Rufus turned to the policeman. 'Happy New Year, officer,' he mumbled.

'Happy New Year, sir. Good luck.'

The chorus of 'Auld Lang Syne' seeped from some of the houses as Rufus and Connie walked towards Devlin's car, parked up the road from the police station. It had begun to drizzle, so Rufus turned up the collar on his suit jacket, and pushed his hands deep into his trouser pockets. There was the leaflet. He grasped it, then slowly began to crumple it into a ball.

THREE LONDON ARTISTS

Jonathan Jones

THE FIRST TIME I met Gustav Metzger we had a rendezvous at the café of the Royal Association of British Architects (RIBA) on Great Portland Street. He ordered a cup of hot water. Tiny and wizened, he was hard to reconcile with his legendary reputation as the 'auto-destructive' artist who inspired the Who to smash their instruments on stage. Metzger at this stage in his life – shortly before a rediscovery that saw him lionised as an avant-garde hero by the art world – was one of London's ghosts. He seemed to belong on the streets, in doorways. An old man with a haunted face and a carrier bag.

Great cities are not just congregations of the living but of the dead. Metzger carried with him a memory of murdered millions, and a childhood stalked by hate. He embodied the fact that when you walk the streets of London you rub shoulders with the history of the world, fragmented into millions of individual narratives of oppression, survival, anger, loss, escape ... songs of innocence and experience. We were sitting over hot drinks just moments away from Oxford Street where people lose themselves in shopping. Perhaps the reason Londoners like to shop is to forget who they used to be.

Metzger was not a happy shopper and he never forgot where he came from. He became an artist only to preach anti-art.

Painting with acid, going on strike, it was as if he protested the fact of being alive by creating art that consumed itself – that refused to be. That day we walked to the Wiener Library, the Holocaust research centre that has been based in London since the 1930s, to see an album compiled by SS Major General Jürgen Stroop as a souvenir for senior Nazis of the 1943 defeat of the Jewish fighters in the Warsaw Ghetto. 'The Jewish quarter of Warsaw is no more!' boasts its title page in black Gothic letters. Inside are more than 50 photographs that document the arrests of the last survivors with a terrifying frankness, as if these crimes against humanity were heroic acts – which indeed the album proclaims them to be.

In Metzger's series of artworks called *Historic Photographs*, these and other horrifying visual records of the Holocaust are blown up to a colossal scale. They are then covered with fabric. To see the photograph you have to go under the cloth, which forces you to look extremely closely at the enlarged image, to engage with it in a physical, immediate way. These pictures are not something to glance at in passing, to consume, then turn the page. They demand your full attention, as they should.

Metzger always chose to meet in anonymous public places in the heart of London. Interviewing him felt a little like being in a John le Carré novel, turning up at a slightly bland location to speak of sombre things under the cover of respectability. A few years later we met in the lobby of the National Theatre. We sat at a white-topped table. This time he spoke in more detail of his childhood.

Metzger was born in Nuremberg in 1926. In 1939 he became one of the approximately 10,000 Jewish children brought to Britain by the *Kindertransport*. By then he had seen a lifetime's worth of history. Picture this: a Jewish childhood in the city where the Nazi movement held its annual gatherings. There on the South Bank, he described to me what it was like to see, year after year as he grew up, Hitler's stormtroopers march through the streets of Nuremberg on their way to camp at their rally grounds on the edge of this old city. You can still see what he saw, in Leni Riefenstahl's film *Triumph of the Will*. The charismatic romanticism of the gathering it records is terrifying because it is seductive and unexpectedly modern, a kind of uniformed Glastonbury. No wonder Metzger became an artist who was intensely suspicious of the power of the aesthetic as such.

Once when Joseph Beuys was speaking at the ICA in the 1970s, he told me, he interrupted the idealistic sculptor's dreamy claim that 'everyone is an artist' by asking: *'Josef Beuys, "Jeder Mensch ein Kunstler" – Adolf Hitler auch?'* (Adolf Hitler too? Was the dictator an artist?). The theorist Walter Benjamin argues in a 1935 essay that fascism preaches art for art's sake. Metzger's lifelong assault on art was, I think, a repudiation of the sinister power of Nazi aesthetics he was forced to see as a Jewish child in Nuremberg.

Orphaned by the Holocaust, adopted in his last years by the art world, Metzger died in 2017. The country where he had found a home of sorts – though he refused to be a citizen of Britain, or anywhere else, and was officially stateless – was itself by then undergoing an identity crisis. After Britain completes its agonising, grinding process of withdrawal from the EU, will this still be a country whose capital is a refuge, a hideaway, an exile's natural home? Of course, people will still come – those who are allowed. Nor should we sentimentalise the past: Metzger certainly didn't. The bright light of the *Kindertransport* distracts us all too easily from the unwelcoming attitude to refugees that prevailed in 1930s Britain. As W H Auden observed in 1939:

Saw a poodle in a jacket fastened with a pin,
Saw a door opened and a cat let in:
But they weren't German Jews, my dear, but they weren't German Jews.

Nevertheless, Brexit is a deliberate narrowing of what Britain means. The vote to secede from 'Europe' has widely been taken as a vote against immigration. The brutal machinery of leaving is itself creating new antipathies. Who knows what hostilities against outsiders might be unleashed by an economically disastrous self-amputation?

For the cosmopolitan London art scene the unnecessary surgery may prove lethal. I find myself thinking of how profoundly the art of London has been shaped by European immigrants. For Metzger is one of a generation of refugees who gave London some of its greatest and most truthful artistic achievements.

*

Frank Auerbach's paintings of London building sites at the start of the 1960s are studies of the city's open wounds. They were made in the years when bombed-out wastes left by the Blitz were being turned into shiny new shops and cinemas. Post-war austerity was soon to be forgotten by Swinging London. Yet Auerbach is in no mood to forget in these visceral churnings of poisoned ground. Oxford Street Building Site I (1959-60) is a faecal stain in which girders and cranes appear to have been slashed with a knife or stick, so forceful are his brushstrokes in the pungent morass. It has the yellow-brown hue and glutinous thickness of the wet mud into which you can almost see the artist peering as he stands beside a vast crater where a new shop's foundations are being dug. Is this a beginning or an end? It resembles an archaeological dig, down into the past. The world is being rebuilt but its optimistic machines balance on the edge of history's pit.

Auerbach was born in Berlin in 1931 and sent to Britain by his parents in 1939. He lived. His mother and father, having got him out, both died in the Holocaust. His early art is scarred and shadowed by this terrible experience. Portraits such as *Head of*

E.O.W. (1957) depict ghostly monochrome relics of a shattered Europe. The weight of history crushes them. His paintings of building sites are even more painful because they portray new life. The agony of rebirth, the horror that the world will go on and bury its dead, that new sensations will destroy memory, is embedded in the filthy earth of these paintings. Like T S Eliot in *The Waste Land*, finding April to be the cruellest month, he shudders at London's renewal:

> ... mixing.
> Memory and desire, stirring.
> Dull roots with spring rain.

Auerbach's long life in painting is in many ways a successful effort to overcome this early sense of overwhelming tragedy. Gradually, in the 1960s, colour comes into his work. The portraits become empathetically human rather than bleakly animal. His London landscapes take on romantic beauty and richness. Instead of holes in the ground he paints the living city and its natural spaces. The work of painting itself becomes his theme, going to the studio his daily epic of survival.

The best collection of Auerbach's work was assembled by Lucian Freud. Among the intimate records of their friendship that Freud kept alongside his superb choice of Auerbach's paintings are comic greetings including a cartoon in which Auerbach portrays Freud leering at Rubens' fleshy masterpiece *Samson and Delilah* in the National Gallery. This dates from when Freud was painting his colossal nude portraits of Leigh Bowery and Sue Tilley.

Freud's rivalry with the Old Masters and unquestioned accomplishment as a painter, climaxing in acceptance by both critics and the marketplace as a blue-chip modern great, may seem a million miles from the radical outsiderdom of Metzger. When Metzger was 'painting' with acid that destroyed the surface he threw it at, Freud was developing what became one of the most powerful and coveted oil painting techniques of modern times. Yet Freud too is a child of history with the sensibility of a refugee.

It would be straining things to see his early life as desperately shadowed. He came to London in less catastrophic circumstances than Metzger or Auerbach. Born in Berlin in 1933, grandson to one of Europe's most celebrated Jewish intellectuals, Freud moved with his parents to Britain as soon as Hitler took power in 1933. His youth seems to have been marked more by delinquency than despair. Yet Freud's London is a city of migrants, a city that people are just passing through.

His portraits are set in his Paddington studio, whose bare floorboards, skylights, mirrors and quirky bits of modern and antique furniture create a permanent impression of impermanence. The whole set-up seems designed so that it could be abandoned tomorrow, should sudden flight prove necessary. Did Freud for all his success sense that he was never quite at home? He certainly goes out of his way to stop his sitters settling in. Some of them seem scarcely to take off their overcoats. *Two Irishmen in W11*, painted in 1984-85, portrays two men both stiffly clad in dark suits and ties. The older one sits in a white armchair looking downward, his meaty hands on the chair arms, like a Pope in a painting by Raphael or Titian. His young companion stands and puts a hand on the back of his seat, loyally. West London floats in the window behind them, houses and a tower block under a grey sky. Is this their city? Is it anyone's city? Here they are, a modern Pope and prelate far from their palace, two 'Irishmen' painted by a Jew in a city full of the restlessness that is modernity.

My favourite of all Freud's paintings, *Girl Sitting in the Attic Doorway*, painted in 1995, portrays a young woman perched naked near the top of a room. The 'doorway' where she sits thinking with her fist to her chin like Rodin's Thinker, echoing the conventional pose of melancholy in medieval and Renaissance art, is really a square hatch just under the ceiling. Why is it there? The walls are worn and stained, the top of the cupboard she climbed up to get here is like a green plinth below her. She is literally in a no-place, a limbo between realities. Just passing through.

Thinking about these three London artists, the barely concealed xenophobia and bigotry of Britain's new course becomes more obvious and more frightening. London is a world city and its art is world art. How can this polyglot cultural capital survive the closing of our mental borders?

NEASDEN LANE

Ben Judah

I CIRCLE THE city.

Days, hours, on random routes that lead nowhere.

Searching.

Rain dapples on the car windscreen into Neasden. Wipers squeak and squeal. The road north from White City unwinds in the colours of a Lowry painting. The curving tarmac is suddenly overcut with vaulting, spectacularly swooshing motorways, as it slices through bleary-eyed depots and railway junctions. Grasping trees thickly border the edges of deserted warehouse service roads; grim perimeters ringed by rusting wire fences and littered shrubs.

Neasden is where row after row of Victorian London finally ends. The mellow Georgian mansions and little cottage-pie lanes in Shepherd's Bush have suddenly gone. Harlesden's endless ladder of cramped, pompous Edwardian terraces, dotted with defunct gin palaces, has given way to bogus Tudor drives. And this is where gentrification ends, too. The English currency of status in this city is Victorian brick – and these niggling suburban semis are far from what the wealthy English dream for in London.

John Betjeman had it in for Neasden. This was the loneliest village in London. The home of the average citizen and the garden gnome. Neasden was Britain in its pebble-dashed conformity. The poet took the train through Metro-land. This was his England.

The kingdom of the privet hedge and the net curtain. The heartland of the garden shed and the fumbling suited commuter. I took the car.

There is trouble in Metro-land. Betjeman's people have gone. The men who went on about Spitfires are mostly dead. Their sons were the ones who hated the suburbs: boys who grew their hair long, resentfully strummed guitars, and only came back for those cold awkward teas and finally to clear out the family house.

The English don't want to live in this borough any more. Betjeman would never recognise Brent. The white British population is now around 18 per cent. South Asians make up 33 per cent. The black population, roughly 19 per cent. Between 2001 and 2011 the white British population of Brent tumbled: losing almost 30 per cent. These net curtains now hide urban poverty. The garden gnomes have gone. The old terraced slums ringing Victorian London from Brick Lane to Frontline Peckham now have soaring wealthy white populations and matching rents. The sexually frustrated children of Neasden want to be close to Shoreditch not the M40 to the Cotswolds.

They want to be central, they want to cycle – they want the city. I think of Betjeman as I park outside a Hindu temple brooding over a car park. Thin lead clouds smear over the blue skies. There is a muggy heat. These are the last days in spring. The cars have begun to pass with windows down. You can sense people are becoming uncomfortable in their clothes. There are a few hours, here and there, when people unzip in the northern sun, but then shiver cold again in the drizzle.

The Neasden outdoors has an indoor gloom: obscuring the temple's hallucinogenic intricacies chiselled into reaching limestone domes. There is a slight smog. Through purring open doors, a chubby, satin-robed man with radiant green eyes stands holding out a pillow topped with a porcelain sleeping Ganesh. Waxed mahogany beams support the ceilings. These folds of wood are woven with frenzied dancing figures, racing animals and psychedelic flowers. Their humming rhythm begins to tingle powerfully inside the heart.

Crippled women slouch towards the sanctum. Dribbling men are lifted out of wheelchairs. This shimmering space contains pure calm. Carved white limestone swirls like a rising whirlpool into the dome. The carving is of such intensity that the whole dome vibrates with colour: hints of soft electric green, blue and red light wash over the point of mystery. This is the most beautiful room in London I know.

But this dome is an exception. Instead of allowing Muslims and Hindus to make dingy terraces sing with minarets and cupolas, planning permission is frustrated at every turn. Ostentatious Oriental designs are blocked by the councils. This means the other London mostly prays in basement mosques, converted cinemas and damp bingo halls, where the lighting is dim and the carpets are scuffed, where the pipes whine and the electricals hum, and every draught creeps in.

'They never wanted us to build this here, but we never gave up ...'

A flake-skinned temple guard clutches me in the car park. He waffles he came north from Croydon because he was pulsed by six heart attacks and paralysed from the neck down; but the temple sanctum has blessed him back to health. The guard shakes his head, wobbling huge drooping ears, and peers expectantly. 'The locals were opposed, of course. But now they think our temple is a great beauty ... They know how powerful it is. This temple has been sending out its energy waves ... and reducing drugs and crime all over Brent.'

The guard shoves his hands in his pockets. Then sighs. 'But England has changed, you know ... When I first came to England much more people were going to church ... now they are not going. I think this very bad. But some whites now come to this temple ...'

I drive further into Neasden. Behind the temple loom two seemingly industrial chimneys backing onto two schools. One, cubic, '80s red-brick, is run by the temple. The other, a fusty old red-brick craning its head into the class system, is not.

Neasden was built mostly in the 1930s. It was somewhat fashionable, even prosperous, for a while. It was the suburb of bird-watchers and Sunday bridge clubs. This was the life sold all over London. They sold it in pamphlets as thatch-cottage serenity, and in posters of rustic bliss, and country rambles – the new-build escape from the infested back-to-back warrens of Whitechapel. This was an architect's urban dream: a middle-school imagination that fetishised the cosy above all else.

But dreams change. I am driving through a failed suburbia of PVC doors and plastic windows. The hedge-clippers and the lawnmowers are silent. The privets are mostly gone. So are the rose bushes and the rhododendrons. The driveways are cracked with weeds and covered in little mounds of broken electricals: I see a smashed old box TV, shoved into the silvery mouth of a scratched washing machine, its hatch door lopped off.

Betjeman's dream is dead. And this is changing the suburbs. Migrants now land at the edges. Poverty now accumulates out of sight. Gabled semis are turning into clammy tenements. Every time Nan dies in Neasden her house gets passed over to a key-jangling landlord. Illegal rentals and overcrowding abound. The fire brigades are worried. Polish builders are hutching-up four or more to a room. Bunks are thrown into Grandad's musty old garden shed and bandit extensions are built on the unkempt lawns. The old working-class suburbs are turning into slums.

Neasden Is A Slum!
It's not so strange that someone gets beaten up there – that's every-
*   day life.*
London: Poles wounded in a night brawl.

The two Poles were wounded in knife fights in London's Neasden. Most likely a group of five Englishmen got into a scuffle with two Poles.

I lived in Neasden where 15 Poles lived in the same house.

This is what the Eastern Europeans think. And this is not hard to find out. To know what Poles really think read their online forums. These are posts stuck up on the newspaper site Gazeta.pl. The thread: *Neasden is a slum!* But there are others too. Threads about overcrowding. Threads about beatings. And accidents at work.

So what that 15 people live in a tiny room, that's not normal. Let immigrants from Africa or Bangladesh live like that, but not people from Europe!

My notebook is full of their stories.

The rain droplets are warm as I wander along Neasden Lane. Black hoods hang around the Quality Fried Chicken. Their empty boxes at their feet. Down the lane urban believers in Nikes, puffa jackets and air-fresh white jubbah robes saunter in and out of the London Fatwa Council by the glowing Kashmiri grocer's. I watch the hoodies come in here with their paranoid shuffle. There are some preachers who will only ever carry those Nokia throwaway phones. Because they are always listening: to every sermon, and to every charity appeal.

They come in themselves sometimes, the watchers, into the basement mosques, and the shisha bars, with little leaflets explaining what the law is and what they have a right to request. They wink at the owners. We know who has the right to remain and who doesn't in the family. We know who is here illegally. So, if anyone we are looking for comes in we are going to hear from you. OK?

I stand outside a clapped-out corner shop. The glass wall inside plastered in 40 biro-scrawled little notes. Rooms available only for Europeans, Sikhs or Hindus. There is work for carers and mobile digits to call. There is work in a massage parlour and the number of the pimp. There is a protest for Gaza.

I wander the lane collecting stories. The walls are plastered with posters to call home. Romania 1p. Pakistan 4p. Poland 1p. The loneliest village in London has become heavily Eastern European. Two Polish village boys in black baseball caps strut up and down clutching after-work beers. A Romanian guy in a fake Armani jacket and joggers does the same. They wear cheap aftershave, but still stink of booze, and sweat slightly with the sudden bursts of sun.

The machines in the Romanian kiosk breathe throatily, cooling dozens of meaty sausages. The white cabinets heave with Transylvanian beers. Behind the checkout a depressive with strained hazel eyes and a huge florid face spends the day fiddling with her phone until it runs out of battery, and then starts again. She is about 35. Her head slumps into pink-fingered hands as we talk, and then: 'This place is horrible. I hate the fights. The moment Friday night starts ... Romanians start beating Poles who start beating Irish ... and they don't stop until Sunday. It's frightening sometimes.'

There are two straight-up Polish mini-markets on Neasden Lane. I find the same stories there. Nervously a big-breasted 20-year-old cashier, with a chewed lip and a locket round her neck, uncomfortable in a pink crop top, fidgets and mumbles – some Romanians raped a Polish girl. 'The Romanians and the Poles ... nobody drinks like us ...' She draws breath tensely in the yellowy gloom: they say, these Romanian bad men were here before they were supposed to be. When they got deported, Poles snaffled up their jobs, and squatted their park-bench hangout. But the Romanians returned: they wanted both the bench and the building work back. The rape was their revenge. The fidgeting cashier wants out of Neasden. I record her stutter. 'They are not fighting ethnic battles, y'see ... they just drink themselves into a stupor and then fights kick off between them and the Irish. Every weekend ... the same thing happens.'

Along mangled Neasden Lane, the Irish pubs still fly sun-faded green-white-orange tricolours. Council posters call to study for the citizenship test. Ghanaian women inspect fruit and veg piled high outside the Kashmiri butchers. Pakistani, African and Eastern European lives float past each other. Barely touching. Men brush up in the festering pub. Women occasionally talk in the Turkish mini-market.

Imagine Neasden as a shop, it would come out like that mini-market: Way2Save. Polish rock music blasts out. The shop smells of flour: fresh Anatolian pide bread is being made round the back. There are sacks of African powders. Pakistani confectioneries and PUSSY energy drinks. Here the obese Polish stacker, packing up the flatbreads, laughs off the fights with her throaty chortle. 'Oh ... Neasden! My little Eastern European village. They are fighting, yes ... but it's not serious. Men will be men. This is perfectly normal ... You know our kind. We can get angry at everyone.'

I HAVE A FRIEND WHO IS POLISH, HE'S VERY NICE

Kinga Burger

THREE THINGS HAPPENED that week; first, Gerald left me; he packed his bags and moved in with his mother; then my bank, after eight years of seamless relationship, blocked all my credit and debit cards without a word of explanation; and finally, I woke up on Friday morning to learn that the people had spoken and they wanted out of the European Union, or perhaps more precisely they wanted us out of here. It was a true hat-trick of betrayal. That should teach me to take things for granted. After sitting on the sofa for about 20 minutes with one sock on, I picked up the phone and called in sick.

Many people, generally women, told me that cleaning calms them down, so I considered doing something about the kitchen, wondering how I had let it get into that state in just a week and without actually cooking anything, but eventually the enormity of the task chased me out of the house.

The café round the corner was the usual Hackney establishment, slightly overpriced but Instagram-friendly – distressed furniture and blackboard signs that told you it cost a lot of money to look this poor. Their menu promised banter, but to everyone's relief normally there wasn't any. People would just buy their coffee and get on with their day without making eye contact.

Today was different, today the news was so unusual, so un-expected, that everyone forgot how to be British for one morn-ing. The good people of Hackney gathered in the café and the atmosphere was that of an enormous, collective hangover. They all looked like they didn't quite remember the night before but they were certain they had done something they would never have done sober, and I thought that if I had looked a little more obvi-ously Polish, someone would have been sure to apologise to me.

'What the actual hell? We are so fucked.'

'You know, it's only advisory, they can ignore the referendum result.'

'How stupid are these people? Who are they?'

No one knew who those people who voted for Brexit were. They swore all their friends voted to remain. Everyone insisted they didn't know anyone who voted to leave, and if they had to quietly disown their own parents to make that claim, then so be it.

'This is not what I wanted to wake up to on a Friday,' I said to no one in particular but within the earshot of a white woman, possibly in her mid-40s, who I judged could be my way into this group.

'There goes my relaxing weekend,' she said. We talked for less than a minute and a half before the inevitable:

'So, where are you from?'

I was tempted to say originally from Peckham, but that I lived in Hackney now, but I had tried that one before and it only ended with an awkward dance of 'oh, your accent sounds … er, European'.

'I'm from Poland.'

'Oh, where in Poland?'

'Gdynia, it's on the coast.'

'Ah. My plumber is from Poland. I've forgotten the name of his town but it's near Warsaw, I think. Maybe it begins with P. Peyno, perhaps?'

This sounded like nothing. It seemed that the British people continued to be amazed to come across another Polish person when they already knew one. Even though there were so many of us here, it wouldn't be difficult to run into five before breakfast.

'Peenoto?' she continued.

It now became vital we establish her plumber's hometown and I was at a loss. I didn't want her to think I was uninterested and rude, so I offered, 'Pułtusk?' which was the only town starting with P, near Warsaw, that I could think of.

We settled on Pułtusk.

'He's a great plumber, always on time, always knows what's wrong and how to fix it. I call him all the time.'

Just how many plumbing jobs can one person need?

'He's such a lovely man.'

All of this was meant as a personal compliment to me. And how could anyone vote for Brexit if the European Union brought them plumbers who were both punctual and lovely?

'Oh, he actually taught me a couple of Polish words!'

She was excited and stretching her mouth in preparation for the flood of consonants. I was mildly curious – my countrymen seem to teach the Brits the oddest things. Just recently a man bragged to me that he knew how to say 'carrot' and 'hedgehog'.

'*Krprpszyz bfrzyrzgrz,*' she said and looked at me expectantly. I wanted to tell her how much I appreciated the effort but that those weren't words. I looked around, hoping for someone to save me from having to guess what they meant. I thought of Gerald, sitting in a café at this very minute telling some other Polish girl that he knows how to say 'I love you'. I should've taught him to say 'Stay away from me. I will make you love me and then I will abandon you and break your heart,' but that was probably too many consonants.

'*Brzbbrzgyrz? byrzybrzyg? brzbrzbrzy?*' She kept making noises at me and I was so sad that I had no idea what they meant. I felt I was failing my side of this small-talk bargain and wanted to go home to check if Gerald hadn't returned while I was out.

*

'Find yourself a one-night stand,' Laura insisted.

It was premature, he had only been gone for five days, all his things were still there, but we went to a club all the same so that, as she joked, I could get under someone else to get over Gerald. Going clubbing hadn't been part of my lifestyle for a few years now, but apparently it was like riding a bike. A neat triangle of going to the bar, discreetly observing everyone around you under the pretence of dancing, and finally the bathroom round. Laura insisted she was having a wonderful time but if any of us genuinely liked clubbing we would be doing it more often and not just as a go-to solution when one of us was broken-hearted.

Ever since smoking had been banned in clubs it had become obvious how much we all perspire. I was pushing past people, picking up their sweat on the way. There was a good-looking guy on the other side of the room and I wanted to get near him, even though I had no plan for what to do next. I kept an eye on his red shirt and dark hair while I circled closer. It took me two more gin and tonics to accept he had no interest in me. I stared at him, openly, as only Polish people can, but he skilfully avoided acknowledging me.

The alcohol was starting to have its effect on me and I got the urge to be dramatic; jump in a cab and go over Gerald's. All of a sudden I knew I had all the words that would make everything alright again, that would make this whole hellish week disappear. I was determined to act on this impulse right after I used the loo. There is no better place to be drunk than a girls' bathroom in a club. The only place the mythical sisterhood can be observed in its unadulterated form.

Uber wouldn't take me to Gerald's as my cards were still blocked. Everything was beginning to look like a nasty conspiracy set up to bring me down. A black girl in front of me in the queue asked me if I was OK, so I told her everything. She told me I was lucky Uber wouldn't let me make the trip.

'Not only would it cost you a fortune to go to fucking Acton Town from Shoreditch, you would also wake up tomorrow and hate yourself.'

She followed it with a bunch of assurances about how smart and pretty I was and we argued for a while about who was more beautiful, she or I.

'Where are you from anyway? I love your accent.'

'Poland. Gdynia. By the coast. Been here for ten years,' I spat out quickly so that we could go back to talking about how men are trash and how we could always do so much better.

'Oh my god, my sister used to date a Polish guy!'

'Oh really?' I acted surprised to learn that there was a Polish person in this girl's life before me.

'He was so gorgeous. Absolutely beautiful and a nice guy too. His name was Paul. I don't understand why she would ever break up with him. A total idiot. You've gotta introduce me to more Polish guys.'

I knew hardly any Polish men and those I did know could not be described as gorgeous by even the most charitable women. The girl and I were best friends by the time we reached the toilet stalls.

*

I spent the rest of the weekend crying and sleeping and didn't hear from Gerald until Tuesday when he called to say he was cancelling all the accounts in his name and that I should set something up for the internet and electricity if I wanted to continue living in the 21st century. He was also taking his name off the lease, so he advised me to find a flatmate for the guest room.

'You're probably gonna have to try to actually fit your clothes inside the wardrobe, then.'

We used to joke about how I turned the guest room into an open closet but maybe he had resented it the whole time. I buried myself in the heap of unfolded clothes in despair. He was making sure I knew it was final, nothing to hang my denial on.

I toyed with the idea of leaving it all and moving back to Poland. I, too, could move in with my mother. Allowing myself a few minutes of self-pity, maybe half an hour, an hour at most, I thought about how much everyone implied they would be just so much better off without me. If I could kindly remove myself, they would be very obliged. Even my bank would do perfectly fine without my custom. Except, of course, my mother and I keep our conversations to five minutes tops, which is how long we can manage without arguing on average, so that idea was doomed from the beginning.

It wasn't so much deciding to stay put and not let anyone chase me out. More a case of not knowing what else to do and where else to go. I called BT and opened a new account under my name. I was lucky to have a name that wasn't a mouthful, Monika Lis. Lis means fox. Way better than, say, Agnieszka Strzelczak.

BT keeps some of its call centres in the UK and I spoke to a nice man from Dundee who asked me about my mother's maiden name to set up my security question. This was when things normally got trickier

'W-O-J-C-I-E-C-H-O-W-S-K-A'

'Oof, where is that from?'

'It's a Polish name. That's where I'm from.'

'Oh, cool. I used to live with a guy from Poland. Great lad. Actually moved down to London now.'

We had made it to Dundee as well, it turned out.

'Seriously. The best flatmate I've ever had,' he added, just in case I didn't believe him at first.

'And that's done for you. Is there anything else I can help you with today?'

I stopped myself from asking more about his ex-flatmate because it had just occurred to me I could turn it into an art project, a catalogue of random Polish people that friends and strangers tell me about. There would be a plumber from Pułtusk or some other P-town, a girl-from-the-bathroom's sister's gorgeous ex-boyfriend named Paul, some dude from Dundee. I could draw sketches of how I imagined those people. It might work. It could bring me fame.

I developed this project in my head while I took a shower and it was looking better to me by the minute. I must've lost track of time because the water got cold. In fact, the shower had been getting progressively colder for the last week or two. It was asking for a cheesy metaphor about Gerald's heart but I resisted it and called the agency the next day to send someone over to check out the boiler. They arranged for someone to come on Thursday morning and I hoped he would be at least half as impressive as Punctual from Pułtusk.

For once, I was not disappointed. Not only did he arrive five minutes early but he was ridiculously good-looking. Truly romantic-comedy cute. He was polite and took his shoes off, which gave me pause.

'Where are you from?' I asked.

'I'm from Poland,' he said.

'But of course!' I replied, as if it all made sense now. I enjoyed and hated the familiarity that would follow, now that we had established we were both Poles away from home. There was an unwritten rule that all Polish immigrants must be up on each other's business two minutes after the 'hello'.

'You're Polish too, aren't you? I can tell.'

'Ah, that unmistakable Slavic bone structure, eh?' I said in Polish, accepting I'd been made.

'You know, each time someone looks familiar to me – like I know them from somewhere – I know they're Polish ... or Czech,' he admitted after a moment.

'Where in Poland are you from?'

'Piaseczno. I normally say Warsaw, because it's close enough and no one knows where Piaseczno is, but really I'm from Piaseczno.'

'A P-town!' I gasped.

'What?'

'Do you have a private customer round here? White, female, mid-40s?'

'Yeah, I have one like that. She calls me all the time. She wants her radiators bled once a month.'

'No kidding!'

I met Punctual from Pułtusk, who was really from Piaseczno, but every bit as amazing as the woman had claimed. He told me it wasn't the boiler but the thermostat in the shower, something about some spring or screw or some such, I wasn't listening. I was only hoping he wouldn't have the right part and would have to come back. And maybe I could make him stay and bleed the radiators too.

As he was leaving I caught sight of the photo of me and Gerald on the mantelpiece and clumsily moved to flip it down. He misunderstood my intention and said, 'Don't worry. I'm not like those other Polish idiots that would give you grief over that. As a matter of fact, I dated a black girl myself. Actually, she broke up with me a couple of weeks ago.'

'Oh, crap. I'm sorry …'

'Nah, don't worry. She just wasn't that into me. Her sister, though. Her sister seemed a lot more into me, so that was awkward. How long do you think before I can ask her sister out?'

He laughed. I must've looked horrified because he quickly added, 'I'm joking. I wasn't going to ask her sister out. I don't even want to date now. London is great when you're single. Don't you think?'

That hadn't been my experience so far but maybe I lacked perspective.

'Trust me. I moved from Dundee a few months ago and that's no place to be single. It's so much better here. You can always stay anonymous in London and disappear into the sea of people if you want to.'

I snorted.

'So, you want to stay here? With Brexit and all? What are we gonna do about that?'

'We? Keep calm and carry on, I guess,' he replied in English. 'Enjoy your hot showers!'

He winked, he smiled, and he left.

FLÂNEUSE: GUMMED EYES

Iain Sinclair

Mysterious grey forms, like reconnaissance photographs of a bombed city, or ruinously deformed eyeballs held against a sunless sky, appeared on huge hoardings in the development zone around London Bridge station. It was impossible to imagine what product they could be advertising. Except art. The universal fixative for the fallout from a project such as the Shard tower, with its satellite rail and retail parasites.

The vampire-green of traffic lights washed the giant London Bridge hoardings with a gothic varnish, before being blooded again. Several pedestrians, manoeuvring to get the most effective iPhone steals from these enigmatic lunar advertisements, came close to being obliterated by an ill-conceived and unnoticed cycle lane.

I was making my way towards a meeting with the photographer responsible for the hoardings, for those gummy eyeballs, the dead planets. Effie Paleologou was discussing her work in the chapel at Guy's Hospital. The old London teaching hospital was now establishing a Science Gallery where art and science would 'collide': CONNECTING ART, SCIENCE & HEALTH INNOVATIONS IN THE HEART OF THE CITY. A post-truth exaggeration, from the wrong side of the river, well beyond the City walls, plastered across fences.

Whenever I am asked about the *flâneuse*, I think of Effie. She came to London from Athens, Paris and New York, already fired by her reading of Walter Benjamin. She found her project in walking at night around the purlieus of railway stations and points of transit. There was a Sebaldian colour to the enterprise, well ahead of *Austerlitz* – a book that she, in some ways, attempted to illustrate before it existed. Her photographs, usually taken at a time when travellers are most vulnerable, most abandoned to the city, were in translation. They were *of* England, but not English. They were London. Which is very different. London is multi-tongued, urgent. Cruel. London is everywhere, eyes wide open: exploited and exploiting.

Liverpool Street station was the heart of Effie's pictorial essay: fugitive faces framed in window panels on Underground trains and late-night buses. Even those who live here, quite legitimately, look like paperless migrants. The waiting. The stretched hours. The achieved photographic capture is made in competition with a burgeoning net of high-angle surveillance cameras. And then the drifting away into the first places where immigrants would settle: blocks of austere flats viewed from a certain distance, that ring of sodium lights around an artificial football pitch.

Effie was securing her images and carrying them home for meticulous processing into prints that could be exhibited or catalogued. But she avoided direct confrontation. She kept her own identity, as photographer/recorder, out of the story. The anecdotes of misadventure, with discretion, were reserved for her friends. London values, but never rewards, anonymity. Effie explored the existential crisis in what she called 'the secret life of cities after dark'. She honed the neurotic rasp of concentration brought about by circumnavigating districts lit by the flare of imminent threat. She avoided the crowd, the monad, and waited for the sets to empty. Her sensibility was theatrical.

Benjamin, Baudelaire and Henry James were cited. Effie

spoke about the *flâneur* as a person, a man, who discovered the city 'through desultory wandering and a trajectory which catches the transitoriness and ephemerality'. James would be the odd one out in that group, a confirmation of Paleologou's wide and informed reading among the classics, European and American. The meandering Jamesian sentence, with its internal logic and feline thrust, was an established part of the Greek photographer's practice: her nocturnal circuits.

*

Taking her son to school, venturing through Bethnal Green, going about her business, daily journeys, Old Street, Liverpool Street station, Effie walked with purpose. And she noticed how the places where she was forced to wait, put on time, were graced with patterns of expelled chewing gum. *She was no longer a stalker, she was a stopper.* She logged the discriminations of gum with the rigour of a research scientist. She used macro-lenses to inflate the microcosm of splat, stiffened boils ridging the tarmac. Like bits of the inside of a cheek, chewed and expectorated. She bent to the fertile dirt. She was no longer anonymous. She had stopped moving, standing in the shadows, losing herself in the crowd. She was now the spectacle: woman as police officer, council snoop or location hunter. An obstacle. Something to be stepped around. While she stooped to her task. 'The aesthetics of the insignificant,' she called it.

The flat world of our city pavements, disregarded by most pedestrians, is revealed, under the obsessive scrutiny of Paleologou, as significant terrain. A carpet of ill-fitting stone slabs, decorated with fast-food detritus, becomes part of the curvature of the universe. The slightest scars – heel scratches, bicycle tracks, spilled blood, yesterday's vomit, sodden leaves embedded in cracks, ice damage – register a pathology that the qualified witness records and exposes.

One of Effie's defining gifts is the ability to work from wherever life chooses to locate her. Or wherever, on impulse, she chooses to locate her life. In the case of the chewing-gum series – *Microcosms, 2014* – the geographical limits the photographer decided to impose formed an occult triangle, lines of attraction and repulsion, between three stations: Bethnal Green, Old Street, Liverpool Street. Each of these active hubs had a freighted back-story. Bethnal Green: a wartime disaster with panicked crowds crushed on the stairs. Liverpool Street: a railway cathedral supported by carbonised columns like an iron forest, where involuntary exiles like Joseph Merrick, the Elephant Man, returned to London. Or where *Kindertransport* trains delivered so many future orphans. W G Sebald, arriving at Liverpool Street from Norwich, took to these streets in quest of postcards that he could infiltrate into the crafted pages of his documentary fiction. The German poet used photographs to authenticate events that never quite happened. Paleologou speaks about uncovering an 'arbitrary cartography', points of arrival and departure. She is hunting for incidents or materials capable of sustaining her anonymity – and, at the same time, confirming the only qualification that will permit her continued London residence: the accumulation of recorded detail making a new map of an old place.

The prints based on that humblest and most intimate metropolitan pestilence, chewing gum, forge a metaphorical connection, worthy of Bataille, between the bulging pregnancy of the glob on the pavement and the blood-veined eye of the observer. It was a brilliant notion: instead of cataloguing, in the traditional fashion of the dandified *flâneur*, shop windows, hats, shoes, advertisements, Effie kept her steady gaze on the unscrolled *mappa mundi* of the London pavement. A monochrome carpet of transience fouled by fossils of gum in patterns like an early star map. As above, so below. There was magic to this exercise. Repetition was part of its charm. From the black spots – in which so much could be read – we can imply a stupendous range of human intercourse.

There is a sexual tenderness in Effie's album of oral rejects. Dry mouths have been salved by the sugary-sweet coating around a capsule of rubber. The stain on the pavement is the DNA of a passing stranger who is now brought inside, into the domestic cell of the studio, by the intimate processes of the darkroom. Paleologou compares gum-chewing to eating and kissing. But here is an oral transaction with no nutritional value. Gum is anti--food. It mimics foreplay – nibble, suck, bite – but it must not be swallowed. To swallow would be to choke. Gum is prophylactic, a shield against human breath, taste, life. Gum is a wartime US import, a gift of cultural imperialism, thrown from the invader's tank to the outstretched hands of children. Expanding pink balloons, puffed from lipsticked Lolita mouths, are unscripted speech bubbles from the Trumpist comic of the world.

What is beautiful is the poetry of reduction that Paleologou imposes on her quest. From her archaeological record of the density of gum sightings, the photographer conjures a narrative of spectral crowds 'forming random constellations as if in a parallel universe'. But the suspect act of photography is never enough. She kneels in the dirt, like a supplicant, a local historian making brass rubbings, to put paper over the sticky traces, to rub them with a pencil. This is an affectionate engagement with 'viral colonies of debris'. It makes no difference if we are seeing these pinpricks as glimmers of million-year-old light from deep space, printed from a telescope, or a pulsing cancer cell enlarged on a slide under a microscope. The fissures are geological.

Effie's images are contemporary in their desperation to reanimate the city by recording its most disposable but enduring detritus. And pre-modern, in the medieval philosophy of humours, in metamorphosis and alchemy. The prints defy category and date of origin. They are Victorian. They hint at the birth of photography, the death of fundamentalist Christianity, the beginnings of psy-choanalysis.

It is not part of the official trajectory of the project, but Effie's image trail leads straight to the gravestone of William Blake in Bunhill Fields. Visitors, sitting on a bench under a drooping fig tree, contemplate the enormity of the poet's residual presence in London. And they spit out gum. The coins, placed every day in tribute on the lip of the gravestone, leave rusty traces. The stone is smoothed by exposure to sunlight and acid rain. Paleologou sees her retrievals as part of an established tradition. A tradition of ac-cidental collaboration between attentive artist and the legions of ordinary citizens going about the business of survival. 'I question not my Corporeal or Vegetative Eye,' said Blake, 'any more than I would Question a Window concerning Sight. I look thro' it and not with it.'

After the event in the chapel, Effie walked me to the colon-nade of the hospital, where a selection of her prints were displayed: moons, deserts, laboratory specimens. All derived from chewing gum. The photographer was eager to present her work as part of a triangulation with the oval tablet recording that short spell, 1941-42, when Ludwig Wittgenstein 'worked incognito at Guy's Hos-pital Pharmacy as Drugs Porter and Ointment Maker', and the unfortunate bronze effigy of John Keats, failed medical student, in one of the stone igloos rescued from old London Bridge.

Before catching a 149 bus at London Bridge station, I mar-velled again at the way gum had been made into art, into adver-tisement, and how the subtlety of Effie's expanded images was barely noticed in the noise of the place. The night-smudged tower of the Shard broadcast its acoustic pulse into the fretful station concourse, where late travellers were talking to themselves, shout-ing at their hands.

FLÂNEUSE: LONDONERS TALK

Michèle Roberts

I'VE ALWAYS ENJOYED wandering around London on my own, by day and by night, exploring, getting lost, finding new routes, sidestreets I don't know. Sometimes, if I pause, people approach me, wanting a brief chat. Sometimes I eavesdrop on their conversations. Back at home I often write down what people have said. Mostly it's men who want to talk to me, hence the paucity of women's voices in this piece. It records stories found between the City of London and the East End over the last ten years. (Michèle Roberts)

I'm a bit up the arse: I've lost my fiancée and I've lost my dog. The fiancée left me and the dog died. To tell you the truth I'm far more cut up about the dog. My world's been turned upside down. I've got a photo of him here, look. I bought him a bed costing £200, a sort of mattress with a buckskin trim. And then I'm a bit up the arse as well because I don't make enough money. This morning I read my stars in the *Sun*. They suggested my financial affairs would be looking up quite soon, so I put £50 on a horse to win. I've just called my mate and the horse lost. That's a bit much. £50 is a lot of money. I can't really afford it. *(Man in overalls, in café, Roman Road)*

She ought to go. Really she ought to go. Well, at least you saw her. For your sake in the future. She just ought to go now. You ought to go. Get onto the motorway. If there's ever a need I would come. So she'd have been proud of me if only she'd been conscious. I know Dad appreciates it. She knew I'd do anything for her. I must go, I must go. We kept thinking, so maybe she'll go now. She's so peaceful, she ought to go. She just ought to fall asleep and not wake up. I know, I know: she must be so strong. I hope they don't do it: all the drips, the tubes to feed her. Just not worth it, at her age, to put her through it, is it. She's over 90. She ought to go. I must go. I must go. *(Woman in pale blue suit, on mobile phone, Approach Road)*

My great-grandmother was called Black Bess because she had the gift of second sight. She passed on tips to my grandmother and she passed them on to me. A robin in the house spells death. It's bad luck to have a hole in the fire. Never put a pair of new shoes on the table. My mother still lives in the old lodge on the edge of the woods, opposite the house in which my great-grandmother lived. Recently she gave me two porcelain swans, which belonged to Black Bess. *(Taxi-driver in blue parka, in layby, Liverpool Street)*

Some of my family, they grew up without me noticing. I was always working. They liked it all right, the money for holidays. One of my daughters didn't want to know me. Ten years on I met this girl and said to her: there's something familiar about you. She said: well, I'm your daughter. To tell you the truth I've been married three times and with a bit of practice in between you've got that helping hand to recognise true love when it comes along. *(Man in blue jeans, in café, Mile End Road)*

I dream of studying astronomy. Perhaps one day in the Open University. My school teacher put me down when I asked a question about atoms, and put me off science. I worked as a guitar teacher for ten years before Maggie Thatcher put an end to all that. I reckon I don't believe in myself enough, having left school at

14 with no qualifications. *(Man in grey tracksuit, in café, Bethnal Green Road)*

Lap-dancing girls. Essex girls. Tarts I'd have to call them. Prostitutes. Two of them got in the cab one night, Liverpool Street, wanting to get home, saying: how much? Fifty quid I told them. Turned out they only had a tenner each. They said to me: come in and we'll lap-dance for you, make up the difference. *(Man in grey fleece, in pub on the Roman Road)*

Virgins, virgins. Buy my virgins. You want one? They are from Fatima, the very famous shrine. You are my first customer today. You will bring me luck. *(Man in pale blue fleece, Brick Lane)*

So you like my chef's trousers, do you? Good. Well, I wouldn't wear a skirt, would I? I am a Master Cellarer. No, a Lady Master Cellarer I should say. I'm getting squiffy with the staff. *(Landlady in pub, Limehouse)*

I used to be a butcher. But I got hit by the recession so I became a cabbie instead. My father abandoned us children when my mother died and got married again, left us boys to fend for ourselves. So I grew up selfish, not wanting to be, but knowing nothing else. I left my own three boys when my butcher business failed and I took to gambling and my marriage broke up. I did the gambling mainly for company because I was lonely. Now I've got a new girlfriend and a new little cub, and I ring my boys every day, and try to see them regularly. I tried to talk to my father but my father won't talk. He's very hard. *(Man in blue jeans, in newsagent's shop, near Cheapside)*

Excuse me, miss, are you praying today? Are you praying as you walk along? Are you praying to Jesus our Saviour today? *(Man in black suit, Moorgate)*

What can I do for you, daughter? In the freezer there are three choices for dinner tonight. Tell your father to defrost a pizza. There must be a pizza in there. If he can't cope with that he deserves to be fired as a father. *(Woman in grey suit, on mobile phone, Liverpool Street station)*

I grew up in Bethnal Green, in Finnis Street, near the old fire station. We were on the third floor, with no bathroom and a lav out on the balcony. So when the Council rehoused us in a tower block we were pleased. Oh if only we'd stayed. That house must be worth a million by now. Should have sold it, made my fortune. Bethnal Green was a bombsite. We played on the half-sunk ships in St Katherine's Dock. *(Man in dark puffa jacket, in betting-shop, Roman Road)*

I always like having a peep through that archway there. Once it was a café. It used to be good for herrings, whelks and winkles. I used to go there of a Saturday. And he was courting that girl for nine years, then they got married, then they was divorced in a year. But they're still together. They started courting again. That furniture shop over there, he bought a suite there, it fell apart in three weeks. Him and his mates they took it back but they wouldn't give him his money back. So they dumped it. Left it there in the street. *(Two women in puffa jackets, bus stop, Bethnal Green Road)*

Those Amish girls he killed, he did it out of revenge. For something that happened to him when he was young. He did it for revenge. They say he had a huge bucket of KY jelly with him, he was going to abuse them before he killed them. Oh yes. They say he only shot them so soon because the police arrived. Apparently the Amish have forgiven him. They've asked his family to the funerals. So there must be something in that God stuff mustn't there. But perhaps not. Me, I'm so cynical. They're just doing it for publicity for the Amish cause. *(Man in olive denim jacket and blue jeans, antique shop, Spitalfields)*

That recent rape case. Ninety-nine per cent of men wouldn't dream of having sex with a drunken woman. You want her to respond, see? You must be anti-men if you think otherwise. *(Man in pinstriped suit, on pavement outside bar off Cheapside)*

If you say hello to people on the towpath they return the hello, much more than people do on a path in the park. Oh, look at her taking the skipper his lunch. Oh, that looks nice that plate of food does. Oh, the skipper's not impressed. He's still mending his prop. He has a load of weed entangled I suspect. Last week I saw some men towing a boat away from where it was moored by the gasworks, just below Sturt's Lock, a seagoing boat, quite rounded, uninsured, hadn't had its safety test, hadn't paid mooring fees, I said oh what a shame to tow it away and the man said: no, it's as rotten as a pear. *(Man in black beret and red windcheater, on canal-side towpath)*

Any tickets left for *Romeo and Juliet*, Saturday night? *(Man in brown monk's habit, red neckerchief and sandals, at theatre kiosk, Liverpool Street)*

Come along, mother, come along. Home is where the heart is. Tra la la! Tra la la! Mind how you go now. Jerusalem the golden! With milk and honey blessed! *(Man in tweed suit and red waistcoat to woman pushing zimmer frame, walkway down to Millennium Bridge)*

LOVERS, LIARS, CONJURERS AND THIEVES (AN ODE TO SOUTHWARK)

Inua Ellams

After five hours tied to break-beats so thick
you could bitch-slap a rapper with, rave-drunk
on bass, funk and melody, I slouch sweat-heavily
by Waterloo Bridge, ready myself to ride home.

Now, from the moment I cross over the bridge
and leave the Southbank's lights sparkling,
the River Thames, with its long lapping
happenings, hi-fives the riverside walls for me.
The road is free (usual for this hour), its silence
stars a shiver that shudders the road sign,
its flow winds by a bin bag, burst like ripe fruit,
two foxes make harvest of its juice. If you look
past their fur you'll hear the soft purr
you might've once poured into your lover's ear,
when caution thrown clear, and under shadow-
cover, were smothered in an alley with his lips.
But lovers tiff, one fox's paw fists
and their battle cries riff with the day's remnants
of torn bags, beer cans, cigarettes and spliffs.

Elephant & Castle is a coral reef, resplendent,
rippling with daredevil kids too schooled
in cool to check the pickpocket whose wrist-flick
shimmers like a blade. A shoal of girls clothed
in tinsel dresses burp and bubble with ale,
their cheap garments ripple like fish scales,
dazzling migrants sailed from a nightly slave
of mop buckets, bathrooms, broom sticks
and piss. Their tired limbs just about miss
drunk cyclists' swim cross traffic, who brake
too late, front wheels smash, chains erupt,
pedals clash, perhaps now they'll admit,
(like the rest of us) to going nowhere fast.

Camberwell is cliché hell. The bars spill out
a steady swell of weed smoke, desperate men
and willing women whose red-tipped fingers,
the same red you have cried into cold mirrors
against loneliness – that darker shade of blush,
stroke their bare arms with 'yes, my place
is yours tonight'. This same crimson rims
the eyes of dry-lipped addicts too fixed
on last fix to catch the faint wisp of endless
hope haunting a lone streetlamp, whose glow
halos the crowns of boys, heads bowed low,
shoulders swaying to and fro, hands folded
to form two fingers barrelled before a cocked
thumb, this cypher's silent guns punch the air,
salute the beat-boxer's steady glare, his pressed
breath: fresh carpet, over which the MC spits
in time, conjures their lives in rhyme.

Rising; the last bastion of breath – Peckham
– rests in south's fortress. By the library, two
unmarked vans park for stop & searches.
For all their stealth, rubber-sole boots, gloves,
high powered torches; all the hours spent bent
on code names, seeking swift results to deep
problems, leads here where metal sticks choke
black throats – for all their stealth and state-
given right, they can't steal the fight from
Peckham's young, whose backs still broad,
heads so rise, skin soak shine of the new blue
moon whose dominance is fractured by
the scattered light of a firework,
out of place, but welcomed.

Close by, a barman toasts his stolen gin,
a night baby gurgles in her plastic cot,
a student pauses before a full-stop,
and the culprit strikes again:
a swift-struck matchstick blooms, the fire
works, blossoming upwards, explodes outwards,
a bouquet of sparkle fire, petalling out against
a sky, so bright it beats the sun back. Two hours
pass before it tries to climb the horizon again,
finds me hunched over my laptop screen, trying
to let my fingers know what my heart means
by this journey mashed of instances where
bin bags splash, cyclists crash, a rapper
freestyles the scene?

Well, this is how it's always been, lovers, liars,
conjurers and thieves; the world is a break-beat
backed by these, over which the poets sing.

MODEL BOATING IN VICTORIA PARK

Travis Elborough

NORMAN LARA IS one of the biggest names in a sport that is all about the little things. For he is a world champion and record-breaking model steam boat racer. Born and bred in Bow, his natural habitat and the scene of many of his greatest triumphs is the model boating lake in Tower Hamlets' Victoria Park where he is often to be found on regatta Sundays directing events from the edge of the lake.

Lara is chair of the Victoria Park Model Steam Boat Club, a post once held by his late father. His mother was also a stalwart member of a club that can trace its roots back to the turn of the last century, when nearly half the world's maritime vessels were registered in London, shipbuilding remained (just about) active on the Thames, and over 20,000 men were employed by the capital's docks.

It began life as the Alexandra Yacht Club – its name a tribute to the soon-to-be queen consort, Princess Alexandra. But with a group of model boat enthusiasts meeting regularly at the lake, yachts graciously gave way to more bantam craft and the Victoria Park Model Steam Boat Club was officially formed in 1904.

Not long after that, its coffers were bolstered by a pound donation from Horatio Bottomley, the Liberal MP for Hackney

South.[1] And within six years of the club's founding, Victoria Park also received the gift of a miniature garden from the Mayor of Tokyo. Created by the Yokohama Nursery Company and first displayed at the Japanese-British exhibition at Shepherd's Bush, it measured nine by four feet and was mounted on a trolley that could be wheeled outside for people to admire on fine days. Both the garden, which contained some tiny trees that were over a hundred years old, and the model boat club, two of Victoria Park's smallest Edwardian additions, proved among its most sizeable attractions.

Home in the park for the Model Steam Boat Club was (and remains) a lake previously used for public bathing. This was laid out despite initial objections by the park's designer James Pennethorne, who believed bathing would lower the tone and 'quite destroy the value of the Park as a place of residence'. But plenty of poorer local residents, especially men from the nearby dye and

---

[1] A local boy made good, largely by doing bad things, Horatio Bottomley was born in Bethnal Green and spent most of his childhood in an orphanage. After serving an apprenticeship as an office boy in a legal shorthand firm, he ventured into finance and publishing. He was a founder of the *Financial Times* and also the owner for a time of the *Sun*, then an evening newspaper. A lover of the high life, he miraculously evaded a conviction for falsely promoting inflated Australian gold mining company shares in his papers, but was bankrupted by debt and forced to stand down as an MP. Blessed with an unwavering faith in his own abilities, he bounced back at the outbreak of the First World War by launching *John Bull*, a virulently anti-German but hugely popular patriotic newspaper. Speaking at dozens of recruiting rallies, for which he pocketed huge fees while encouraging hundreds, possibly thousands, to step towards their deaths in the trenches, he was described by the *Daily Mirror* as 'London's answer to the Zeps' – a phrase that was unfortunately possibly truer than anyone could perhaps have realised when it came to the final body count. He was re-elected to Hackney South as an independent after the war, but was eventually sentenced to seven years' hard labour for fraud, having, among several other misdemeanours, promoted a bogus Victory Bonds banking scheme. He emerged from Wormwood Scrubs to tread the boards, telling his colourful life story in whatever tawdry flea pit or gin palace would pay him, before dying in penury in 1933.

tanning works, who had recourse to little other than the working canal to spruce themselves up on the way to and from the factory, certainly appreciated it nonetheless. And in 1898, when recalling his years as the park supervisor for Municipal Board of Works, LT Colonel J J Sexby claimed that he'd once seen as many as 2,500 men and young boys taking a pre-work dip there on one early summer morning alone. Little wonder then that William Morris, after visiting Victoria Park to speak at a political rally on 8 August 1886, reported that while the park was 'rather a pretty place with water', the water itself was 'dirty'.

In Victoria Park, labour and boating have long gone hand in hand, with the first vessel ever to sail on its lakes belonging to the original park superintendent, Samuel Curtis, who requested a rowing boat so he could trim the foliage around the island for the pagoda. The model boaters' first clubhouse was an old gardening hut.

Lacking the means to buy ready-made engines by firms such as Basset-Lowke, from West End department stores such as Gamages, most model steam boats raced at Victoria Park were custom-built from scratch. Their creators, more often than not, were engineers by profession. Local East Enders for whom tinkering about on a lathe in leisure hours was second nature, as manufacturing itself then was to the area. Men, and it was mostly men, who prided themselves on their mechanical ingenuity, preferring a hobby that combined getting their fingers oily and wading about in water, and for whom the phrase busman's holiday could have perhaps been coined.

Early club photos in bleached-out sepia depict Lowry-esque figures all in hats (flat caps, trilbies and bowlers), and, regardless of the weather, heavy woollen three-piece suits and shirts and ties, standing beside Lilliputian steamers perched on hefty, hand-carved-looking wooden frames. Arthur Evans. Bill Morse. Stan Clifford. Ted and Daisy Vanner: sturdy-sounding names that can be imagined appearing above ironmongers' shops or on musical hall bills, live on. Uttered reverentially by older boaters who recall them as fondly as hazy childhood summers. But also kept alive by the presence within the club of some of their boats: passed down through the generations, many are still running, with the oldest working steamer, All Alone, dating from 1924. A less arcane model, Potential Threat, owes its name to a lyric from an Abba song, and its compellingly sinister, sort of Dark Knight-ish, all-black livery to the colour-blindness of its owner, the modern club's secretary Keith Reynolds.

Whereas Victoria Park was once one of a network of model boat clubs across London, most have gone. East End rivals at Forest Gate and Hollow Ponds, Walthamstow, are no more and competitions are as likely to take them to St Albans, Welwyn Garden City, Birmingham or Norwich, or even Paris, as Blackheath – one of the other remaining clubs in the capital. Beyond these shores, the hobby especially thrives in Bulgaria, thanks to an array of first-rate model boating facilities bequeathed to it under the Soviet Union's command economy, which established specialist centres of excellence for any, each and every kind of competitive game or sport.

But while members at Victoria Park were once drawn from the surrounding area, often inducted into the club by their parents or joining as teenagers, having caught the bug after admiring the action on the lake, a significant proportion are now based outside London entirely. Many of the park's most dedicated weekend boaters today travel in from places as diverse and far-flung as Basildon in Essex and Littlehampton on the Sussex coast, their loyalty to the club evidently undiminished by distance.

While it does have younger members, some of them women too, it is probably fair to say that not everyone in the club is quite in the first flush of youth. A particular concern expressed by a couple of grizzled enthusiasts is the dearth of provision for engineering in schools. Youngsters, they argue, rarely come face to face with a drill bit, and probably know more about bandwidths than bandsaws. Model boats might be dinky, but they are functional machines, ones whose engines must be cared for to be kept going. To do that, at least a basic grasp of mechanics is required. That grasp, or so they maintain, is not so often gifted to those educated in an era where apps feature more prominently in the national curriculum than arc welding.

Here already for 111 years, the Victoria Park Model Steam Boat Club is not going anywhere any time soon though, and could easily last for another century. Its clubhouse by the lake, heavily shuttered to prevent break-ins, is a listed building. Its members (and the park itself) are committed to its continuing success, and Lara currently holds the world speed record for hydroplane racing.

This especially whizzy form of motor model boating involves marine craft that look like a cross between a pond-skater and a Scalextric slot car. Hydroplanes are tethered to a line fixed at the centre of the pond. Once set going on the water, they spin rapidly round and round. Frothing up the lake, they emit a high-pitched waspy buzz until finally, out of fuel, they fizzle out like spent rockets. In the hands of Lara, such boats have now exceeded speeds of 140 mph.

Ruddy-faced and usually dressed in tracksuit and Adidas wind cheater, the universal mufti of the touchline, Lara has the style and demeanour of a Conference League football manager whose team are on the cusp of promotion. Exuding paternalistic bonhomie, he smiles at boaters and spectators alike, gently ribs wader-clad members waist-deep in the water, and dishes out sage advice to fellow hydroplaners when their boats stubbornly fail to jerk into life, despite concerted yanks on starting cords.

The other thing quickly noticed about Lara is that his mobile goes off often. And when it does, it plays the opening bars to 'Stairway to Heaven'. The phone renders the Led Zeppelin rock epic as rinky-dink as an ice cream van chime. But in terms of scale, a pocket-sized Jimmy Page could hardly be more apt as a ringtone for a record-breaking model boater going about his hobby at a pond in Victoria Park.

DOWN CEMETERY ROW

David McKie

'TIME, LIKE AN ever-rolling stream,' wrote the celebrated hymn-odist Isaac Watts. 'Bears all its sons away; /They fly, forgotten, as a dream /Dies at the opening day.' True of most of us, maybe – daughters as well as sons – yet not entirely true of Isaac himself. His hymns, especially this one, are still lustily belted out in Christian places of worship. And here even now is the great man himself, nine foot high and commanding all he surveys, at the heart of Abney Park Cemetery in north London.

He isn't buried here. He died in 1748, almost a century before the fine estate where he had lived for many years as the guest of Lady Abney was transformed into a parkland cemetery – one of a chain of new creations inspired by a general revulsion at the way so many Londoners had been disposed of before.

Coffins, *The Times* reported in 1843, were hardly in the ground before they were disinterred and broken up to fuel the stove in the workmen's hut. New graves were dug by cutting down recent burials, severing arms, legs and heads in the process. A gravedigger told the paper he had been 'up to my knees in human flesh by jumping on the bodies, so as to cram them in the least possible space at the bottom of the graves, into which fresh bodies were afterwards placed'. Not fresh for long, however: quite apart from the moral outrage at the dead being treated this way there were fears for the health of the public; all the more so, no doubt, when passers-by, and sometimes worshippers, had to hold their noses to keep out the stench emanating from a nearby churchyard, or when a grave at St Mark's shattered the peace of fashionable North Audley Street by exploding.

Nineteenth-century London, with its unflagging zest for improvement, was not going to stomach that. Legislation was progressively introduced to forbid urban burials (as Paris had done years before), and seven modern cemeteries were created, mostly in unblemished countryside. In order of their appearance, these were Kensal Green in 1832, West Norwood in 1836, Highgate in 1839, Abney Park, Brompton and Nunhead in 1840, and Tower Hamlets in 1841. Today they are frequently if somewhat incongruously classed together as the capital's 'magnificent seven'.

At the head of the magnificence league came Highgate, still the most famous and most visited of them all, though that isn't exclusively for the original cemetery west of Swain's Lane. Perhaps the most celebrated incumbent now is Karl Marx, buried in 1893 in the overspill cemetery east of the lane – at first, in an insignificant plot, but promoted in 1954 to somewhere grander, with the grave now crowned by a ferocious head of the prophet created by a Marxist admirer. In 2017 a very different cult figure was installed in the western cemetery: George Michael. Unlike Marx's fans, Michael's cannot go there to pay homage: his grave is excluded from the conducted tours that are mandatory at Highgate West, for fear that unfettered access might create an N6 equivalent of Elvis Presley's Graceland.

In most respects, however, Highgate is exuberantly and shamelessly over the top. Above all, perhaps in its Egyptian Avenue, entered between two mighty ominous portals – a dark and rather creepy place, even after its original roof was removed – and the nearby catacombs, with family names, and often past addresses, proudly displayed at the doors. These catacombs survive in several early cemeteries. Here the dead are laid out on a kind of funereal equivalent of trays. They were often created under the cemetery chapel, with the dead winched down to their new locations, though that isn't the case at Highgate, where you walk in at ground level. Yet even this is topped by the mausoleum built by the German-born financier and later proprietor of the *Observer*, Julius Beer; initially to commemorate his daughter Ada, who died at eight, but no doubt coloured by the sure and certain knowledge it would come to commemorate Julius too.

Installed at the highest point of the cemetery, it cost him £5,000, the equivalent, as the tour guides will tell you, of some £3million now. It was modelled on the Mausoleum of Halicarnassus, one of the Seven Wonders of the Ancient World. Though you cannot go in, you're permitted to peer through a window at the even more lavish interior, which is also the subject of a virtual tour on the internet.

*

One gets the sense in such places of a kind of posthumous competition: my tomb is bigger and better than most – it's equipped with more angels or crosses or urns than yours. Beer at Highgate is taking out an insurance against oblivion. 'The glories of our blood and state,' wrote the 17th century dramatist James Shirley in a poem he called 'Death the Leveller', 'are shadows, not substantial things; There is no armour against Fate; Death lays his icy hand on kings: Sceptre and crown Must tumble down, And in the dust be equal made With the poor crooked scythe and spade.' People like Beer were not having that. Their achievements, their unquestioned eminence, were not to be swept away by the mere fact of death.

That is also true of Kensal Green and West Norwood, but the feeling here is notably less vainglorious. Certainly the architects and the monumental masons whose establishments clustered at the gates of the cemetery, as some still do, have had a fine chance to express themselves: so many angels – demure angels, downcast angels, defiant angels, militant angels with imperious arms upraised (avenging angels perhaps), and angels, at Abney especially, whose arms, uplifted or otherwise, have gone missing. And everywhere, so many crosses, conventional, Celtic and otherwise; so many urns and pillars and obelisks and minor towers.

More ambitious monuments, too, some evoking the role the deceased played in life. At Highgate West, a lion sleeps on top of the tomb of Thomas Wombwell, a menagerist (exhibitor of animals); there's another on the tomb of his fellow menagerist Frank Bostock, at Abney Park. Elsewhere military men, from generals to private soldiers, are sometimes remembered with helmets and rifles and similar tools of their trade. One of the most entertaining monuments at West Norwood, that of a notable banker called James William Gilbart, incorporates an image of a squirrel storing nuts for a rainy day. Streatham Park, a far less ostentatious place than these, housed the grave of a man of whom it was said, 'he died as he lived, a cyclist', complete with images both of the man and his bike.

Yet in these other graveyards, there isn't the sense, as there is at Highgate, of a community sealed off from the busy world. Bakerloo trains rattle by to the north of Kensal Green cemetery, while those of the old Great Western Railway (Brunel's railway: he is buried here) thunder past to the south. Flats and what look like old factories look down on the graves; there are gasholders on the boundary – all giving the sense that the dead of Kensal Green and to a lesser extent of West Norwood are still in the midst of life. It helps too that here you are permitted to browse rather than being directed to what has been selected for you, as in Highgate West (only by failing to pay attention to what we were being told did I manage to spot Beryl Bainbridge).

You're also less likely on a conducted tour to come upon the kind of family story you find in so many cemeteries, including Highgate East, where I chanced on the family grave of the Motes, Joseph and Eliza. They lost Joseph James at two weeks (he is buried at Kensal Green), Rhoda Mary at seven ('a child of faith and prayer'), Alice Elizabeth at five; Rowland Edward at one year, eight months, a second Rowland Edward ('he loved Jesus') at six. Eliza died at 52; Joseph's second wife, Hannah, died some 20 years later; Joseph himself lasted till he was 88.

Kensal Green owed its early success to royalty. The Duke of Sussex turned down his chance to be buried at Windsor; Dickens commended him for his acknowledgment of 'the equality of death', but the Duke's main concerns seem more to have been to avoid the chaotic circumstance of the funeral at Windsor of his brother King William IV, and his determination that a favourite mistress should one day be buried beside him. He was royalty, even so. Well-to-do Victorian Londoners making their wills clamoured to join him.

It was customary in these cemeteries to keep dutiful Anglicans apart from the rest. Burial places were segregated; sometimes a deterrent ditch was dug between them. There were also separate cemeteries across London for Roman Catholic dead (one adjoins Kensal Green) and for Jewish dead, though some Jewish-born families – like the Beers – were destined for Highgate. There is one mausoleum at Highgate West which straddles the great divide, since some of the Hawes family were Methodists but the rest were Anglican converts. Anglicans would be given one chapel, dissenters another. Near the main gate at Kensal Green you will find the well-restored ruins of the old Dissenters' Chapel, which include a panel commemorating those whose graves were destroyed by enemy action.

Enemy action was far from alone in destroying cemeteries. Neglect was a much more prevalent cause. Families who had once tended graves moved out, or lost interest. Impertinent weed and rampant unsupervised foliage spread, until some graves were no longer accessible. Though some, especially Abney Park, had always been meant to mix man's work with nature's, resources no longer ran to controlling the balance. Other menaces, though, were always apparent. Vandals loved to deface memorials and clip the limbs off angels. Given the chance, some still do. But at least we are nowadays spared the robbers and body-snatchers who raided graves for the treasures that might be buried with the deceased, or made off with the corpse to sell for dissection by medical schools.

In time, the private companies who had founded these cemeteries foundered. In the late 20th century, some sites had become unmanageable, deteriorating into metropolitan wilderness. Essential buildings too fell derelict, ceased to function. One of the saddest sights is at Abney Park where the chapel behind Watts's back was long ago abandoned – though since I first went there, what's left has been tidied up: trees no longer sprout through the roof. This is now an orderly ruin. Once carefully tended mausolea in some cemeteries are now in effect abandoned. The names of those installed there are still legible over the doors but the doors themselves are bricked or concreted up.

Two groups came to the rescue of these places as they declined: local councils, and volunteers who declared themselves the Friends of the cemetery and set about living up to that claim. Such interventions were not always easy. At West Norwood, Lambeth Council, having engineered a compulsory purchase, sought to make the cemetery a place for the present rather than for the past. In the hope of creating the kind of park they wanted, they tore down gravestones and monuments – more than ten thousand, the Friends of the cemetery say – and sold old graves which were not their property to those who sought new ones. In 1994 that process was stopped by the Archdeacon of Lambeth, allied with the Friends, and the council was ordered to restore some of what it had extirpated; although most of what had been lost could not by then be restored.

There is still, even so, a sense of continuity here, with favourite graves and memorials visited and admired as they have always been. Some of the most conspicuous commemorate people less remembered now than others around them. At Kensal Green the grave of the Duke of Cambridge, grandson of George III, famously incompetent commander-in-chief of the army and comprehensive reactionary, is overshadowed by the mausoleum of a lesser general next to it. At West Norwood the simple tomb of Hiram Maxim, inventor of the Maxim gun, a device which must have sped many men to their graves, is heavily outscored by a neighbour whose name is no longer legible.

The literature of the cemeteries makes much of the great men and women who have honoured them by their presence – West Norwood seems especially proud of having signed Mrs Beeton – though it's easy to be misled when you look at the simple guides that cemeteries give away free. Highgate East has many occupants, apart from Marx, who might be the subject of pilgrimage – including George Eliot, buried both under her pen name and the married name in which she died, Mary Ann Cross. But its Dean Swift is a City man, not a writer, and its Elgar is not Sir Edward, the composer. At Kensal Green there are monuments celebrating reformers, one to Robert Owen and the second to a host of others, created by Joseph W Corfield, with further names attached by Emma Corfield – perhaps his daughter? But few of his heroes are buried here, and neither is he: he is at Abney Park.

Lambeth's ambitions to empark West Norwood were echoed elsewhere. Tower Hamlets today – taken over by the Greater London Council and then by Tower Hamlets – is much more of a park than a cemetery. Graves survive on a take it or leave it basis. For the joggers and strollers who frequent its wooded paths and those who come to sit and read, or just contemplate in its gentle meadows, they are incidental at best. Notices posted round the park – except for one recording that a particular space was once a turning circle for horse-drawn hearses – are mainly to do with the flowers and the trees. Not many celebrities finished their days here. Fork right at the tomb of Ebenezer Caleb Shepherd, close to the entrance, and you may come across a small congregation of better-off people, several with names that suggest successful immigration breeding later prosperity nearby in the City: Bockelmann, Bullwinkel, Kremer, Schwenk.

That's in line with what is evident across London cemeteries: they represent a truly cosmopolitan city. Here and there you may find what amount almost to separate cemeteries, such as the Greek necropolis within Norwood, which looms up like a sudden eruption of Athens in London SE27. Sometimes such incomers cluster together in discreet little patches: Italians, Africans, West Indians, and the rest. There are also memorials to the Commonwealth dead of two wars. And at Abney, one to more than 90 people who died when a German bomb fell on Coronation Avenue N16 in 1940. Names like Cooperstein, Danzinger, Krakowski, suggesting Jewish refugees from Nazi Germany, are intermixed with Ballards and Beams and Bulls and, inevitably, Smiths. In all these cemeteries, quite modest memorials greatly outnumber the showy ones.

It's necessary, too, to remember, as one browses them, that much of London has always died uncommemorated. Most could never have paid the swanky prices that architects and masons charged. In 1850, 80 per cent of burials were in paupers' graves. Nor are the famous sites representative. The classic guide to these places, *London Cemeteries: an Illustrated Guide and Gazetteer* by Hugh Meller and Brian Parsons, lists 126 cemeteries in today's capital city, and even they appear to have missed a few. Many of these are modest, even minute – and they are the likeliest destinations for Londoners today, whether for burial or, increasingly, cremation.

From the railway that runs south-west out of Waterloo, just before you reach Earlsfield station, you may get a swift glimpse

of Wandsworth cemetery, locally known more often as Earlsfield. When councils in older parts of London found themselves
banned from burying their townspeople on their own territory,
they bought sites elsewhere where no such restrictions applied,
which is why St Pancras Cemetery is in Finchley and the City of
London cemetery is at Manor Park, E12. The boroughs that made
up what is now Wandsworth were a popular choice, so that both
Lambeth and Streatham cemeteries were established in what was
then Tooting.

Wandsworth/Earlsfield began as 12 acres in 1878; it now covers 34. This is very much a 20th-21st century place: all carefully
cultured and orderly, the very reverse of the wider stretches of
places like Kensal Green. There is nothing here of what Highgate
calls the 'romantic decay' that is so prolific in the 'magnificent sev-
en'. But given the fate and state of the older cemeteries, it's easy to
see what's at work here. Upkeep comes first. To let such places run
wild would be asking for trouble.

Yet well-ordered Earlsfield too has invited controversy. On
the western side of the cemetery, below the incessant trains bus-
ily heading south-westwards, there's a mound above the general
level with nominal railings round it, full of the shiny black stones
which are now the popular choice. This is where in the 1980s the
council turfed over existing graves to install new ones above them.
Higher up the hill towards the cemetery's grim neighbour, Wandsworth Prison, the stones are uniformly grey and you begin to
encounter the crosses and angels – one of whom has been there
long enough to have lost her left hand – so familiar from previous
peregrinations.

There's another powerful distinction too, to be noted here, between how we died then and how we die now. Most people today
are remembered for who they were, not what they achieved; for
their private lives, not for public ones.

There have always been standard expressions of loss and grief, but they seem more numerous here. 'If tears could build a stairway, And memories a lane, We would walk right up to Heaven And bring you back again': author unknown, but a verse long familiar in death notices in local newspapers.

Still, as in more devout Victorian London, there's the constant assertion of what the funeral service calls the sure and certain hope of resurrection. Long-married couples are 'together again'; 'reunited'. Innumerable people have 'fallen asleep', even been 'taken by angels'. Just occasionally there's an acceptance that the process of death is not always so gentle and peaceful. A wife at Tower Hamlets 'fell asleep with much suffering'. At Earlsfield, it's recorded of a husband who died at 47, 'He suffered much, But murmured not/ We watched him day by day/ With aching hearts/ Grow less and less/ Until he passed away.' Reality creeping in.

So, 300 years on from Watts's hymn, the great majority of Earlsfield's incumbents seem to conform to his bleak assessment: they are gone and forgotten as if they had never been. These are people who by Highgate's aspirational standards were never of any great consequence. They never became great bankers, or politicians or admirals or major generals, or directors of the East India Company. Yet their epitaphs attest their overwhelming consequence for those they left behind. In this sense, simple cemeteries like Earlsfield reflect the nature of London more truly than the magnificent seven.

ALMOST THE EQUINOX

Sarah Maguire

and the Thames so emptied of current
it shows bare flanks of sand. Beige sand. A beach.
The sudden vertigo of hardness when we're cupped
over the walls of the Embankment

examining the strange cream stones below,
driftwood, bottle-tops, crockery, one sodden boot.
And the slow mud opens its mouth.
Jets long departed, their con-trails fire

across the fierce blue skies, unfurling
into breath. The very last weather of a summer
spent impatient for change,
waiting for a sign, an alignment.

Beneath our feet, a hemisphere away,
the full moon tugs fluids into tides, and stops
another night in its tracks,
hours before it climbs over London –

the constant pull of elsewhere
mooring us outside ourselves. The colchicums

come naked into the early autumn air.
Bruised into mauve and purple,

their frail blooms admit the memory of harm
in their risky flight to beauty. Packed bulbs
underground harbour their secrets.
Now that we have witnessed

the flare of that ginkgo spilling up
besides St Paul's – its roots woven
deep beneath a graveyard of graves,
its slim knotted branches, sleeved

with airy, fantail leaves –
it will return to us, suddenly,
years from now. Anomalous Jurassic relic,
its origins are as ancient as these slabs

of blackening Whitbed Portland Stone,
set here by Wren to stamp out Fire and Plague.
As a child, I climbed all the stairs
to the Whispering Gallery, laid my cheek

against the painted plaster of the dome,
and let those perfected acoustics bear my changed voice
back to myself. The huge nave
reminds you of the Great Mosque in Kabul –

sunlight falling on pillars of stone, the hushed intentness
of prayer. Shattered, war-torn, it's still standing,
somehow, next to the river by the Bridge of Bricks,
just as Wren's great dome once soared above the Blitz,

    intact. Tonight, we will look up to see
Mars, that old harbinger of war, come so close to us
    it rivets the southern sky with its furious,
    amber flare. Sixty-thousand years ago it lit

        these heavens and looked down
on ice. Next convergence, nothing will be left of us
leaning on this bridge of wires and tempered steel,
    wondering at the river and the city and the stars,

here, on the last hot night before this planet tilts us
    into darkness, our cold season underground.
The tide has turned, the Thames comes inching back,
    drowning everything it will reveal again.

ABOUT THE CONTRIBUTORS

The **Akwaaba Writing Group** is based at a social centre for migrants and refugees in Dalston. Contributors are Olufunmilayo Aguda (Olu), Omolola Alhul (Lola), Juliana Ezekiel, Kenny, Remmie Najjuma, Anthony Kwame Ntem, Ola Oyewusi, Hadil Ben Soltana, Warda Ben Soltana. This story cycle was compiled/edited by Benjamin Morgan, Kiare Ludner, Alice Tilche and Luke Williams.

Arifa Akbar is a British Pakistani journalist and critic. Born in London in 1972, she worked for the *Independent* for fifteen years as a news reporter, leading its news-team in the aftermath of the 7/7 attacks, and then as its arts correspondent and literary editor, until April 2016. She has regularly written for the *Financial Times*, the *London Evening Standard*, and appeared on Sky News and BBC Radio. She is currently head of content at the publisher, Unbound, and launch editor of its long-form literary website, *Boundless*. She is working on her first novel, *The Memory Book*.

Memed Aksoy was born in Istanbul to Kurdish parents and moved with his family to London in 1989. 'A Story in Three Languages' was written as part of a creative writing partnership between Stoke Newington Literary Festival and the Halkevi Kurdish and Turkish Community Centre in Dalston. Memed was killed in northern Syria on 26 September 2017, while documenting the battle for Raqqa.

Omar Alfrouh is a student at Newman Catholic College in Brent. He was born in Syria and arrived in London in 2017. 'My House in Harra' was produced as part of English PEN's Brave New Voices project for young immigrants and refugees, and was published in the anthology *Imagine Your Shadow* (English PEN, 2017).

Sophie Baggott is a Welsh journalist specialising in human rights, based in south London.

Kinga Burger is a Warsaw-born, London-based writer, currently working on her first novel.

Duncan Campbell is a former crime correspondent for the *Guardian*. He is the author of two novels, *If It Bleeds* and *The Paradise Trail*, and five non-fiction books, including *The Underworld, That Was Business, This Is Personal*, and *We'll All be Murdered in Our Beds* (Elliott & Thompson).

John Crace is a parliamentary sketch-writer, author and super-fan. His books include *Vertigo: One Football Fan's Fear of Success* (Constable), *I Never Promised You a Rose Garden: A Short Guide to Modern Politics, the Coalition and the General Election* (Corgi), *I, Maybot: The Rise and Fall* (Guardian Faber) and, with John Sutherland, the *Incomplete Shakespeare* series.

Tom Dyckhoff is a writer, broadcaster and historian on architecture, design and cities. He has worked in television, radio, exhibitions, print and online media. He is best known for being a BBC TV presenter of *The Great Interior Design Challenge* and *The Culture Show*. 'The Circus Comes to Town' is from *The Age of Spectacle: Adventures in Architecture and the 21st-century City* (Picador, 2017).

Travis Elborough is an author whose books include *Wish You Were Here: England on Sea* (2010), *London Bridge in America: The Tall Story of a Transatlantic Crossing* (2013) and *A Walk in the Park: The Life and Times of a People's Institution* (Vintage, 2017).

Inua Ellams is a poet, playwright, performer, graphic artist and designer who was born in Nigeria in 1984 and is now based in London. He has published four books of poetry. His show, *An Evening with an Immigrant*, has toured widely. His play *Barber Shop Chronicles* was premiered at the National Theatre in June 2017.

Jo Glanville has written for the *London Review of Books*, the *TLS*, the *Guardian*, the *Independent* and the *Bookseller*, amongst other publications. She has been director of English PEN, an award-winning editor of *Index on Censorship* and a news and documentary producer at the BBC. She is currently a visiting fellow at Giessen University.

Stephen Griffith is the senior youth worker and Project Director at the Copenhagen Youth Project in Islington.

Lynsey Hanley is an author, journalist and broadcaster. Her books are *Estates: An Intimate History* (Granta 2007, new edition 2017) and *Respectable: The Experience of Class* (Allen Lane, 2016). She is a regular contributor to the *Guardian* and the *TLS*.

Jonathan Jones is an art critic for the *Guardian*. His books include *The Lost Battles: Leonardo, Michelangelo and the Artistic Duel That Defined the Renaissance* (2010), *The Loves of the Artists: Art and Passion in the Renaissance* (2013) and *Tracey Emin. Works 2007–2017* (2017).

Nicolette Jones is an author and journalist. She is children's books editor of the *Sunday Times* and the author of *The Plimsoll Sensation: The Great Campaign to Save Lives at Sea* (Abacus).

Ben Judah is a journalist and author of two books, *Fragile Empire: How Russia Fell in and Out of Love with Vladimir Putin* (2013) and *This is London* (2016). Neasden Lane is extracted from *This is London* (Picador).

Sarah Maguire is the author of *Spilt Milk* (1991), *The Invisible Mender* (1997), *The Florist's at Midnight* (2001) and *The Pomegranates of Kandahar*

(2007), which was shortlisted for the T S Eliot Prize. 'Almost the Equinox' is the title poem of her selected poems (2015).

David McKie is a former deputy editor and political reporter for the *Guardian*. His books include *Jabez: the Rise and Fall of a Victorian Rogue* (Atlantic, 2005), *Great British Bus Journeys: Travels through Unfamous Places* (Atlantic, 2007), *McKie's Gazetteer: a Local History of Britain* (Atlantic, 2010), *What's in a Surname: a Journey from Abercrombie to Zwicker* (Windmill Books, 2014), and *Riding Route 94: An Accidental Journey Through the Story of Britain* (Pimpernel Press, 2017).

Rowan Moore is architecture critic for the *Observer*. He is the author of *Why We Build* (2012) and *Anatomy of a Building* (2014). 'New Sybaris' is extracted from his latest book, *Slow Burn City: London in the 21st Century* (Picador, 2017).

Daljit Nagra is a British poet and broadcaster of Punjabi origin. He is the author of four books of poetry: *Look We Have Coming to Dover!* (2007) which won the Forward Prize for best first collection, *Tippoo Sultan's Incredible White-Man-Eating Tiger Toy-Machine!!!* (2012), *Ramayana* (2013) and *British Museum* (Faber, 2017). He presents *Poetry Extra* on Radio 4 Extra.

Richard Norton-Taylor is an editor, journalist and playwright. He was security editor of the *Guardian*. His plays, based on transcripts of public inquiries, are published as *The Tricycle: The Complete Tribunal Plays 1994-2012 (Oberon Books)*.

Andrew O'Hagan is a novelist and essayist who has three times been nominated for the Man Booker Prize. His novels include *Personality* (2003), *Our Fathers* (2004), *The Illuminations* (2005), *Be Near Me* (2006) and *The Life and Opinions of Maf the Dog, and of His Friend Marilyn Monroe* (2010). His essay collection *The Secret Life* has recently been published by Faber & Faber.

Ruth Padel is a poet, novelist and author of non-fiction whose books include *Tigers in Red Weather* (2005) and *Darwin: A Life in Poems* (2009). 'Walking the Fleet' came out of work on her most recent poetry collection, *Tidings: A Christmas Journey* (Chatto & Windus), a London story of a small girl, a homeless man and a fox.

Alex Rhys-Taylor is a senior lecturer and researcher in the Centre for Urban and Community Research at Goldsmiths, University of London. His work looks at the intersection of taste, disgust, urban development, race, class and multiculture. His recent books include *Food and Multiculture* (Bloomsbury, 2017) and Walking Through Social Research (Routledge, 2017).

Michèle Roberts is a novelist, poet, and short story writer. Her 16th novel, *The Walworth Beauty* (Bloomsbury), is set in the streets near her south London home in the 19th and 21st centuries.

Jacob Ross is a Grenada-born poet, playwright and novelist based in London. He won the inaugural Jhalak Prize for book of the year by a writer of colour in 2017 for *The Bone Reader*, the first novel of a new crime series. 'A Better Man' is from his collected short stories, *Tell No-one About This* (Peepal Tree Press, 2017).

Ferdous Sadat is a 23-year-old asylum seeker from Afghanistan who arrived in the UK in 2010. He is an active member of Migrants Organise Youth Group. 'The Leaflets' was written as part of English PEN's Brave New Voices programme and published in the *A City Imagined* anthology (2016).

Jane Shilling is an author and journalist. Her books include *The Fox in the Cupboard: A Memoir* (1995) and *The Stranger in the Mirror: A Memoir of Middle Age* (Vintage, 2011).

Helen Simpson has published six collections of short stories: *Four Legs in a Bed* (1991), *Dear George and Other Stories* (1995), *Hey Yeah Right Get*

A Life (2000), *Constitutional* (2005), *In-Flight Entertainment* (2010) and Cockfosters (Vintage, 2015).

Iain Sinclair is a writer and filmmaker who is a leading light in the 'psychogeography' movement. His books include an account of walking the M25, *London Orbital* (book and film, 2002) and *Hackney, That Rose-Red Empire* (2009). His most recent book is *The Last London: True Fictions from an Unreal City* (Oneworld).

Ali Smith is award-winning writer of novels, plays and short stories. She has been shortlisted four times for the Booker Prize. *How To Be Both* (2014) won the Baileys Women's Prize, the Folio Prize and the Goldsmiths Prize. Her latest novel is *Winter*, the second in a four part series which opened with the Booker nominated *Autumn* (Hamish Hamilton).

Lisa Smith is studying for an MA in Creative and Life Writing at Goldsmiths, University of London and is working on her first novel. She has previously worked as a documentary filmmaker. 'Auld Lang Syne' won the *Guardian* 4th Estate BAME Short Story Prize in 2017.

Jon Snow has been the presenter of Channel 4 News since 1989.

Yomi Sode is a London-based spoken word artist who was born in Nigeria. He performs under the moniker GREEdS. His show *COAT* sold out at the Roundhouse in 2017.

Ed Vulliamy is an author and journalist whose books inclusde *Amexica: War Along the Borderline* (Bodley Head, 2010) and *The War is Dead, Long Live the War: Bosnia: the Reckoning* (Bodley Head, 2012).

Ewa Winnicka is a Polish journalist, author, and documentary filmmaker. Twice-winner of Poland's Grand Press Award, she has written on social affairs for *Polityka*, and been a regular contributor to the Polish weeklies *Tygodnik Powszechny* and *Duży Format*, as well as the Italian publication *Internazionale*. This piece is from *Angole* (2014), her book of reportage on Polish immigrants in the UK, which won the 2015 Gryfia

Literary Prize and was shortlisted for the 2015 Nike Award and the 2015 Ryszard Kapuściński Award, Poland's highest award for literary journalism.

Penny Woolcock is a filmmaker, opera director, and screenwriter. Her films include *Tina Goes Shopping* (1999), the grime musical *One Day* (2009) and *One Mile Away* (2012), about the UK's postcode wars. In 2016, her production of Bach's St Matthew Passion for Streetwise Opera, performed predominantly by the formerly homeless with a new finale by Sir James MacMillan, was broadcast on BBC Four.

ABOUT THE EDITOR

Claire Armitstead was born in south London and spent her early years in northern Nigeria. She read English at St Hilda's College, Oxford, and began her journalistic career as a trainee reporter on the *South Wales Argus*, responsible for covering the Welsh valleys during the miners' strike. She joined the *Hampstead & Highgate Express* as a theatre critic and sub editor, moving on to the *Financial Times*, and then to the *Guardian*, where she has worked as arts editor, literary editor, head of books and most recently, Associate Editor (Culture). She presents the weekly Guardian Books podcast. She is a regular speaker at festivals around the world and lectures both nationally and internationally. She was on the board of *The Political Quarterly* for three years and has been a trustee of English Pen since 2013.